IMAGES
of Rail

NORTHWESTERN PACIFIC RAILROAD
EUREKA TO WILLITS

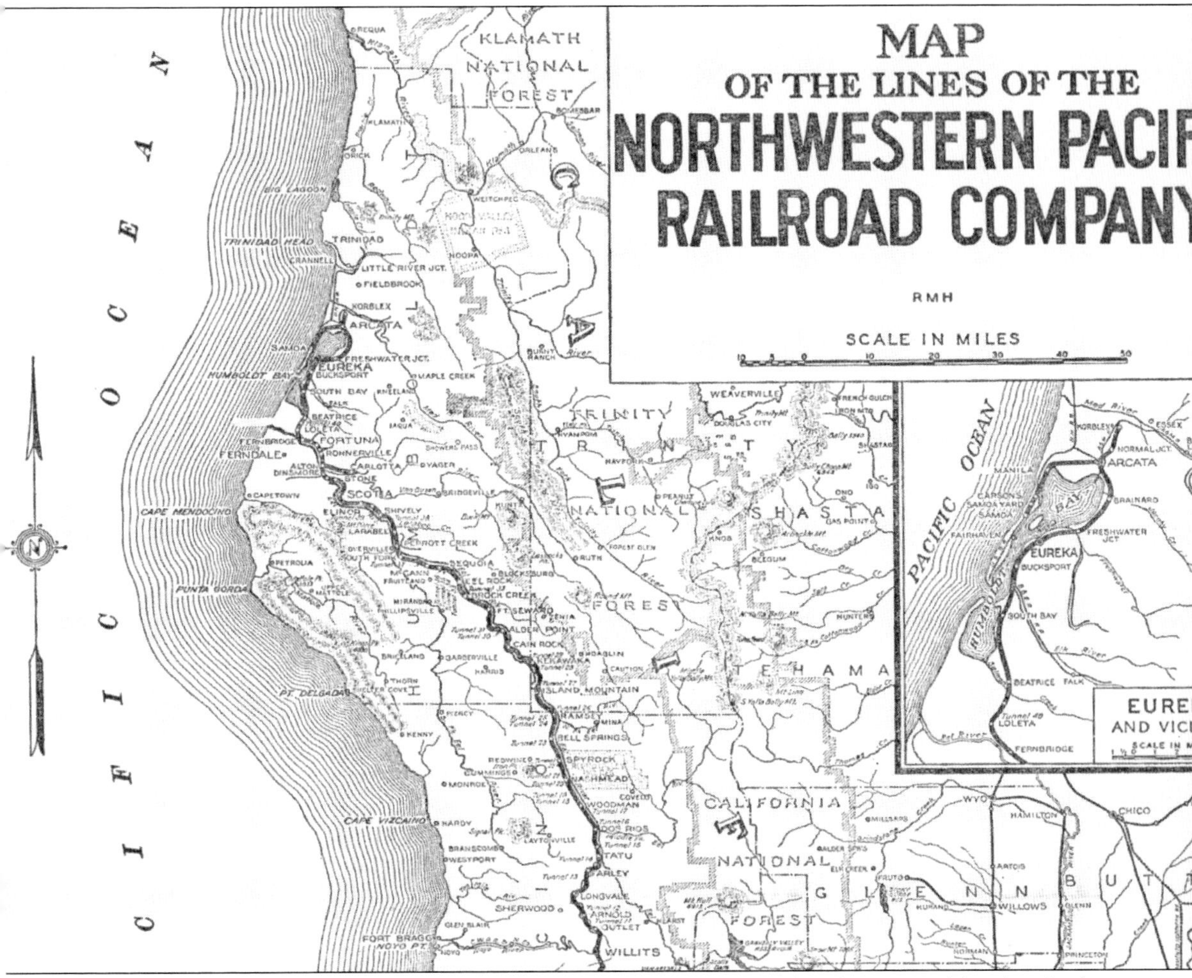

In 1908, the united company of the Northwestern Pacific Railroad—created by the Atchison, Topeka & Santa Fe Railroad and the Southern Pacific Railroad—began construction to connect Eureka with the San Francisco Bay Area. Although it was yet to be completed, the 100-mile section through remote southern Humboldt and northern Mendocino Counties is shown on this map. (Courtesy of the Fortuna Depot Museum.)

On the Cover: On October 23, 1914, crowds gathered at remote Cain Rock to witness a golden spike being driven into a redwood railroad tie to mark the completion of construction of the Northwestern Pacific Railroad (NWP). The crews building south from Eureka and those building north from Willits met at Cain Rock, which is south of Alderpoint along the main fork of the Eel River and still remains inaccessible by car. (Courtesy of Humboldt State University Library.)

IMAGES *of Rail*

Northwestern Pacific Railroad Eureka to Willits

Susan J.P. O'Hara, Alex Service,
and the Fortuna Depot Museum

ARCADIA PUBLISHING

ISBN 978-1-4671-3062-2

Published by Arcadia Publishing
Charleston, South Carolina

Printed in the United States of America

Library of Congress Control Number: 2013935602

For all general information, please contact Arcadia Publishing:
Telephone 843-853-2070
Fax 843-853-0044
E-mail sales@arcadiapublishing.com
For customer service and orders:
Toll-Free 1-888-313-2665

Visit us on the Internet at www.arcadiapublishing.com

The authors dedicate this book to their mothers, Margaret Pritchard and Pam Service. They shared the excitement of researching, instilling in their daughters a love of history.

CONTENTS

Acknowledgments

The authors would like to thank the Fortuna City Council and the Fortuna Historical Commission for their ongoing support of the Fortuna Depot Museum.

Many images in this book are from the collections of the Humboldt Room, Humboldt State University Library (HSU); the Northwestern Pacific Railroad Historical Society (NWPRRHS); and the Humboldt Redwoods Interpretive Association (HRIA). Unless otherwise noted, all images in the book are from the Fortuna Depot Museum.

The Fortuna Depot Museum is enriched by the photograph collections of many people who worked for the NWP and many who dedicated themselves to preserving local history. We wish to thank these individuals and their families for creating this photographic record and saving it for future generations. Collections at the Fortuna Depot Museum, which made this book possible, include those of P.E. Bandy, Ray Barkhurst, Bill Bish, L.E. DuBose, Fred Elliott, Joe Lockhart, Marguerita Nichols, Neil Paulson, Guy B. Rhodes, Evelyn Kruse Swanson, and Francee White. We apologize for any omissions in this list and want to thank those who devoted their lives to the railroad and who have preserved its history.

Introduction

In Northwest California lie Humboldt and Mendocino Counties. The region, with its steep terrain and large redwood forests, remained isolated from the rest of California until the completion of the Northwestern Pacific Railroad (NWP) in 1914. After being settled by immigrants in the 1850s, the coastal regions of both counties were easily accessed by sea, although the overland route was slow and difficult to traverse. The ocean route was dangerous, too; many ships wrecked along the rugged coastline. Moreover, steam-powered ships took several days to reach San Francisco. In Humboldt County, the sandbar across the entrance to Humboldt Bay was very hazardous. Ships often could not enter the bay or were wrecked due to violent, erratic waves.

In addition to communication and travel, shipping was critical to the economic livelihood of both counties. In the 1850s, the usefulness of redwood lumber, often referred to as "red gold," was brought to light. Mills sprang up near the towns of Mendocino, Fort Bragg, Eureka, and Arcata. Mills, a common sight along the coast, were supplied by loggers working in the nearby, seemingly endless forests. However, mill owners were only compensated when they got their products to markets in the San Francisco Bay Area or elsewhere. Sailing vessels utilized small "doghole" ports to ship lumber along the Mendocino coast. Ports were located at Rockport, Westport, Caspar, Mendocino, and other mill sites. Humboldt County utilized the large bay near Eureka for shipping. The Humboldt Bay entrance was improved by the construction of jetties in the 1880s, and ships were locally built with a shallow draft—especially at Bendixson's shipyard near Samoa—to cross the sandbar. While this meant more lumber could be taken south, it also meant that each load was limited by the size of the smaller ships.

Railroads, under construction in both counties, were initially used to bring logs to mills around larger communities. The Union Wharf and Plank Walk Company built the first railroad in Humboldt County on the Arcata wharf in the 1850s. The wharf stretched two miles out into the bay, where the water was deep enough for vessels to navigate. A white horse called "Spanking Fury" served as the "locomotive" for this rail system in the early years and remained in service until the 1870s.

Other rail lines, either regular or narrow gauge, built in both counties were used to access remote forests after lumber companies harvested the trees closest to communities. As each stand of trees was depleted, the companies would extend the railroads. Large lumber companies operated their own engines and cars and had employees devoted to operating their rail systems. These lines were not built to a high degree of engineering, and they frequently had accidents. The lines also needed large bridges to span ravines and creeks. Since these bridges were made of redwood, they burned easily; the workers at the Caspar Mill frequently found themselves fighting fires and replacing bridges as their locomotive, the "Daisy," a 0-4-2 engine, had a tendency to set her bridges aflame. The Caspar Lumber Company was one of many mills along the Mendocino coast with its own logging trains.

In 1884, two important Humboldt mill owners, William Carson and John Vance, joined forces to begin a railroad they hoped would eventually connect Eureka with the outside world. Dubbed the Eel River & Eureka Railroad (ER&ERR), the line linked Eureka to the new railroad town of Alton. The ER&ERR was used for passenger transportation and to haul logs, lumber, livestock, and agricultural produce. Residents of Fortuna and Rohnerville used the line to travel to the county seat of Eureka. The Pacific Lumber Company (T.P.L. Co.), incorporated in 1869, soon extended the line to its company town of Scotia and signed a contract with the ER&ERR to haul lumber to its shipping port at Fields Landing. Other mills in the region, including the Dodge Lumber Company, also extended logging railroads to connect with the new ER&ERR line.

In the early 20th century, the small logging railroads of Humboldt County captured the attention of the Southern Pacific and the Atchison, Topeka & Santa Fe (Santa Fe) Railroads. In 1904, the Santa Fe purchased the ER&ERR, running it as the San Francisco & Northwestern. Vance had extended the line north to Arcata, connecting it with the Arcata & Mad River Railroad. The conglomerates also worked to acquire port space around Humboldt Bay, and both large railroads began making plans to extend railroad lines south to San Francisco.

Meanwhile, the Pacific Lumber Company had been extending a railroad south from Scotia to harvest redwoods growing along the Eel River's main fork. After the railroad reached Shively in the early 1900s, it sparked the growth of the community. Shively met the needs of the many workers in the surrounding logging camps, offering several hotels, bars, stores, and houses of ill repute. As the end of the line, Shively also served as a departing point for those heading south. Travelers left by stage to traverse the rough overland route to reach Willits; in the summer, they could use automobiles, but since wet winters prevented early cars from traveling on rutted, muddy roads, they utilized horse-drawn stagecoaches instead.

After acquiring the rights to the many small lines south of Willits near the end of the 19th century, the Southern Pacific had created one railroad. The owners of the Santa Fe and Southern Pacific met in 1906 after concluding that closing the gap between Willits and Eureka would not be economically feasible for two different companies. They created a subsidiary company—the Northwestern Pacific. Although the NWP drew up plans, they were destroyed in the devastating earthquake and fire that struck San Francisco in 1906. The next year, construction began but was soon halted because of money woes and government challenges arguing that the NWP would be a violation of fair market practice.

Throughout 1907, construction was sporadic on the NWP. During this time, the *Arcata Union* ran an editorial titled "No Place for a Railroad Track." The editorial focused on the route taken by the railroad along the Rio Dell-Scotia Bluffs, prophetically commenting, "that strip of road never should have been laid where it is, and it is no surprise to pioneers along upper Eel River to witness the fulfillment of their predictions that no road could be built there that would ever prove free from damage to life and property in any month of the year." The *Union* was not opposed to the railroad but rather to the selected route. They recommended building bridges across to Rio Dell, thus avoiding the treacherous bluffs, where landslides were a constant threat; this exact location would be the site of one of the fatal wrecks on the NWP line.

Local photographer Edwin Freeman documented other details of the route for the Northwestern Pacific. He photographed scenes along the "gap" between Willits and Shively, helping the NWP promote the idea of a railroad to San Francisco. Freeman moved to Humboldt County after the 1906 San Francisco earthquake and opened a photography studio in 1910. A strong proponent of the railroad, he believed it would bring more tourists to the region. In 1913, he and local newspaperman Charles H. Roberts explored the gap. Roberts wrote the following for the *Humboldt Times*: "From Willits to South Fork we traveled through a country of hills and canyons and ravines, creeks and rivers always with some stream in stone's throw from the path. There is practically no open country from Willits until you arrive at Fort Seward, and no place that the camera cannot be set up at random, and a beautiful picture procured." Using his pictures, Freeman created a slide show that he exhibited at local theaters, creating community interest in the construction and eagerness for the ultimate completion of the new railroad.

Construction of the line was divided into 10 sections, with each section building to connect with the one ahead. Line engineers decided to follow the Eel River's main fork south while simultaneously following Outlet Creek north from Willits. The first obstacle on the north end was boring through Bryan's Bluff to create what would become the second-longest tunnel on the northern section of the railroad. Between 1908 and 1910, construction was intermittent and often bogged down by a lack of funds. Also, the rugged territory through which the line was being built required many bridges and several more tunnels. The greatest challenge lay 11 miles south of Alderpoint. There, Island Mountain caused a large oxbow bend in the river, requiring a tunnel over one mile long with a bridge on the south side. Residents of both Humboldt and Mendocino Counties closely followed the news reports of railroad construction, eager to hear when the railroad would open. The 1911 Fortuna High School *Megaphone* yearbook captured the hopes and optimism of the region as the seniors wrote: "With the advent of the railroad connecting with San Francisco, Fortuna, by virtue of its climate and location will become one of the largest cities on the Pacific Coast."

The NWP finally completed construction—at a cost of nearly $14 million—in October 1914. The railroad soon recouped this expense as companies began shipping redwood lumber on the line. On October 23, 1914, NWP president and general manager Warren S. Palmer drove a golden spike into a special redwood birdseye burl railroad tie to commemorate the event. Three trainloads of well-wishers gathered at Cain Rock, a remote site three miles south of Alderpoint. The mayors of Eureka and San Francisco gave speeches, as did dignitaries from the NWP and its parent companies. Celebrants were thrilled to partake in the completion of the railroad that would finally link Eureka to the rest of California.

Unfortunately, in a foretelling of challenges that would later beset the railroad, a landslide delayed the golden-spike party's plan to travel to Eureka that day. The Eel River's erosive power contributed to many landslides. Additionally, the increase in logging on the hillsides along the railroad route triggered many slides, which plagued the line every winter, causing stoppages on the route and requiring a maintenance crew that had to constantly rebuild the line.

Since it started as a logging railroad, the NWP line followed the river, so the route was not subject to many changes in elevation. The line was built below the Eel River's flood stage along most of the route, but builders had no serious concerns about flooding, because the river had not experienced significant floods since the 1860s. Storms in the early 1900s raised the river's levels, which dismayed some residents but did not deter railroad engineers. One of the first disasters on the line occurred in 1913 with the first of numerous major floods. This flood greatly damaged the unfinished line. Much of the rail bed had to be relaid, and many bridges had to be rebuilt, including the one crossing the Van Duzen River. At Dyerville, the river almost rose to the level of the bridge. Landslides also covered the line in many places, including along the Scotia Bluffs. Seven sections of railroad were destroyed in a major slide at Nanning Creek following the flood of 1913.

The 20th century saw several more floods, including the disastrous floods of 1955 and 1964. The 1955 flood caused significant damage that was easily repaired by railroad crews. The 1964 flood, however, required the complete rebuilding of the line through the Eel River Canyon, where entire sections of the railroad were washed away. Additionally, many railroad bridges had to be rebuilt, including the long bridges at Dyerville, Cain Rock, and Island Mountain. Reconstruction was required to such an extent that another golden spike ceremony was held in June 1965 at South Fork. Other disasters, including fires and derailments, caused frequent line closures.

One of these disasters led to the shutdown of the railroad in the mid-1980s. In 1978, the tunnel at Island Mountain caught on fire, possibly as a result of arson. The redwood beams that supported the roof of the tunnel burned readily, as did the redwood ties. A substandard coal in the rocks also burned, adding to the conflagration. Railroad employees could not put out the intense fire that burned to such an extent that rock was fractured 300 feet high inside the mountain. When the fire was finally extinguished, Southern Pacific (sole owner of the railroad since 1929) considered closing the line. Southern Pacific began moving rolling stock south by truck, including eight locomotives. By this time, the NWP was in competition with the trucking industry and was not seeing the same profits they experienced earlier in the century. Southern Pacific eventually hired the Morrison and Knudsen Company to repair and rebuild the Island Mountain tunnel, and rail traffic resumed, but in a desultory manner. The last NWP train ran on the northern line in 1984.

Since that time, the line has been deteriorating while various agencies have sought to reopen the railroad. One issue preventing the reopening is that numerous mills have closed in Humboldt County, and the current mills no longer produce multiple profitable carloads of lumber. Another reason is that the line has suffered from neglect and would require extensive, costly repairs. The expense of these repairs would require a large payload in order for the railroad to make a profit.

In this book, authors Susan J.P. O'Hara and Alex Service have chosen a thematic approach to cover the history of the NWP. The book will cover origins of the line and its construction, people who worked for the line, places that were connected by the railroad, rolling stock, the many disasters that plagued the route, and the uncertain future of the NWP. The goal is to share the historical importance the line has had to the region and the events that befell it. The authors are donating their royalties to the Fortuna Depot Museum.

One

Redwoods and Railroads

In 1850, the first vessel carrying prospective settlers to the region, the *Laura Virginia*, sailed into what expedition members named Humboldt Bay. As settlers began to harvest and mill the redwoods surrounding the bay, it soon became obvious to the new arrivals that the trees held the potential for great wealth. The settlers soon coined the phrase "red gold" to describe the fortunes that could be found in the reddish wood.

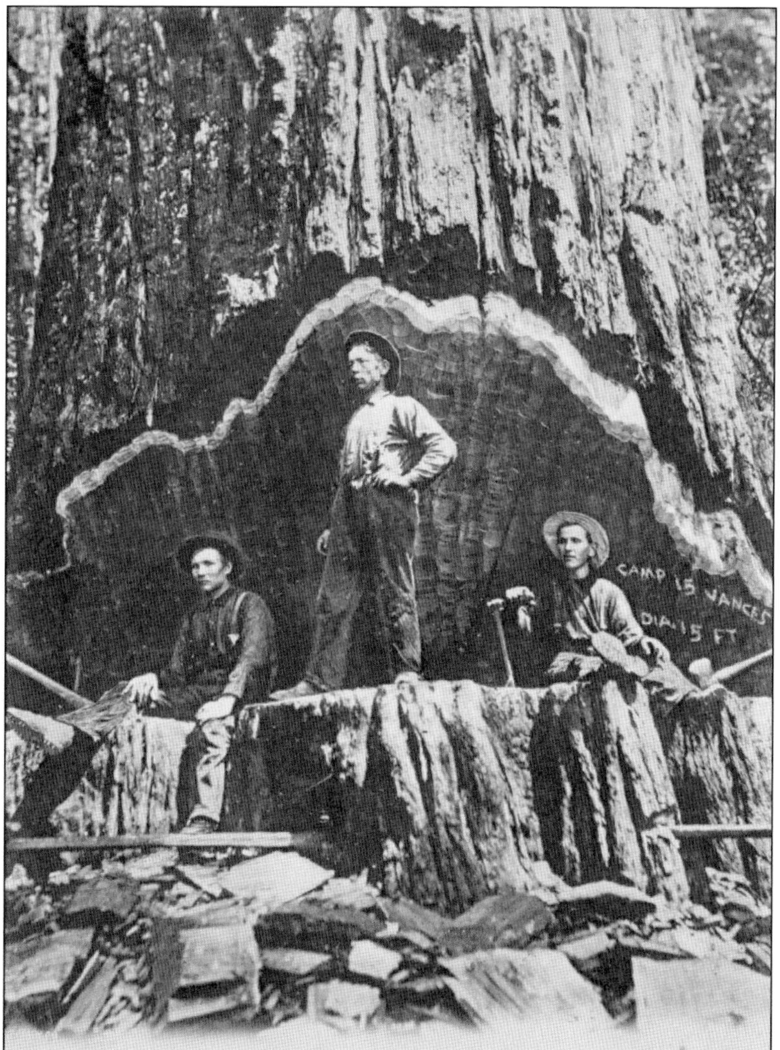

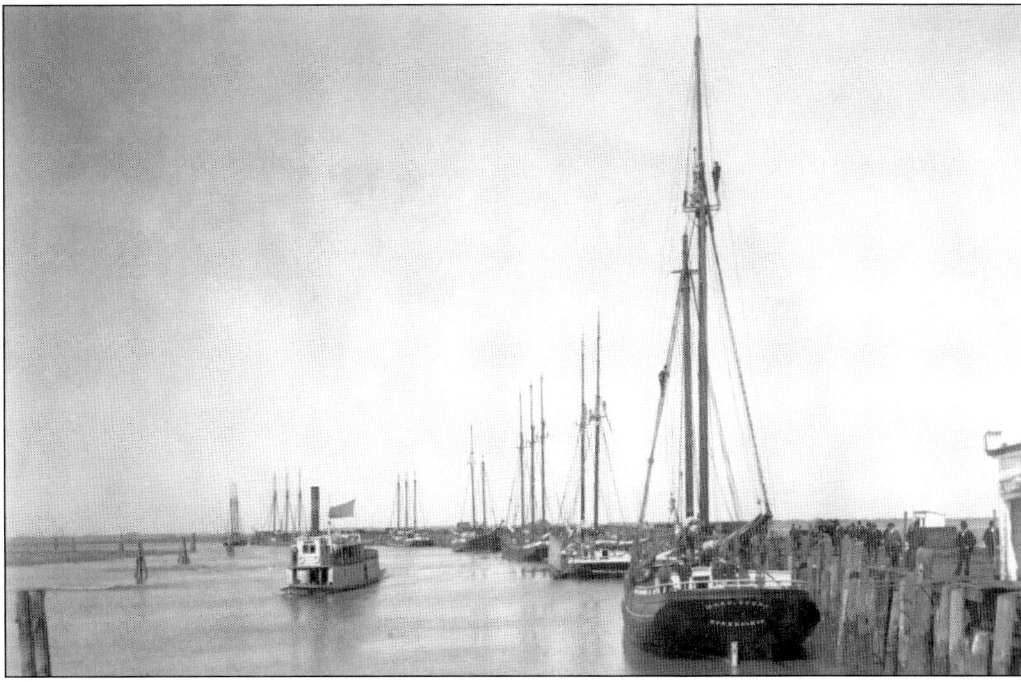

Lumber companies in Humboldt and Mendocino Counties built railroads to transport logs to mills and lumber to ships. Humboldt County's first railroad was on the two-mile-long dock near Arcata (or Union, as it was originally named). The Arcata wharf train, used for nearly 30 years, was initially powered by a white horse named Spanking Fury. (Courtesy of HSU.)

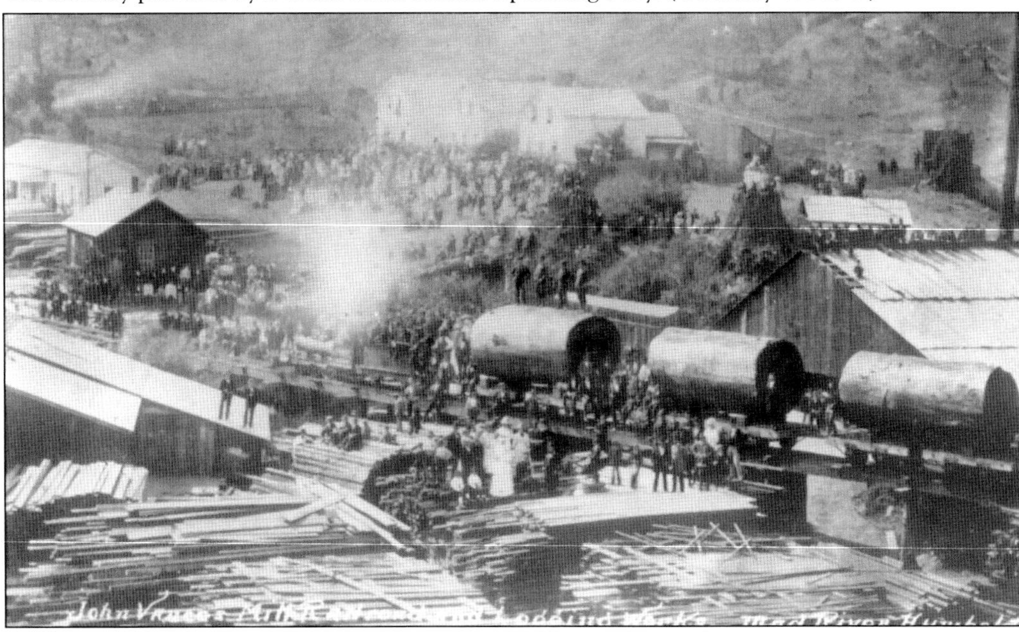

John Vance, an early mill owner on Humboldt Bay, opened his first mill in Eureka in 1857. After depleting resources near Eureka, he moved operations to the Big Bonanza mill along Lindsey Creek near Mad River. This is one of his logging locomotives used to connect the tall stands of redwoods to the mill and then to take lumber to the docks at Arcata for shipping.

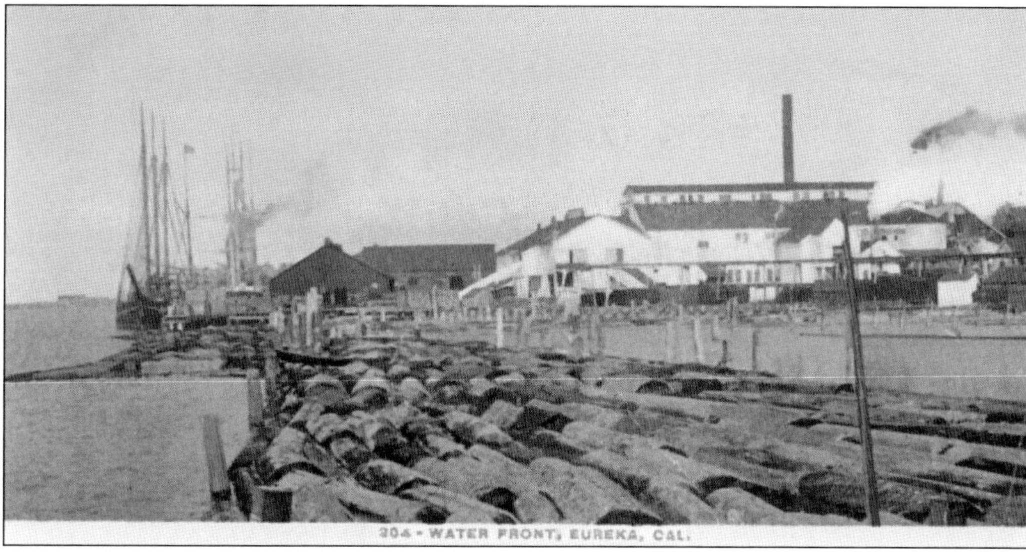

William Carson also had large mills beside Humboldt Bay. Carson used part of the bay for his millpond, storing logs in the bay until they were sawn into lumber. Carson also found railroads necessary to connect his woods operations to his mill. As the lumber industry grew, so did the need to travel farther distances to find tall timber to log.

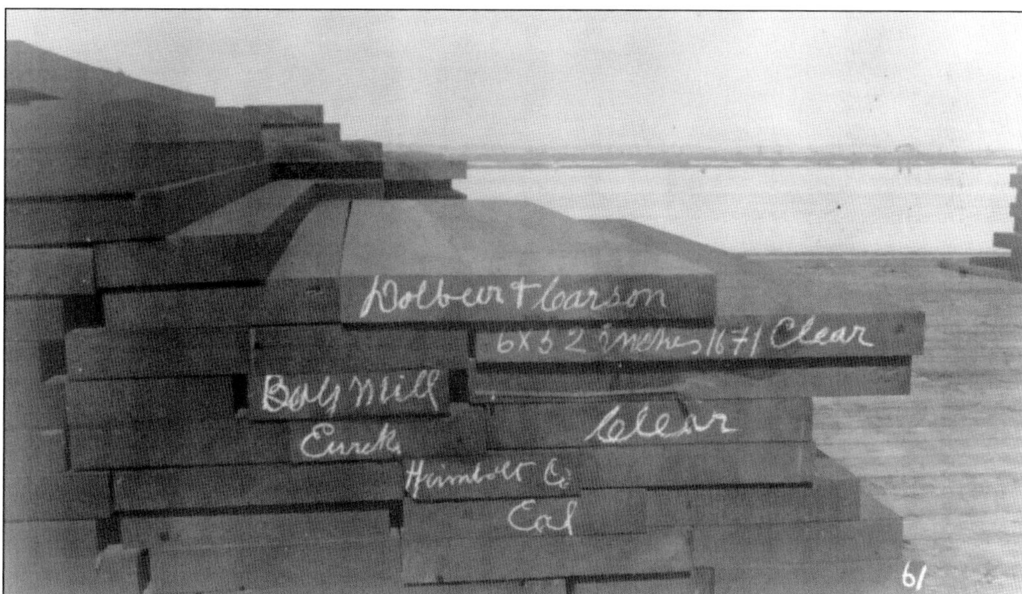

Stacked lumber, ready to be shipped, was a common sight at each mill and at the docks around the bay. From 1850 to 1914, the only way to ship this lumber was across the sandbar at the mouth of the bay. Early sea captains maintained that the Humboldt Bay bar had the most dangerous waters to cross in the Pacific Ocean, except the crossing around Cape Horn. (Courtesy of HSU.)

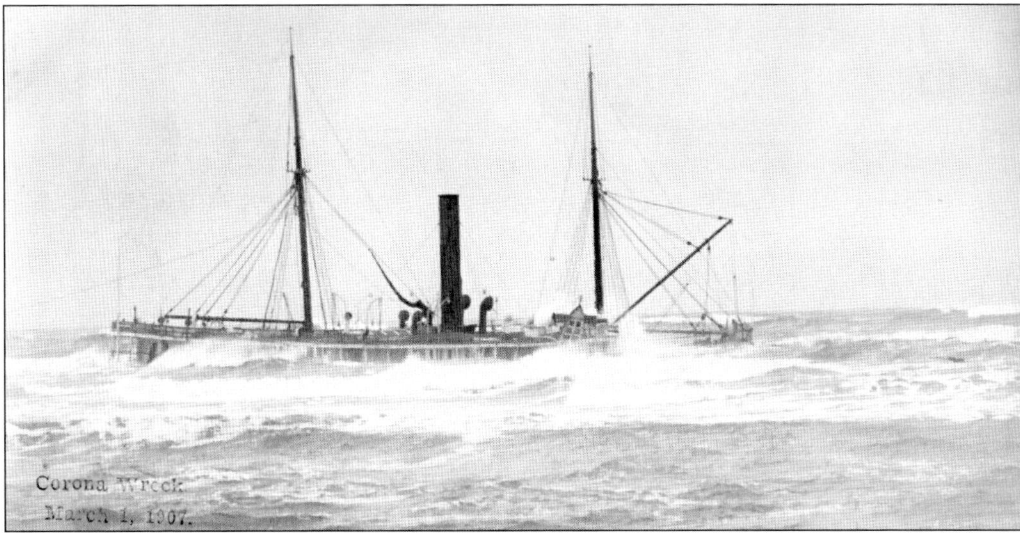

The Humboldt Bay entrance was so dangerous because of a sandbar that blocked the entrance and shifted with each storm. The difficulty of finding the narrow navigable channel contributed to the many wrecks. The wife of a lieutenant stationed at Fort Humboldt remarked on the number of wrecked vessels indicating the entrance to the bay in the 1850s, when she crossed the bar into the bay. The *Corona* (pictured) wrecked in March 1907 while trying to cross the bar.

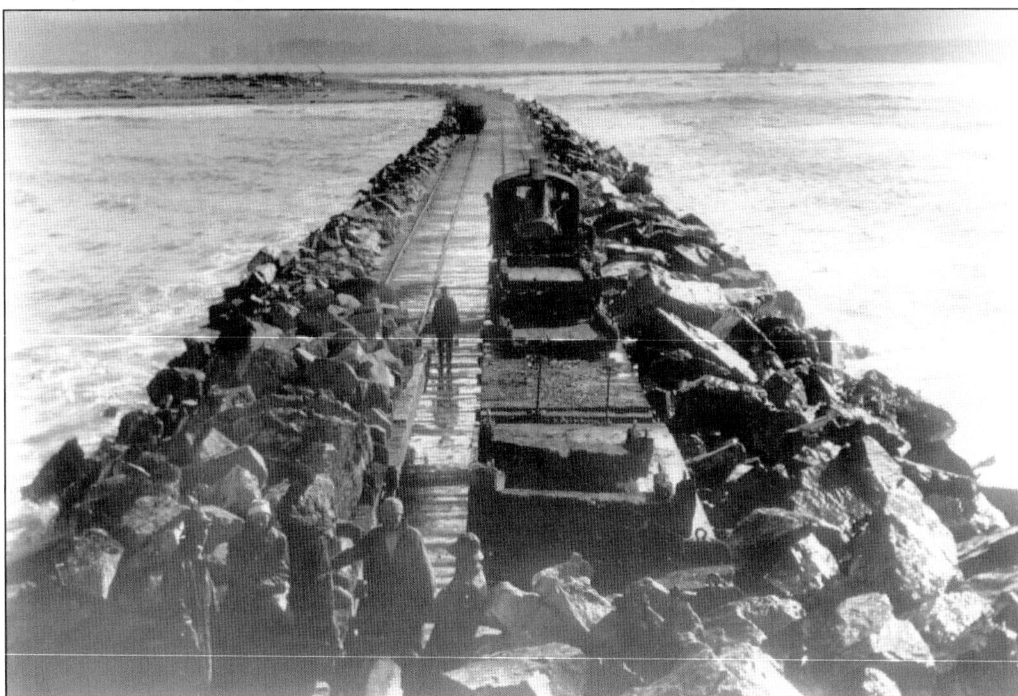

Near the end of the 19th century, the US Army Corps of Engineers came up with a solution to improve the entrance to Humboldt Bay—the construction of two jetties. They built the jetties by placing brush mats on the sandy ocean floor, then dumping rocks on top that were brought by rail. Although the corps completed the jetties in 1899, fierce wave action at the mouth of the bay caused the jetties to erode and become ineffective by 1905.

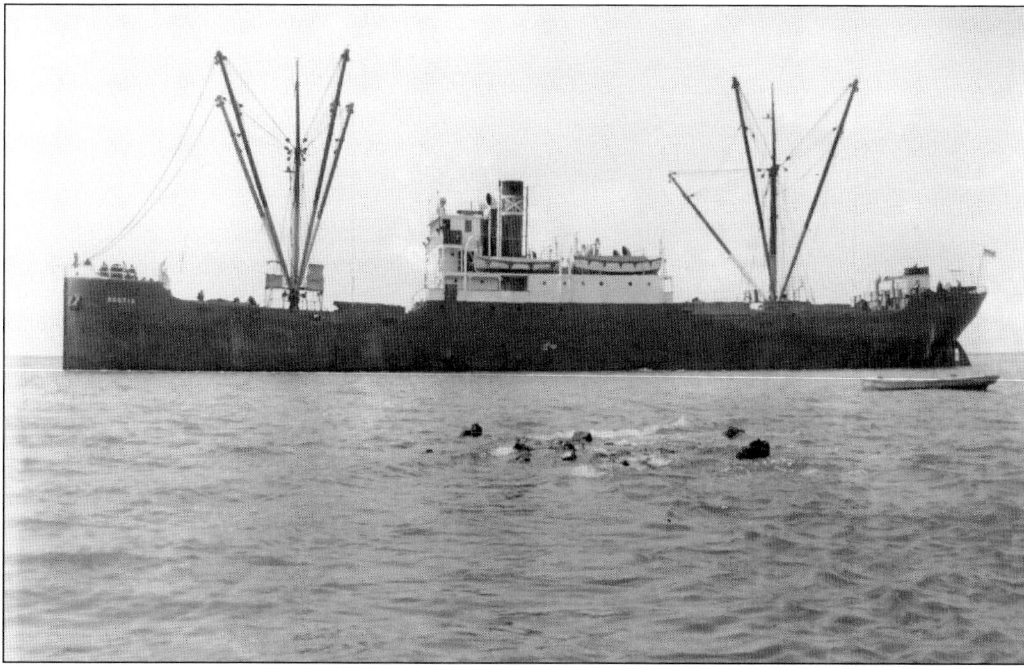

Throughout the 20th century, the jetties continually eroded and were continually repaired—at great cost. In this 1939 image, the S.S. *Scotia* steams past the remains of the jetties. The *Scotia*, owned by the Pacific Lumber Company, was loaded with lumber brought to Fields Landing by rail.

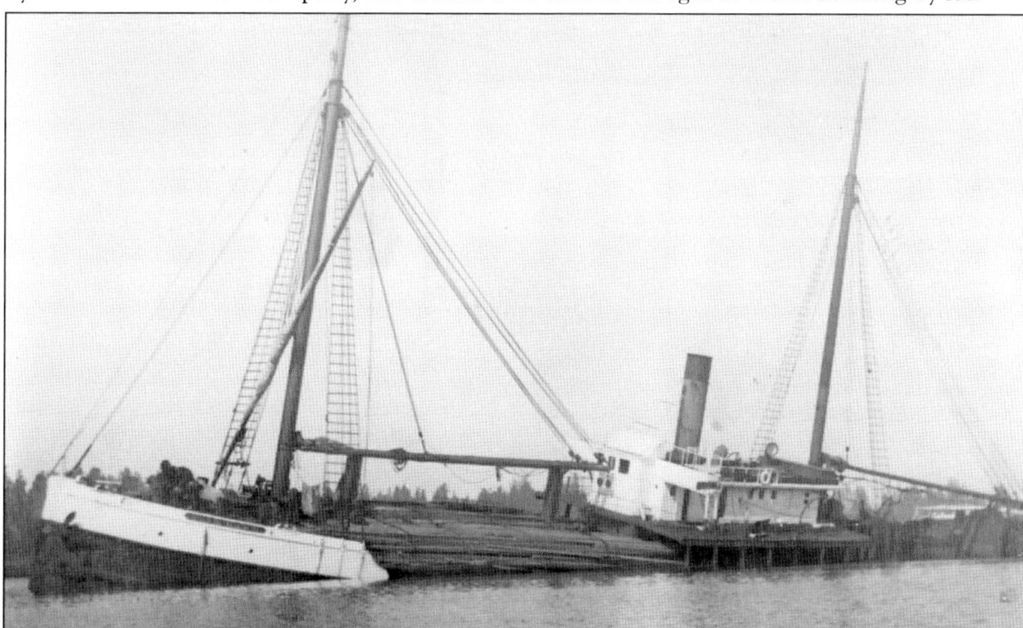

Ultimately, ocean-based shipping was fraught with problems. Ships wrecked, as illustrated by the S.S. *Fair Oaks* (pictured). There were also limits on how much they could haul and how long they took to get to markets. After taking two or more days to make the journey south to San Francisco, vessels could also be prevented from entering or leaving Humboldt Bay for several weeks at a time during winter storms.

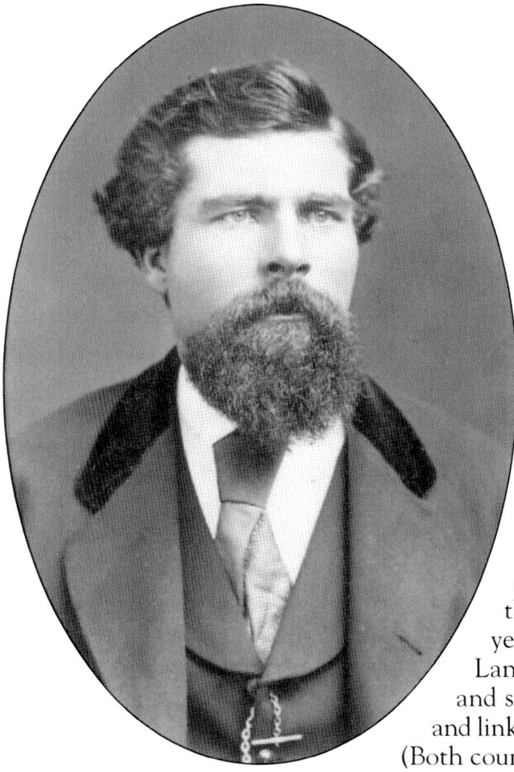

In 1882, a group of businessmen and mill owners, including William Carson (left) and John Vance (below) formed the Eel River & Eureka Railroad (ER&ERR). Carson became president, and Vance vice president, of the new line. Wanting access to the rich stands of timber to the south, they hoped to eventually have a line that would reach San Francisco. Since both owned large mills, they were aware of the value of "red gold." Carson is credited with cutting down the first redwood to be used as lumber in 1850. In 1884, construction began on the railroad. When it was completed the following year, the new line connected present-day Fields Landing and Fortuna and had one tunnel, a trestle, and several bridges. It traveled as far south as Alton and linked with lines from mills at Carlotta and Newburg. (Both courtesy of HSU.)

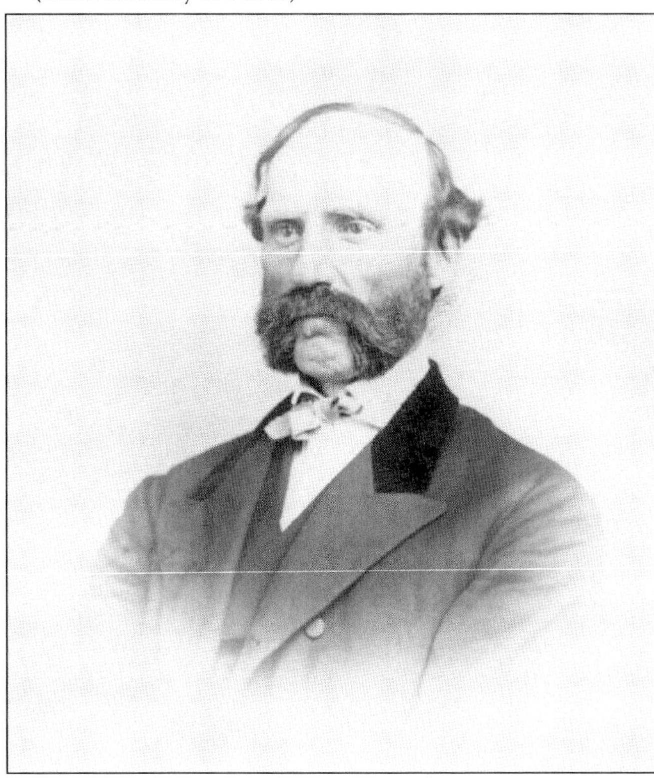

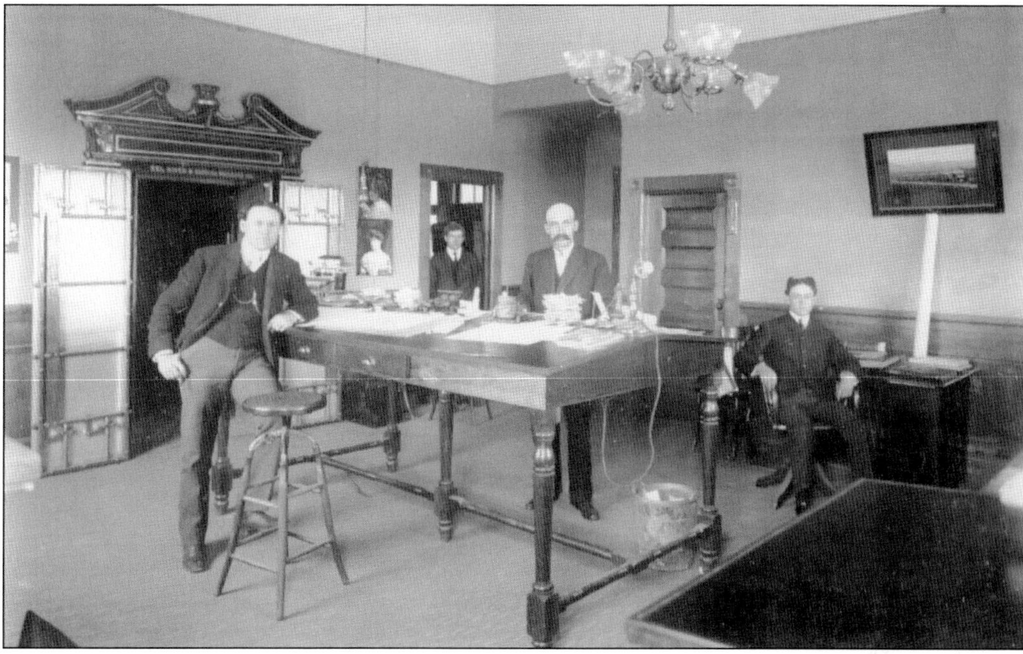

This rare photograph reveals the interior of the offices of the Eel River & Eureka Railroad. William Carson and John Vance's 22-mile line was a profitable one, hauling produce from the Eel River valley and lumber products from area mills to Eureka. The ER&ERR also provided passenger service, offering residents easy, rapid transportation. In 1886, Vance purchased a controlling interest in the railroad. (Courtesy of HSU.)

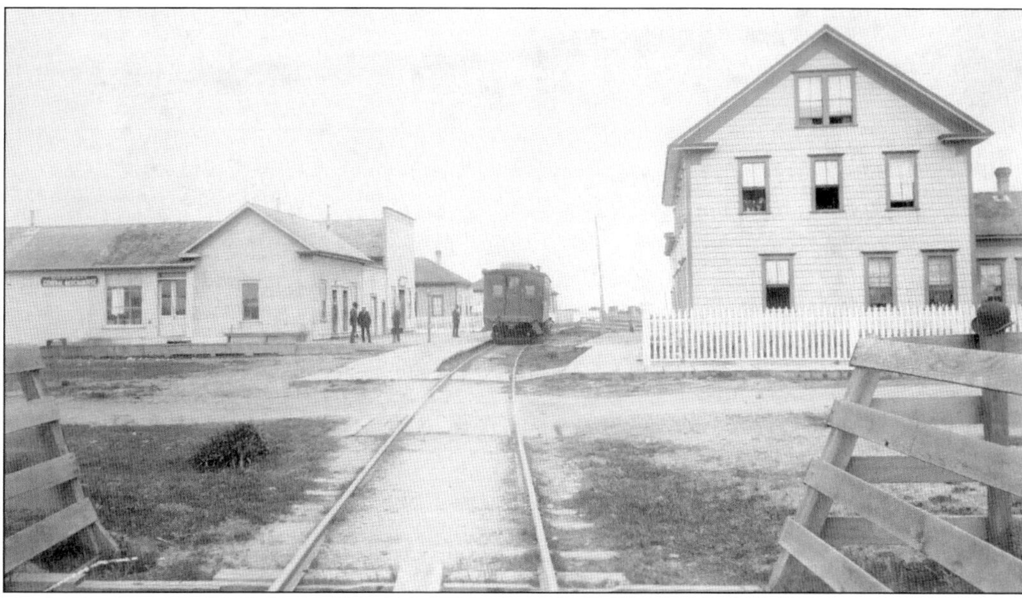

In 1886, Vance wanted to connect the line to Eureka. However, he was unable to purchase the right-of-way through land belonging to Waterman Field in an area known as Fields Landing. In spite, Vance moved his railroad east, away from Field's land. After building a depot and a new hotel (the building at right in this image), Vance had the post office moved from Fields Landing to his new nearby community of South Bay (pictured). (Courtesy of HSU.)

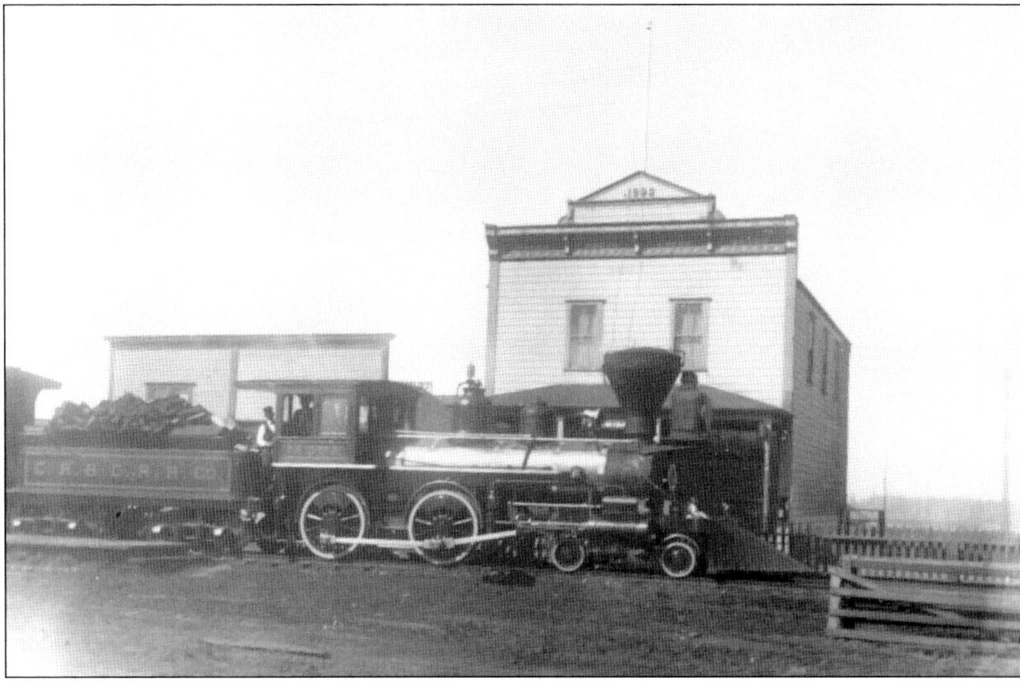

Towns flourished around the railroad. This community, originally called Swauger's Station (the stop was located on Samuel Swauger's land), was renamed Loleta in 1898. The ER&ERR built a new depot, encouraging residents to select a new name. They picked Loleta, believing it to be a Wiyot word meaning "a pleasant place at the end of the water." (Courtesy of HSU.)

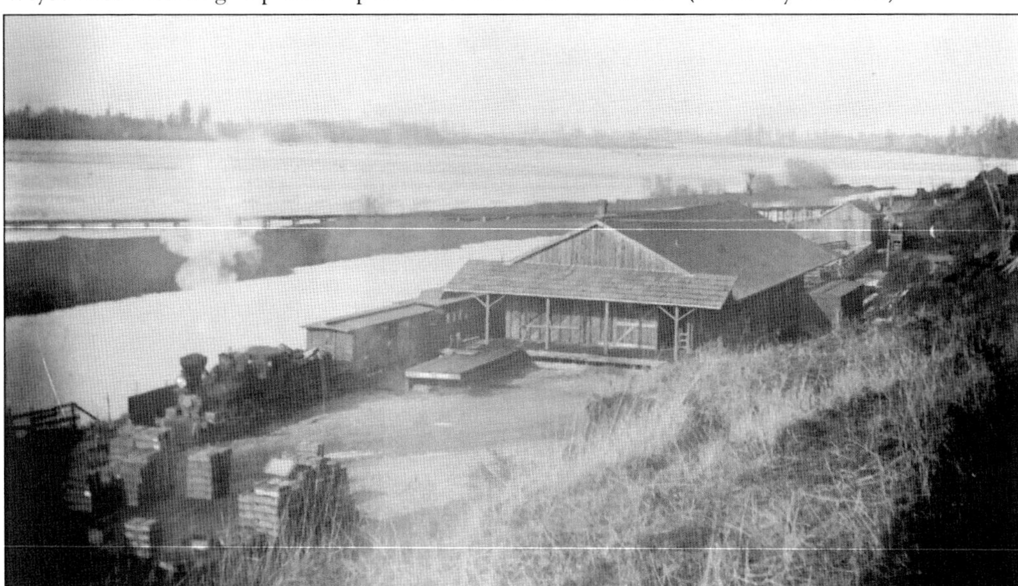

South of Loleta, the train stopped at Singley's Ferry, also known as Ferndale Junction because Ferndale residents crossed the river at Singley's Ferry in order to reach the rail line. This settlement was renamed Fernbridge after the construction of the bridge in 1911. Singley's was one of many ferries that crossed the Eel River. The railroad allowed anglers from Eureka easy access to this popular fishing spot.

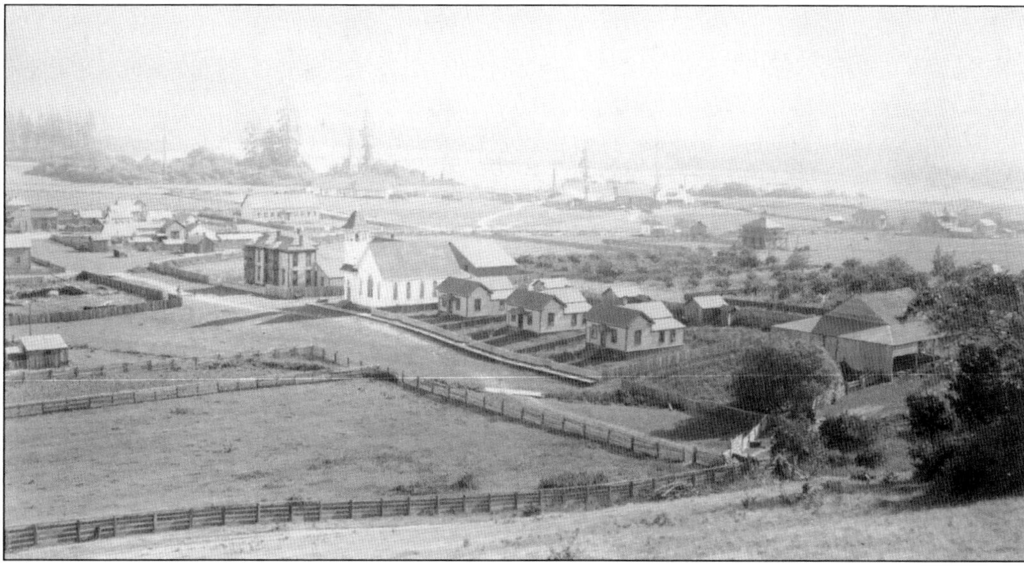

Fortuna, a thriving community south of Eureka, was home to several lumber, shingle, and moulding mills in the 1880s. During this early period, Fortuna was sometimes referred to by railroad employees as "Slide," because landslides north of town necessitated regular repairs on the line in that location. The depot is visible in the background beyond the church spire to the left of center in this photograph.

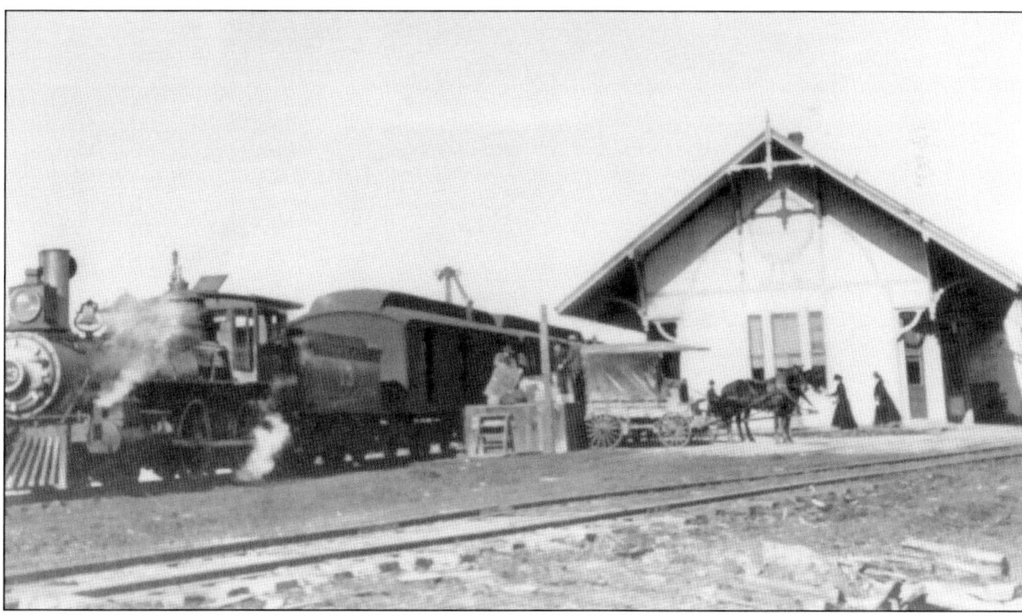

The Fortuna depot was a hub of activity when trains pulled into the station. This depot was built in the late 1880s by the ER&ERR and featured a waiting room and baggage storage area. The railroad provided the most reliable and quickest way to travel within the Eel River valley.

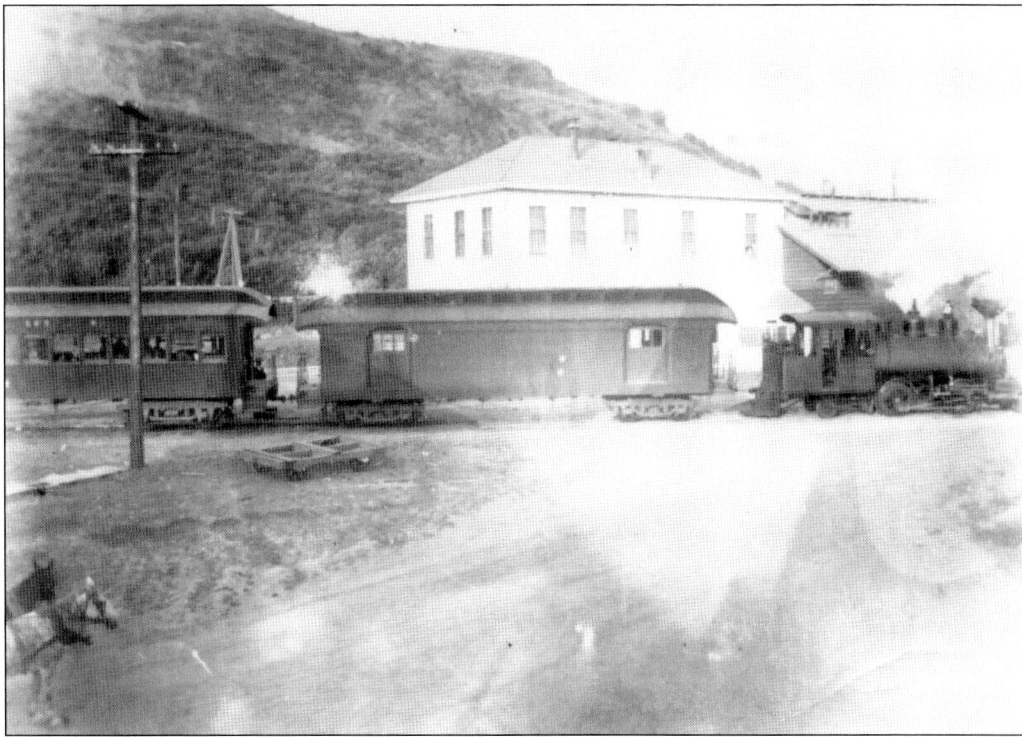

Alton, located four miles south of Fortuna, was the terminus of the ER&ERR, although lines from mills at Newburg and Carlotta extended east. The Pacific Lumber Company (T.P.L. Co.), located five miles farther south, extended a line north from Scotia in 1885 to connect its mill to its seaport at Fields Landing for use in shipping lumber and transporting employees.

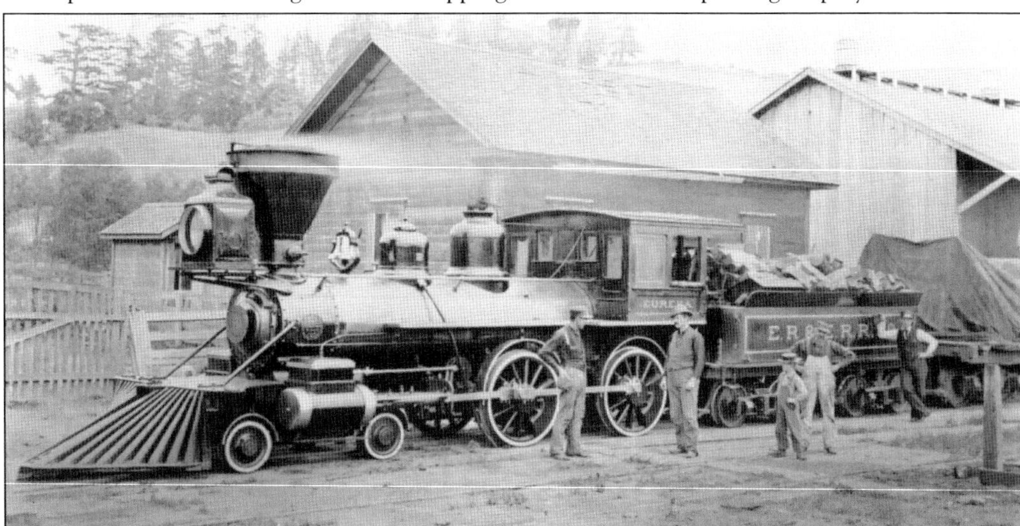

The Pacific Lumber Company began construction of its own railroad in 1882, attracting the interest of Santa Fe Railroad officials who were considering building a railroad in the region. To avoid competition, the ER&ERR offered to charge a nominal fee for T.P.L. Co. to use the ER&ERR. T.P.L. Co.'s lumber was brought on its railroad to Joel Burnell's ranch near Alton, then connected to an ER&ERR engine, as shown here, to continue to T.P.L. Co.'s wharf at Fields Landing.

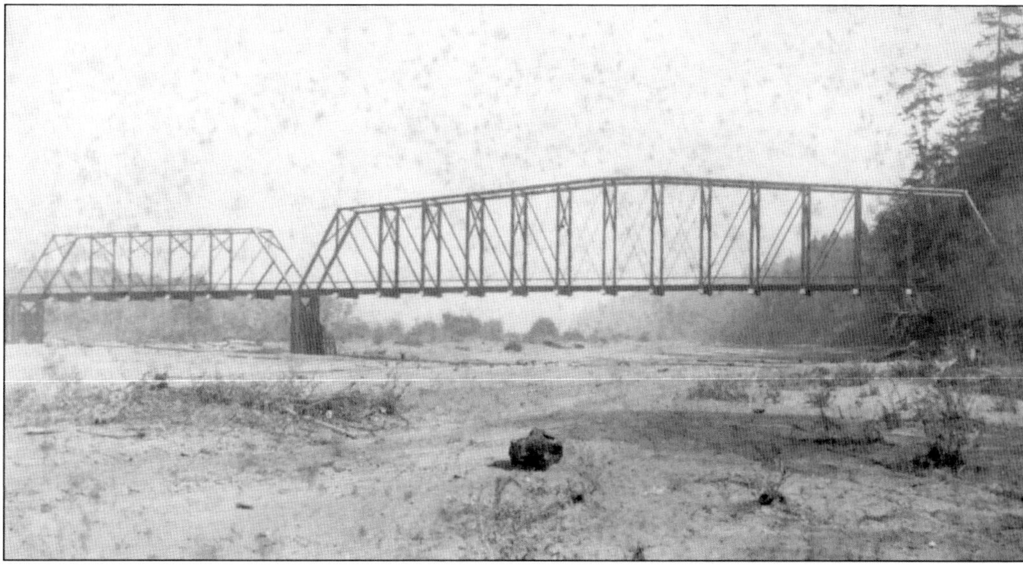

In extending the line north, one obstacle encountered by the Pacific Lumber Company involved crossing the Van Duzen River. In 1884, the company built a steel girder bridge spanning the river. This 1887 photograph reflects the low summertime water levels of the Van Duzen River. This bridge was replaced in 1913 after a large flood in the winter of that year. (Courtesy of HSU.)

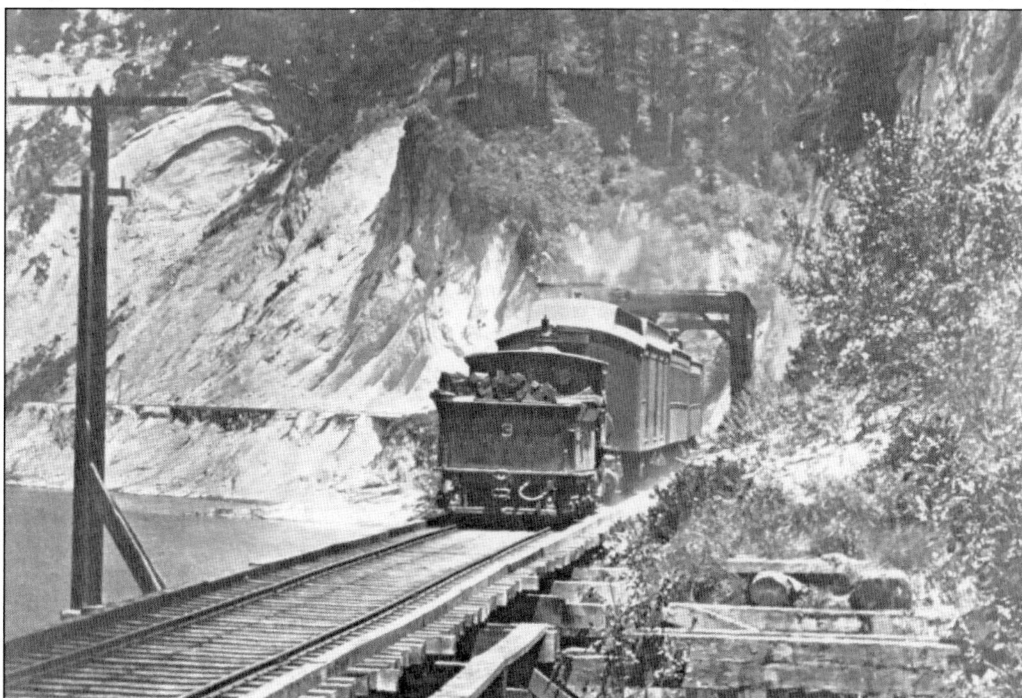

Continuing south, builders of the Pacific Lumber Company line chose to skirt the Eel River on its eastern side, instead constructing two bridges—one on the north end of Rio Dell and one between Rio Dell and Scotia. Advantages of this included access to large redwoods along Nanning Creek. This decision had serious consequences for the line, however, as the route along the Scotia-Rio Dell Bluffs was subject to landslides, which sometimes proved fatal.

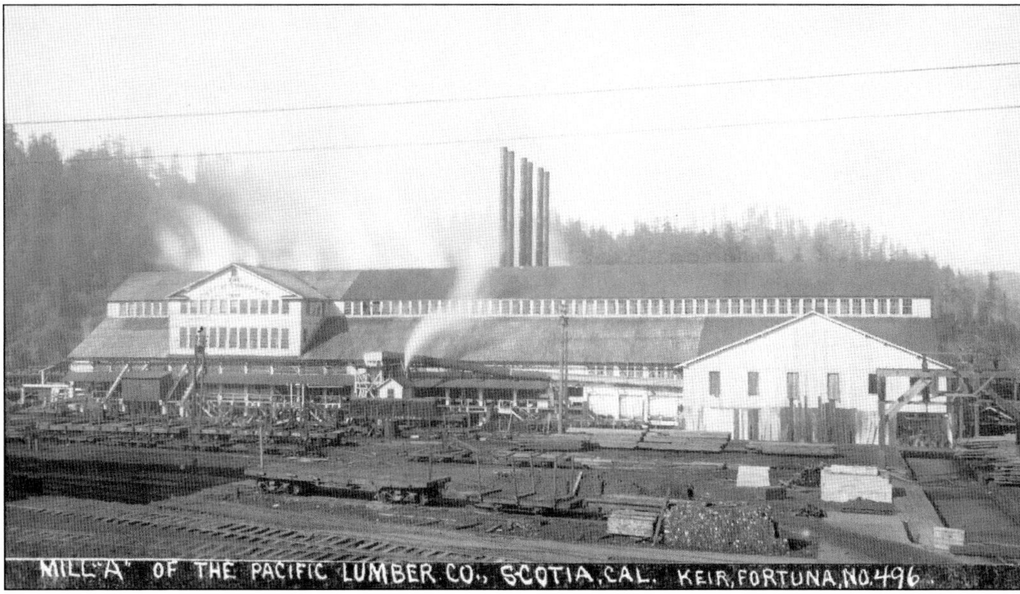

Although it was incorporated in 1869, the Pacific Lumber Company (T.P.L. Co.) did not begin operations until the 1880s. The town of Scotia, originally called Forestville, was the site of this large T.P.L. Co. lumber mill. The company owned 10,000 acres of timber, and the rail line enabled T.P.L. Co. to ship lumber by sea even though the mill was some 25 miles from the port at Fields Landing.

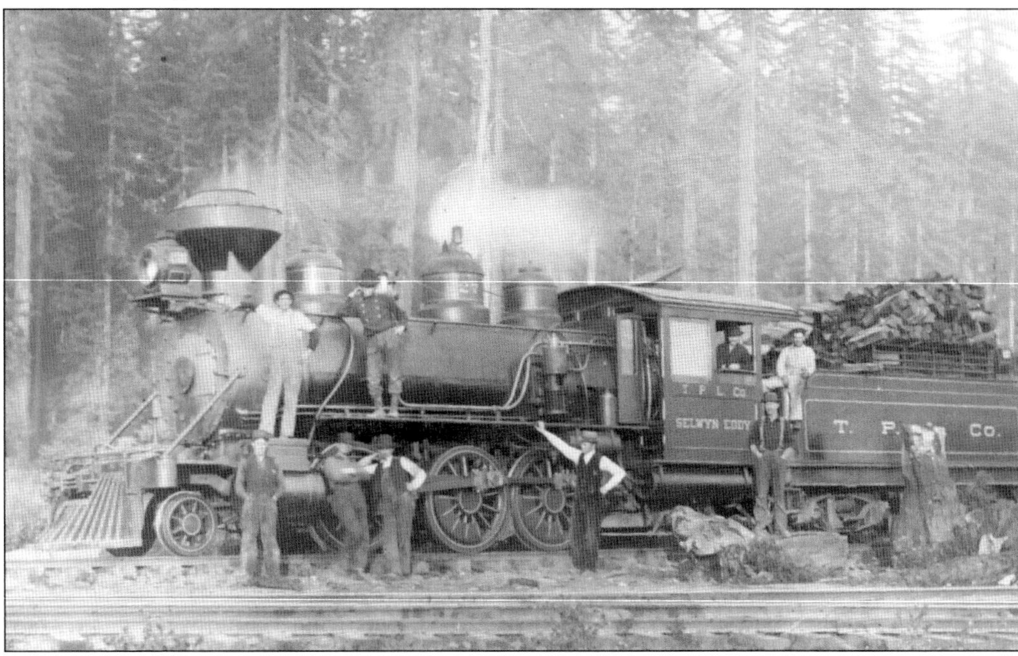

One of the Pacific Lumber Company's locomotives was uniquely known as the "Selwyn Eddy." Both Selwyn and his son, Hiram Eddy, served as presidents of the Pacific Lumber Company in the early 1900s. Manufactured by the Baldwin Company, this locomotive was specifically designed to haul logging trains. In 1909, the *Timberman* described the engine as "a steady riding locomotive which is easy on both rails and flanges when traversing curves."

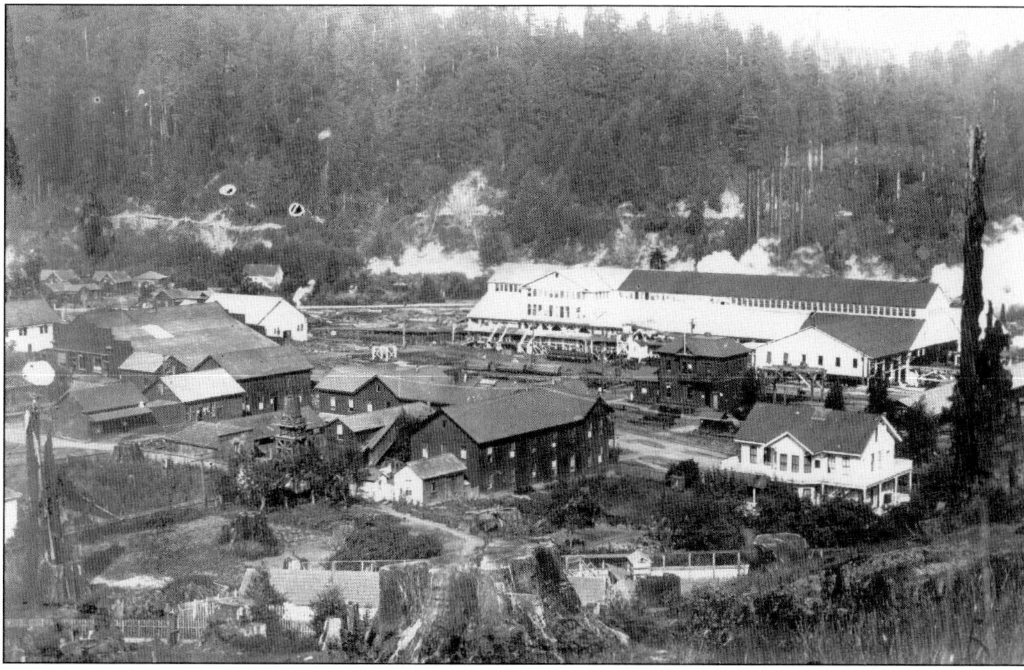

The Pacific Lumber Company, like many other lumber companies at the time, owned its town and rented houses to employees. They also let Scotia residents travel on the railroad, which connected north to Fortuna and Eureka. Passenger trains ran twice a day—a contrast to the more frequent trains bringing logs to the mill or taking lumber north for shipping.

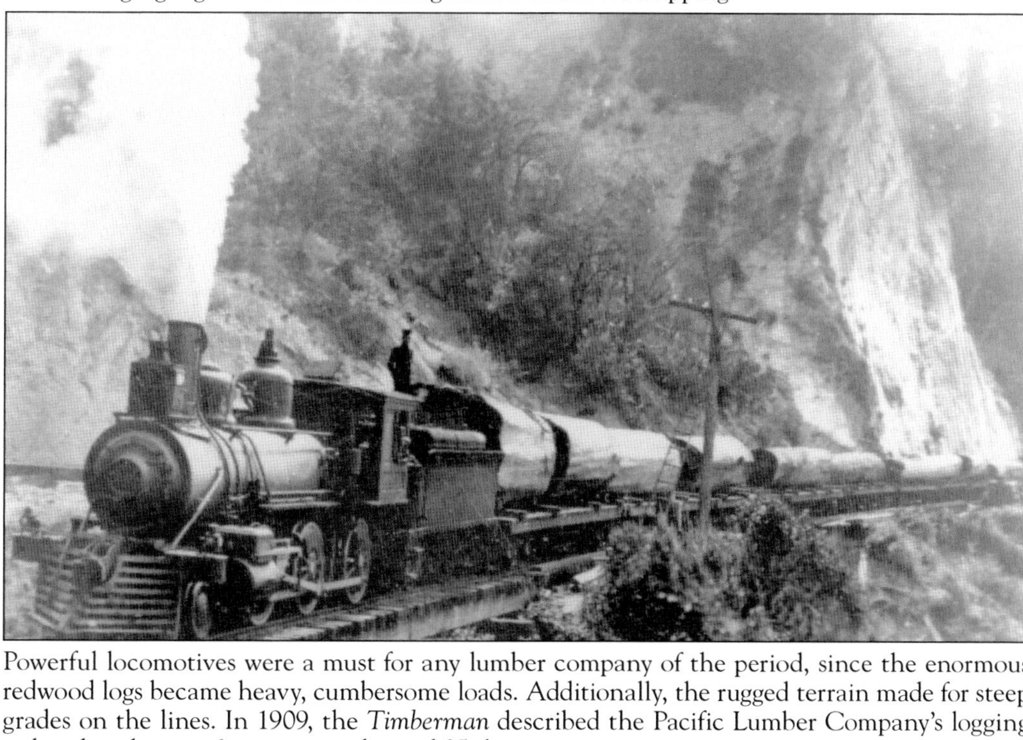

Powerful locomotives were a must for any lumber company of the period, since the enormous redwood logs became heavy, cumbersome loads. Additionally, the rugged terrain made for steep grades on the lines. In 1909, the *Timberman* described the Pacific Lumber Company's logging railroads as having 6-percent grades and 35-degree curves.

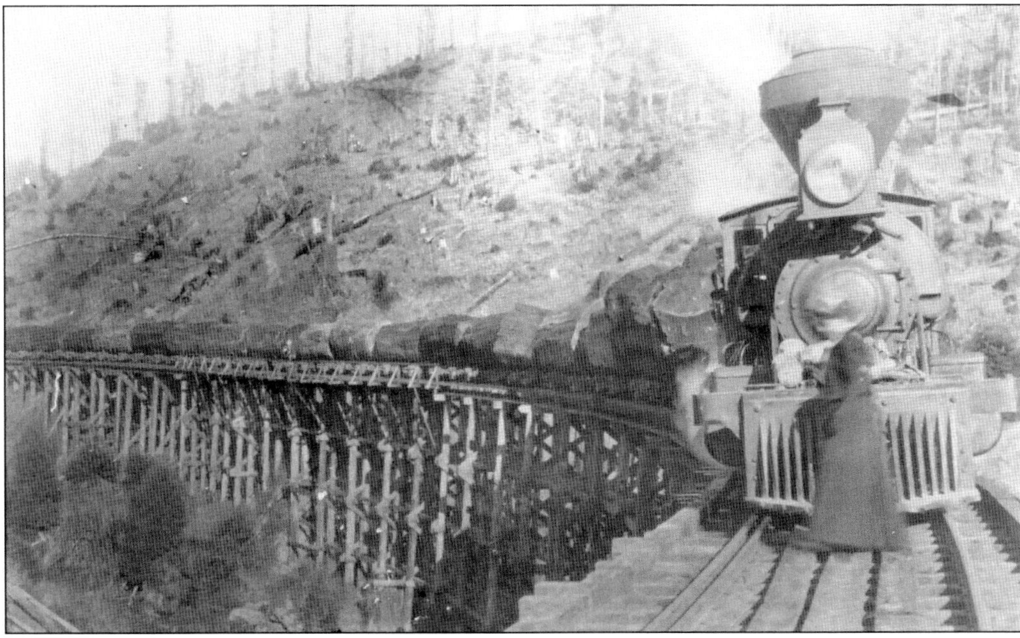

In order to meet the ever-growing demand for lumber, the Pacific Lumber Company built a rail line south along the east side of the Eel River to access towering stands of redwoods. This photograph, which shows a long log train parked while a woman crosses in front of it near Stitz Creek south of Scotia, illustrates the thoroughness with which logging companies cleared hillsides of timber.

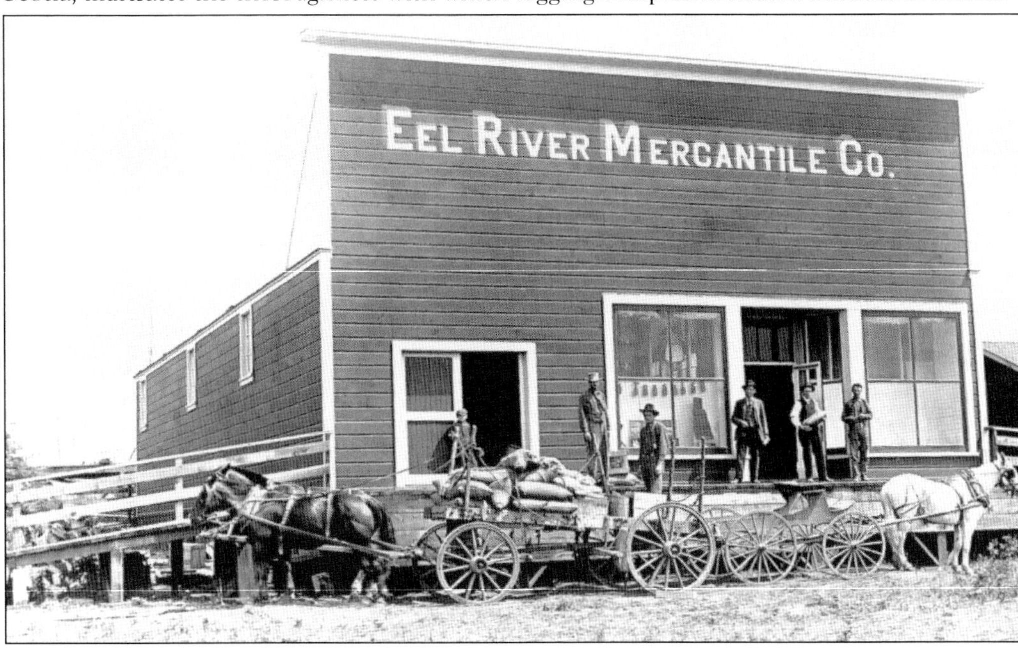

In 1906, T.P.L. Co.'s railroad reached Shively. The Eel River Mercantile was just one of the stores that supplied logging camps in the area. Shively, which became the southern terminus of the railroad, contained 11 houses of ill repute, 12 bars, several hotels, and other businesses. When the railroad was completed to Willits, Shively became a farming community and never regained the prominence it had in the early 20th century.

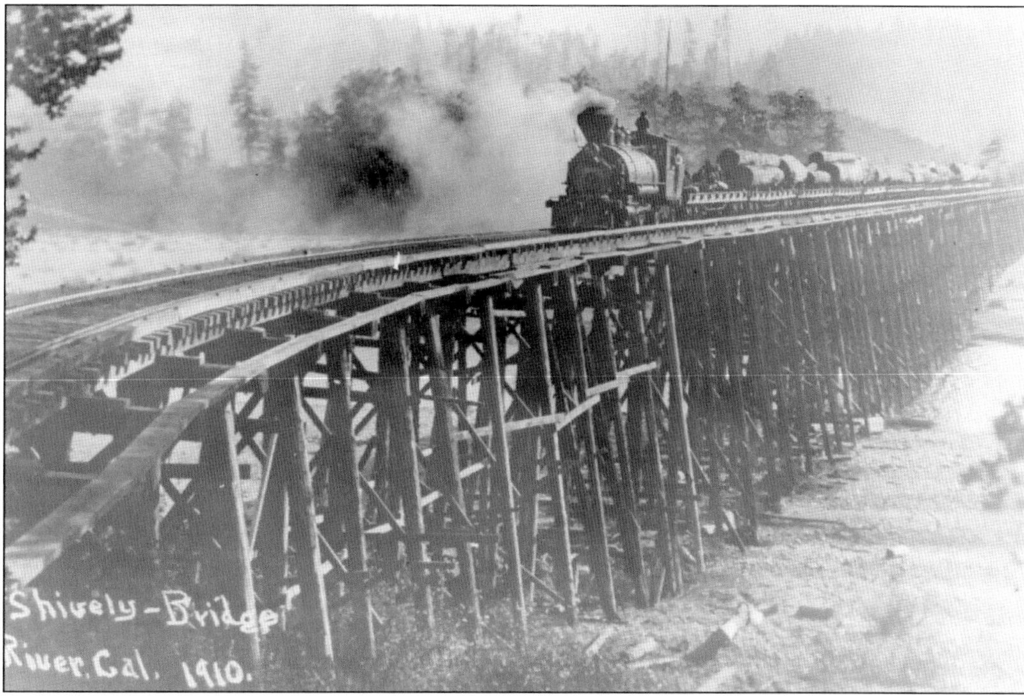

This image features the Pacific Lumber Company's locomotive No. 25. Purchased by the company in 1904, the steam locomotive was sold shortly afterward to Holmes Eureka Lumber Company. The bridge in this photograph demonstrates how redwood lumber was not only shipped on the line but also used to build it. Redwood does not rapidly decay and is easy to split into railroad ties. The remains of this bridge can be seen today between Shively and Holmes Flat.

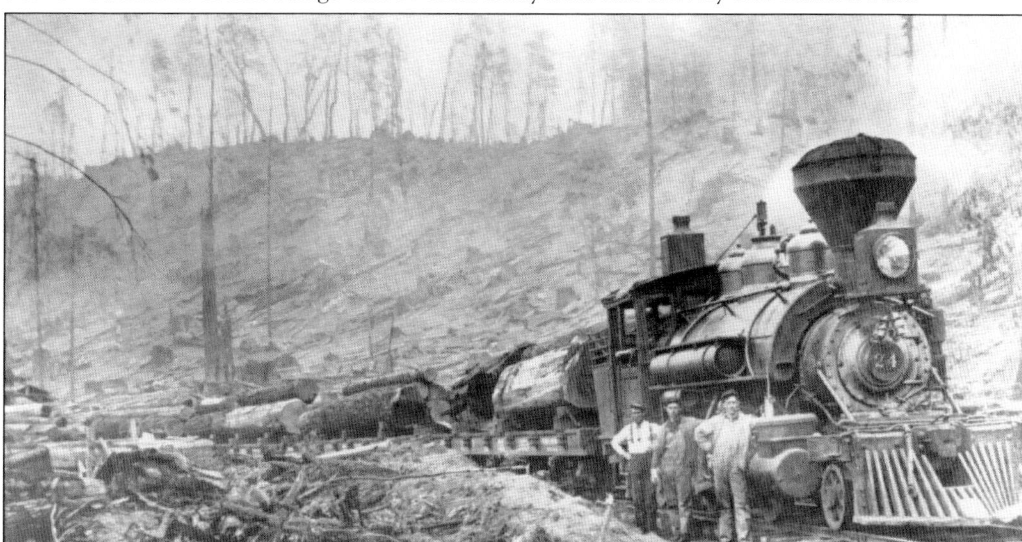

The early logging railroads also served as training grounds for future employees of the Northwestern Pacific. This photograph of T.P.L. Co.'s engine No. 24 at the company's logging operations in Shively shows Ed Weatherby (right), as well as Harry O'Conn and Henry Allen. Weatherby went on to be an engineer for the NWP and was tragically killed in a train wreck in 1937. (Courtesy of HSU.)

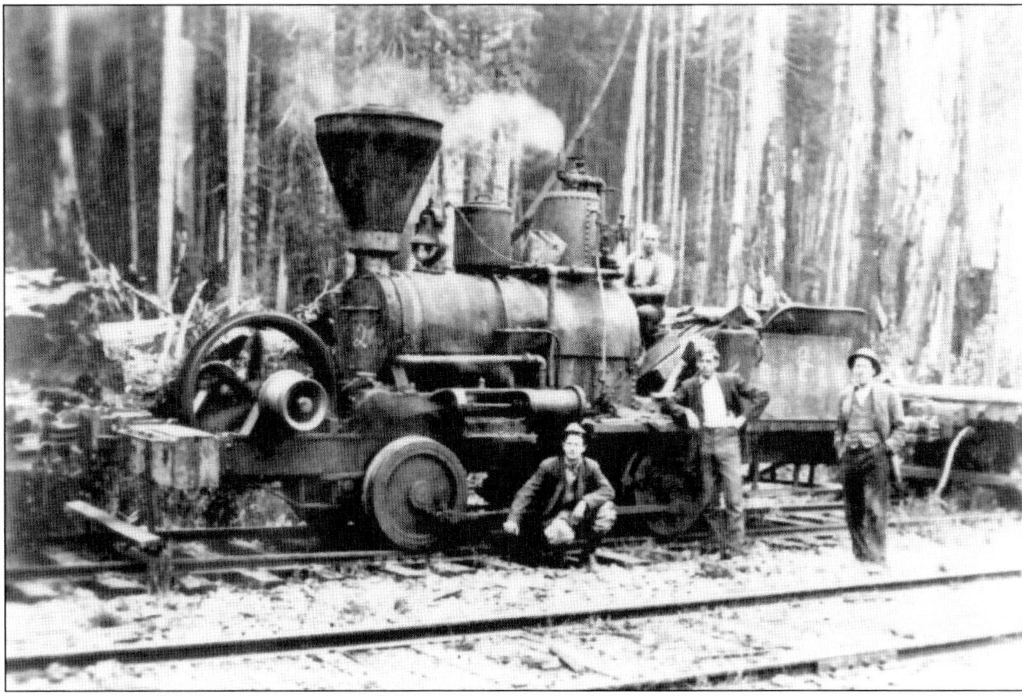

In the early years of the 20th century, the logging railroads and the ER&ERR captured the attention of two large railroad conglomerates—the Santa Fe and the Southern Pacific. The Santa Fe purchased the rights and lines of the ER&ERR, which then stretched from Eureka to Shively. To block further expansion, Henry Huntington, one of the magnates of the Southern Pacific and a major shareholder in the Hammond Lumber Company, purchased rail lines operated by Hammond as the Eureka & Klamath Railroad and the Humboldt Railroad. In 1903, he renamed the line the Oregon & Eureka Railroad. Huntington then leased the line back for the sole use of the Hammond Lumber Company. By 1905, the O&E had 9 locomotives and 212 freight cars.

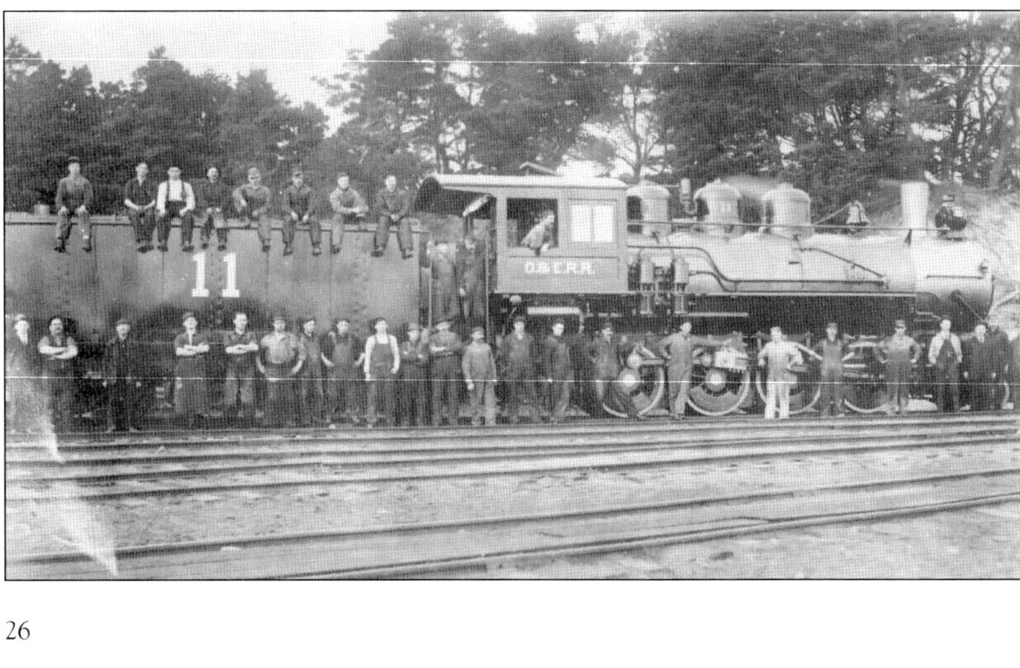

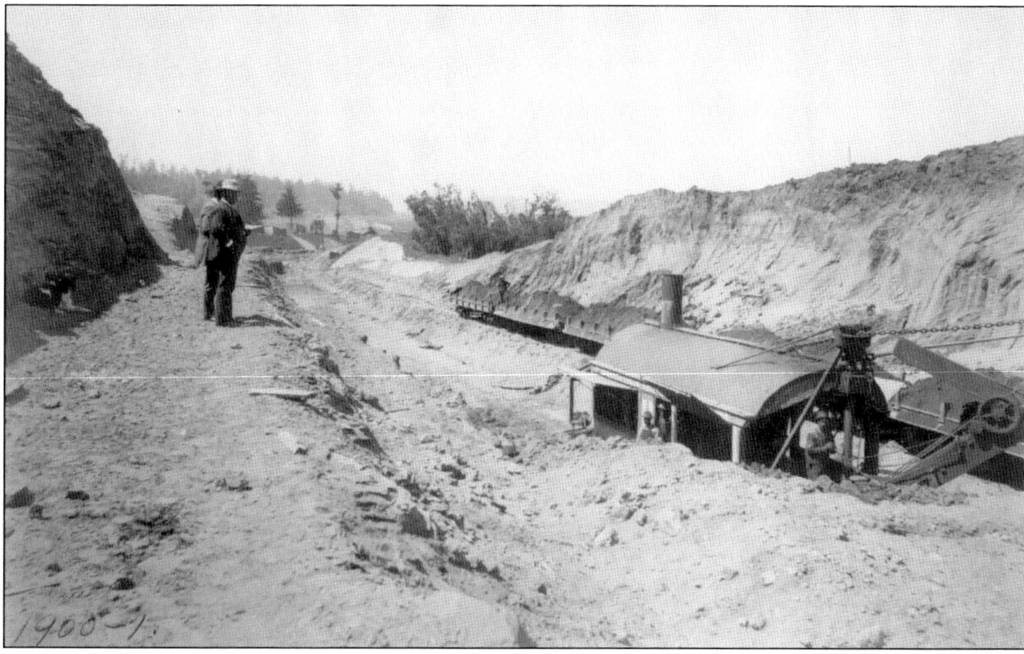

Railroad lines had also been constructed north of Eureka. In 1900, John Vance—now the sole owner of the ER&ERR—pushed the line north toward Arcata. One of the areas the line cut through was Brainard's Point, a name later shortened to Bra-Cut. Here, a large steam shovel is cutting through the sand to create the level surface required for trains. (Courtesy of HSU.)

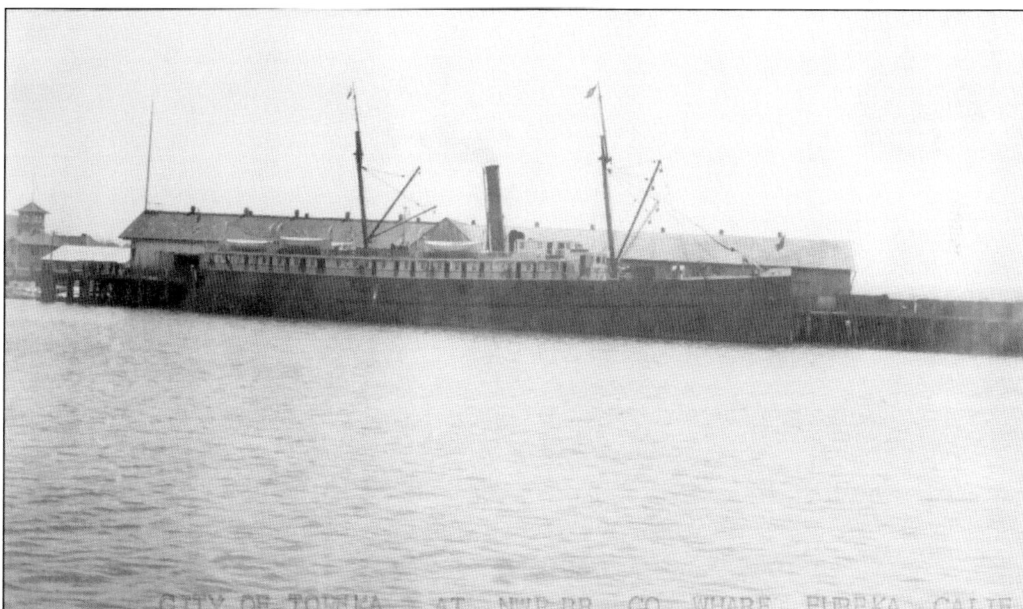

In addition to wanting to build a line south, railroad magnates were also interested in creating a monopoly on shipping by sea. Therefore, the large railroad companies focused most intensely on acquiring rights to rail lines by purchasing waterfront property along Humboldt Bay. Here, the *City of Topeka* is tied up at the NWP wharf in Eureka. In the background, the Santa Fe emblem is visible on the Eureka depot.

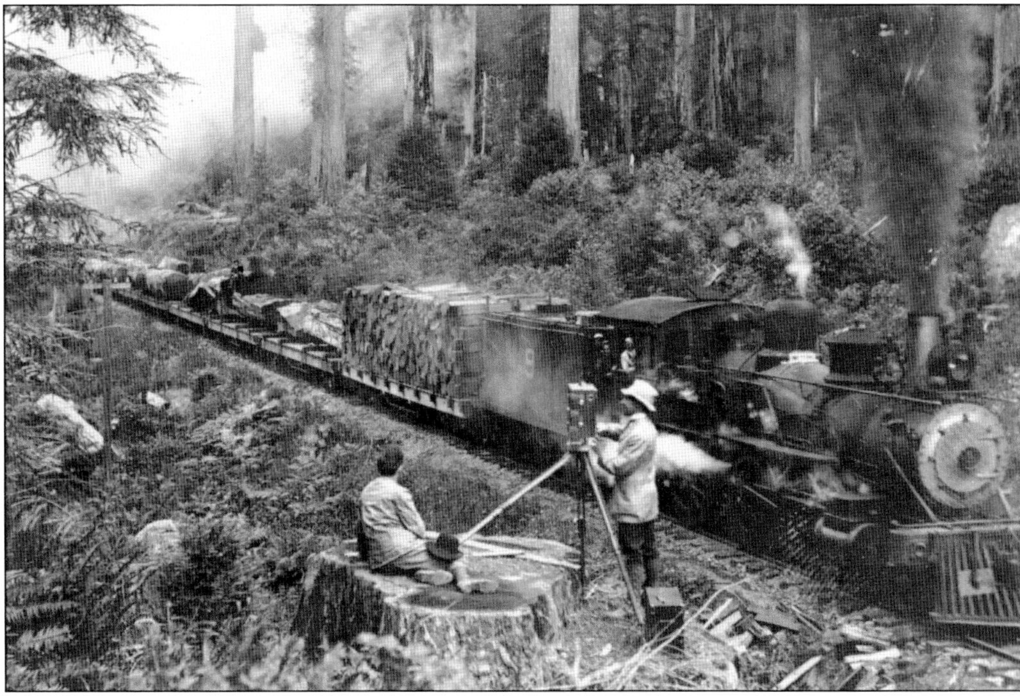

In addition to uniting his logging lines with the ER&ERR, John Vance also wanted to link Arcata and Eureka. Other lumber companies soon took advantage of Vance's expanded line. The Hammond Lumber Company purchased Vance's mill and logging railroad operations in 1902. This is Hammond's locomotive No. 9, purchased from the Eureka & Klamath Railroad. (Courtesy of HSU.)

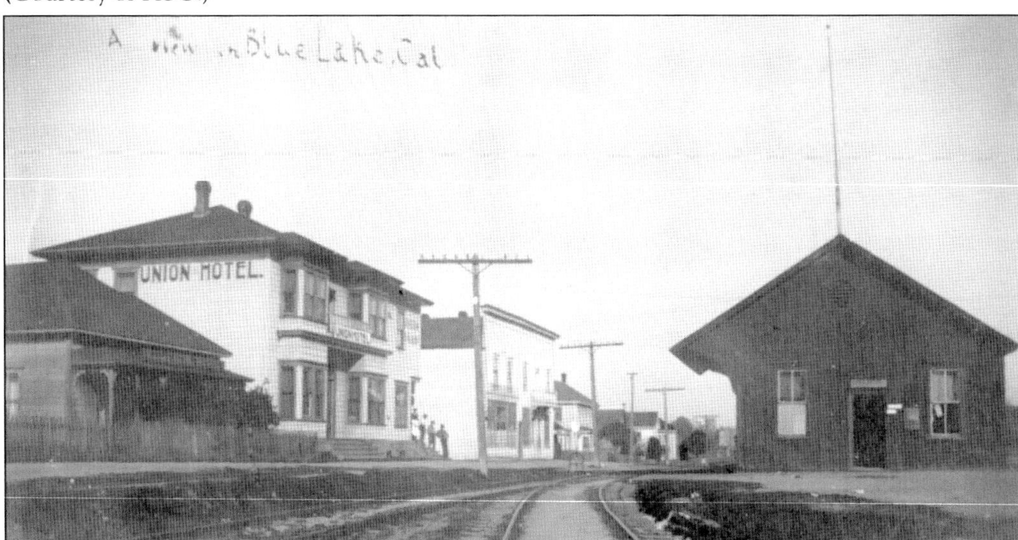

Blue Lake started as a ranching community. By the early 1900s, it was surrounded by mills, notably the large operation of the Korbel brothers to the north. In 1883, the owners of the Korbel Lumber Company connected Blue Lake to Humboldt Bay by rail. Named the Arcata & Mad River Railroad, it was commonly called the Annie & Mary after two secretaries who worked for the railroad. (Courtesy of HSU.)

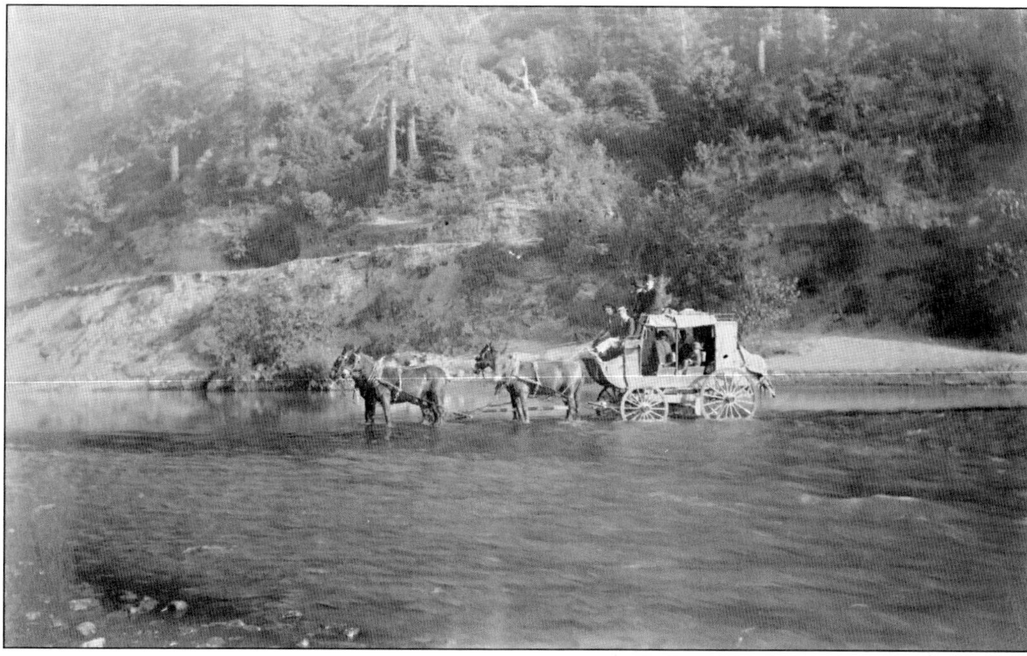

Despite numerous railroads built in Humboldt County, it remained isolated at the start of the 20th century. Annual articles about the county in the *San Francisco Chronicle* constantly remarked that the region needed a railroad south. Transportation to San Francisco was limited to boat or stagecoaches. Residents could travel by rail within the county but had to face river crossings and muddy roads if they wanted to travel south.

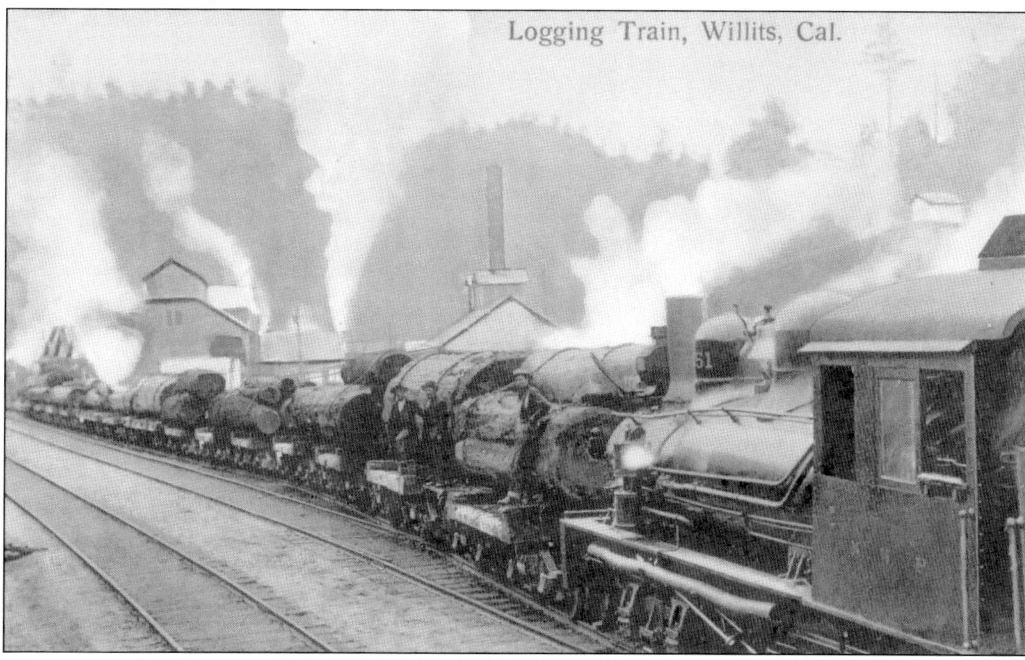

The town of Willits is 100 miles south of Shively. Willits was linked to San Francisco as the northern terminus of the railroads operated by the Southern Pacific. The line was constructed in a piecemeal fashion in the late 1800s to ship lumber, livestock, and fruit, as well as passengers.

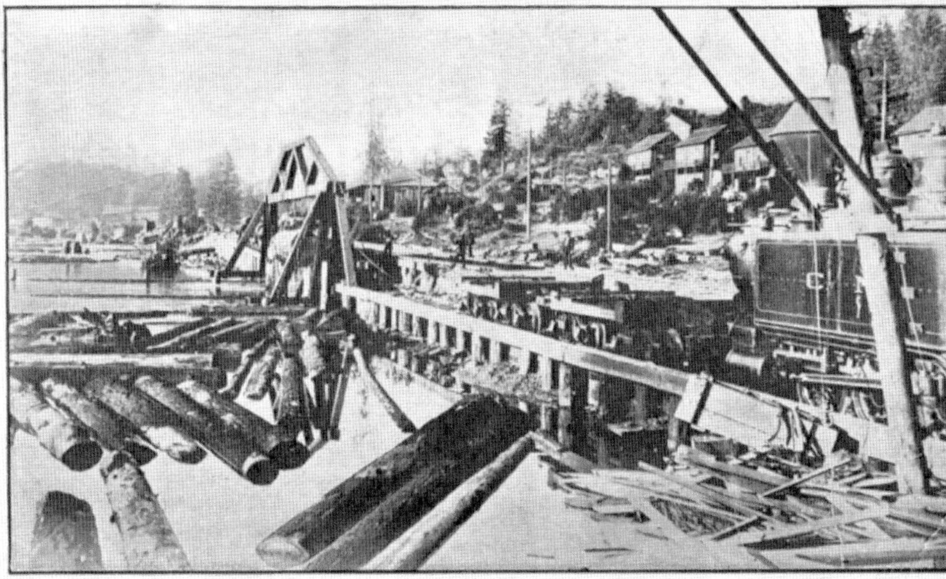

UNLOADING LOGS AT DIAMOND D MILL, WILLITS, CALIF.

Willits had several mills around town and was connected to Fort Bragg by rail in 1911 via the California Western Railroad. In the early 20th century, Willits was becoming a prosperous community with mills and railroads bringing many new residents to the region. Signs of wealth could be found in the many new buildings—especially Craftsman-style bungalows—constructed in the town.

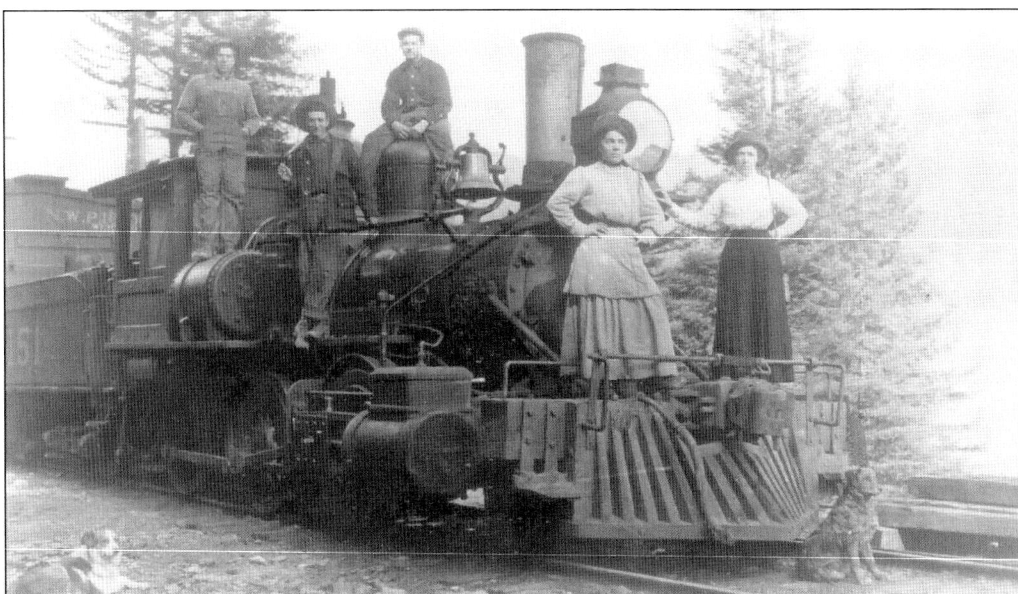

In 1906, officials from the Santa Fe and Southern Pacific Railroads realized that there was not enough profit available to sustain two lines. They created a subsidiary, the Northwestern Pacific Railroad, to unite Eureka and Willits and ultimately construct a line that would run from Sausalito (on the San Francisco Bay) to Trinidad (north of Humboldt Bay). NWP engine No. 151 is pictured here near Eureka in 1910. (Courtesy of NWPRRHS.)

Two

Construction of the NWP

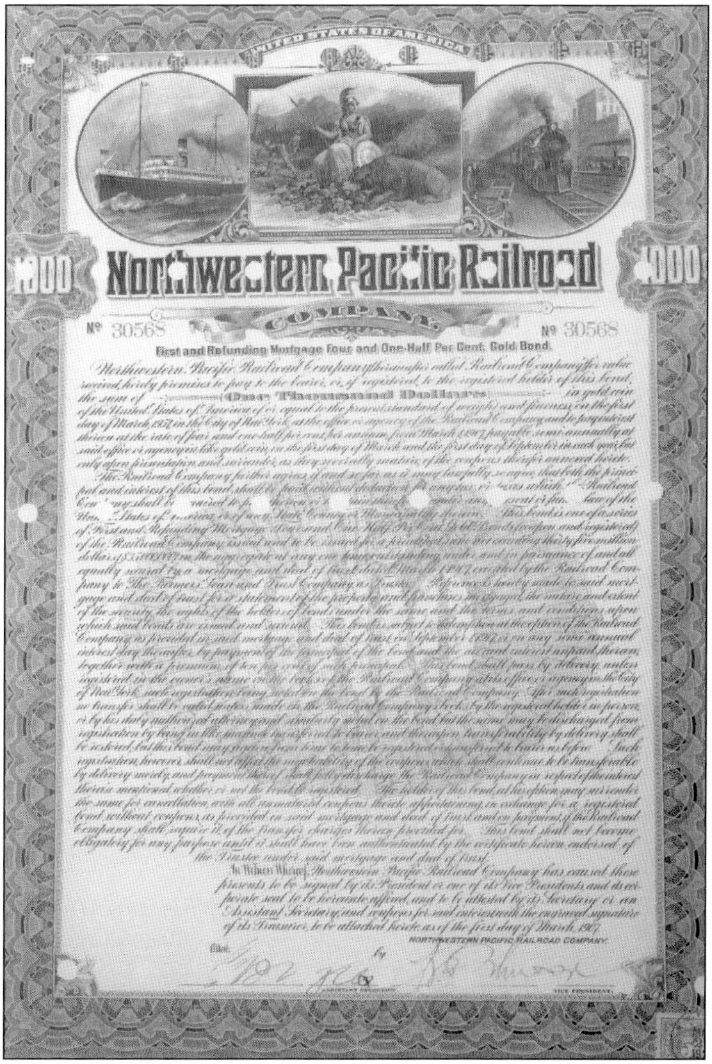
UNITED STATES OF AMERICA

1000 Northwestern Pacific Railroad Company 1000

Nº 30568 Nº 30568

First and Refunding Mortgage Four and One-Half Per Cent. Gold Bond.

One Thousand Dollars

NORTHWESTERN PACIFIC RAILROAD COMPANY.

In September 1906, power brokers from the Santa Fe and Southern Pacific railroads created the Northwestern Pacific Railroad to run from Trinidad to Sausalito. The nascent company needed to build nearly 110 miles of railroad, and that construction required money. In 1907, the NWP sold bonds to raise $35 million toward building costs. In April 1906, plans for the line had been destroyed in the San Francisco earthquake and fire.

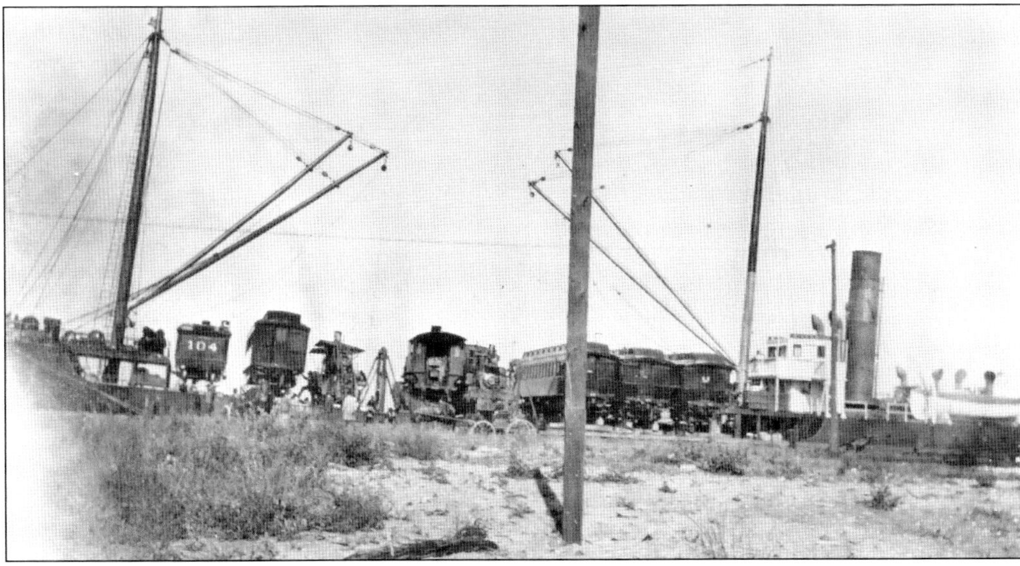

One of the first signs of NWP construction on the northern end was the arrival of rolling stock by sea, shown being unloaded at Fields Landing. Passenger cars, locomotives, and tenders were all shipped for use on the northern end. The locomotives would also help bring supplies to worksites as they pushed south from Shively.

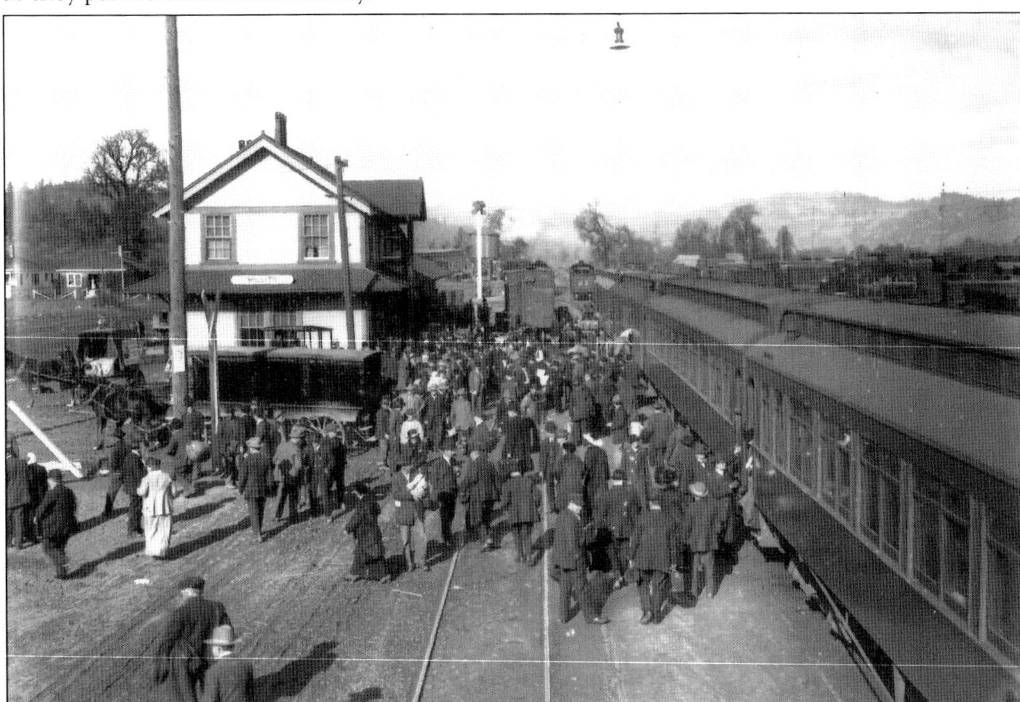

The first phase of construction from Willits was building north along Outlet Creek toward Longvale. The Willits depot is pictured here at the beginning of the 20th century. Built according to specifications for the "Two-story Combination Depot Number 22" of the Southern Pacific, it was replaced with a unique redwood Craftsman-style building that is still used today by the California Western Railroad, which connects Willits with Fort Bragg. (Courtesy of NWPRRHS.)

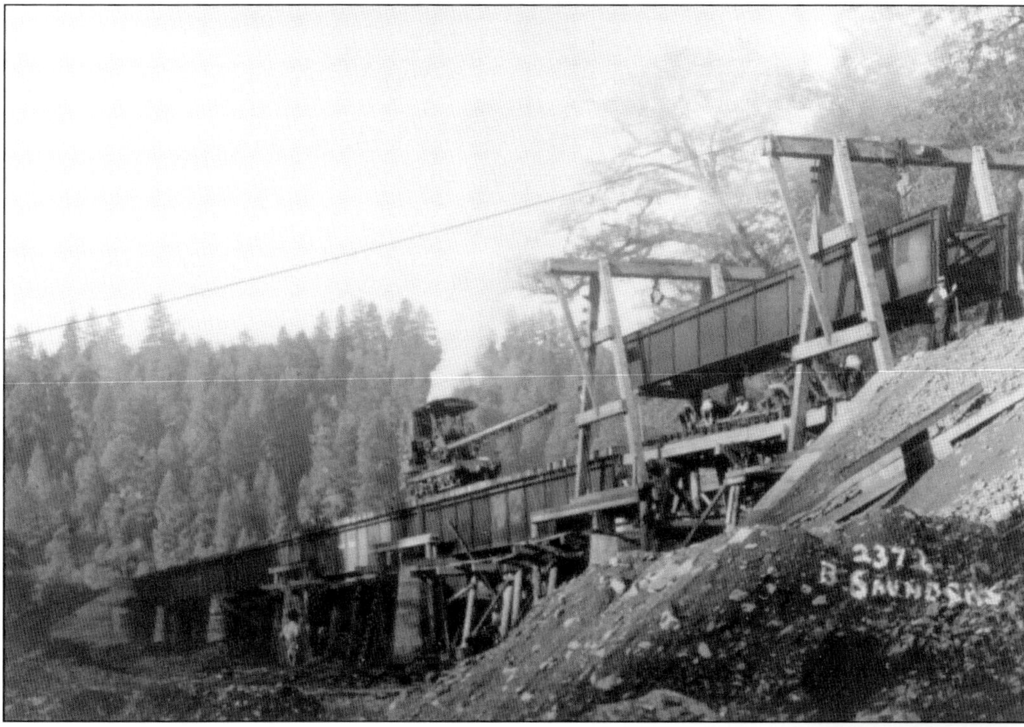

Construction of the NWP was divided into 10 sections with the intent, according to a report in a 1907 edition of the *Ukiah Dispatch Democrat*, "that the grading of each section (be done) separately in order that the work might be completed in the least possible time. It is the intention of the company to complete the work within a year." This goal proved optimistic, as weather, rough terrain, and economic woes delayed construction.

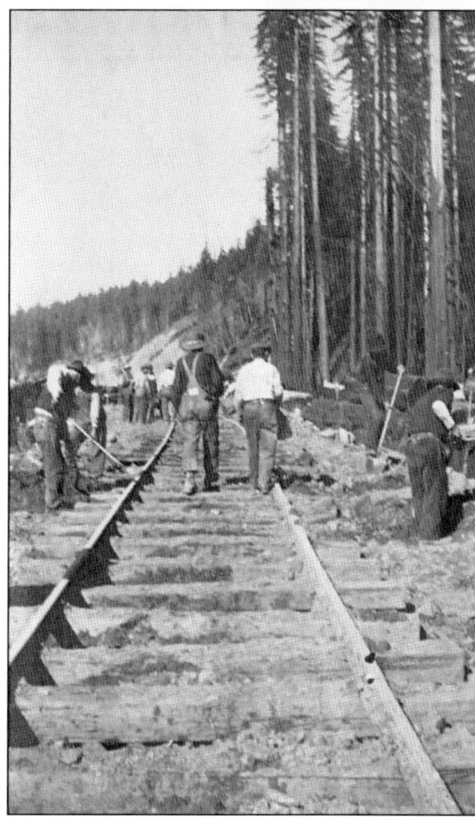

Later in 1907, the *Ukiah Dispatch Democrat* reported that "the first scenes of operations will be on the most difficult part of the route, below Pepperwood, in Humboldt County. It is expected that sufficient progress will be made on the tunnels and bridges in that locality to enable the entire extension to be finished by the end of the year." Willett and Burr, a San Francisco-based company, was responsible for the construction.

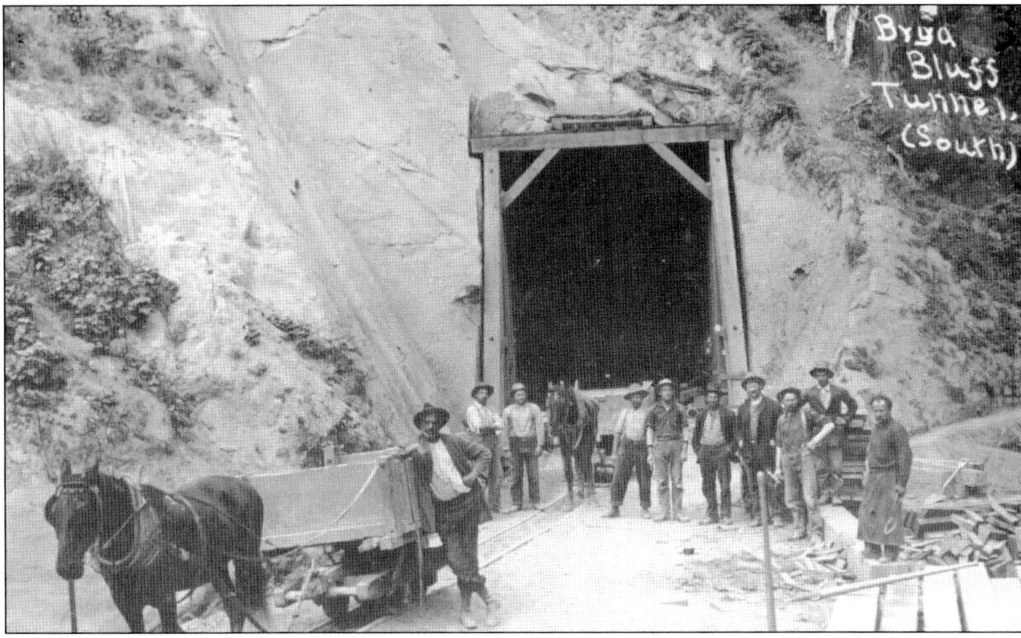

In the fall of 1907, work stopped on the expansion due to a lawsuit, filed in federal court, concerning the perceived monopoly of railroads in California. Work recommenced in 1909, with the *Ukiah Dispatch Democrat* noting in February that the tunnel between Shively and Larabee—Bryan's Bluff Tunnel—had been excavated some 25 feet of the needed 1,200 feet and was being bored in sandstone. (Courtesy of HSU.)

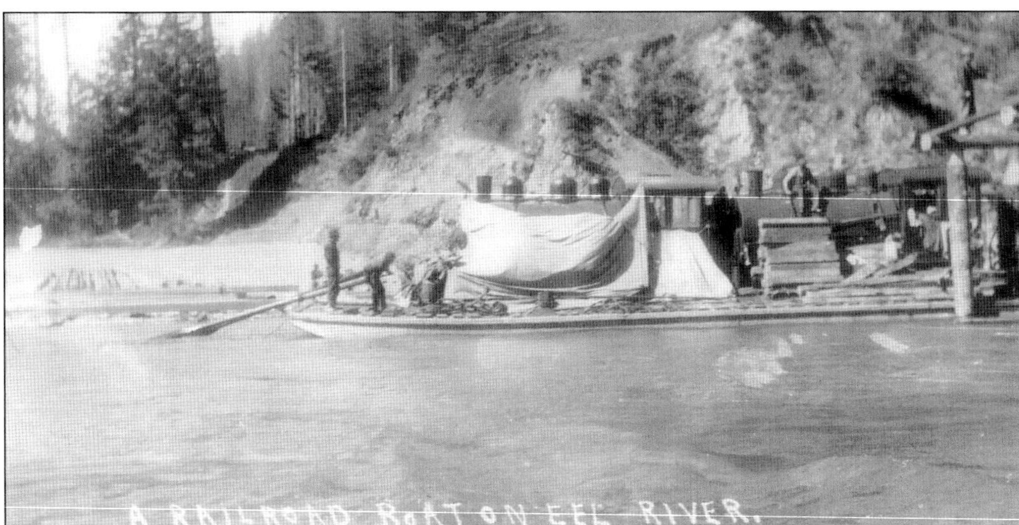

Another obstacle the NWP faced was how to transport men and supplies to where they were needed. In the remote Eel River canyon, the problem was solved when, as the *Ukiah Daily Journal* reported in December 1910, "one of the scows which are to be used in the manner of canal boats in transporting material up Eel River was shipped from this city yesterday . . . with the aid of power boats . . . there will be no difficulty in keeping many of the camps along the river supplied with necessities throughout the winter."

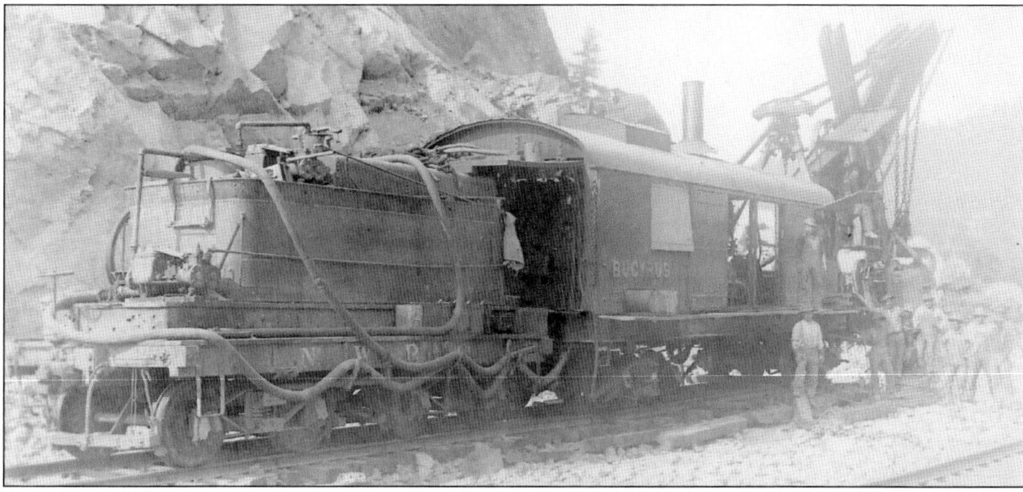

In February 1910, the *Ukiah Dispatch Democrat* reported that at the Shively work site "two large steam shovels, one of them a cumbersome seventy-ton affair, have arrived from San Francisco Iron Works . . . and with their arrival the force of men at work in Shively will be considerably increased." In April of that year, the *Ukiah Dispatch Herald* noted, "one steam shovel is throwing dirt and the other will begin work within the week at the Shively Tunnel." The operation of the larger steam shovel was hindered by the failure to ship parts necessary for operation. The delay in making the larger shovel operational also slowed construction, because the smaller shovel only moved dirt from the track, whereas the larger shovel cleared the entire right-of-way. (Above, courtesy of NWPRRHS.)

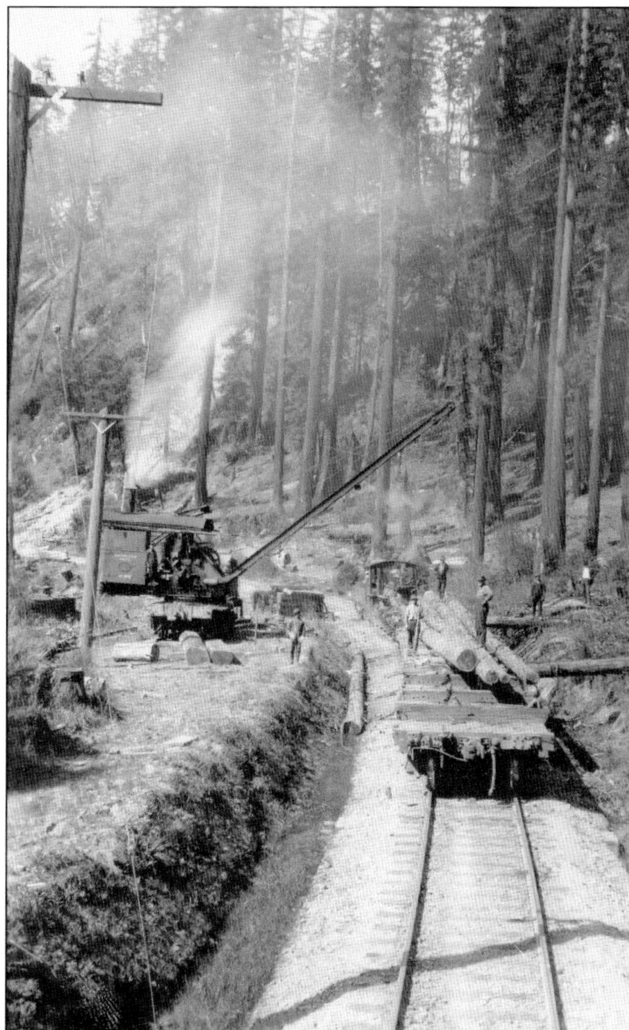

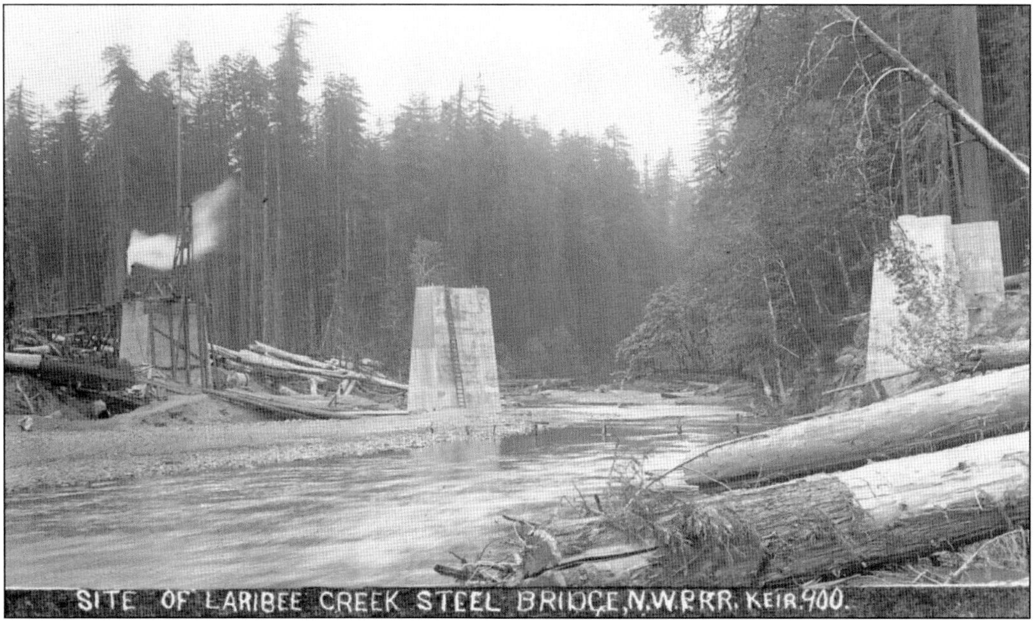

In 1910, $11 million was allocated for construction—much of it needed for bridgework. After completing Bryan's Bluff Tunnel, construction crews reached Laribee (or Larabee) Valley, where they needed to build a bridge in order to cross Laribee Creek. This image shows the all-purpose steam donkey engine, developed by James Dolbeer of Eureka for use in logging, on the concrete bridge pier. The upright steam engine could be used for many purposes, including as a pile driver. (Courtesy of HSU.)

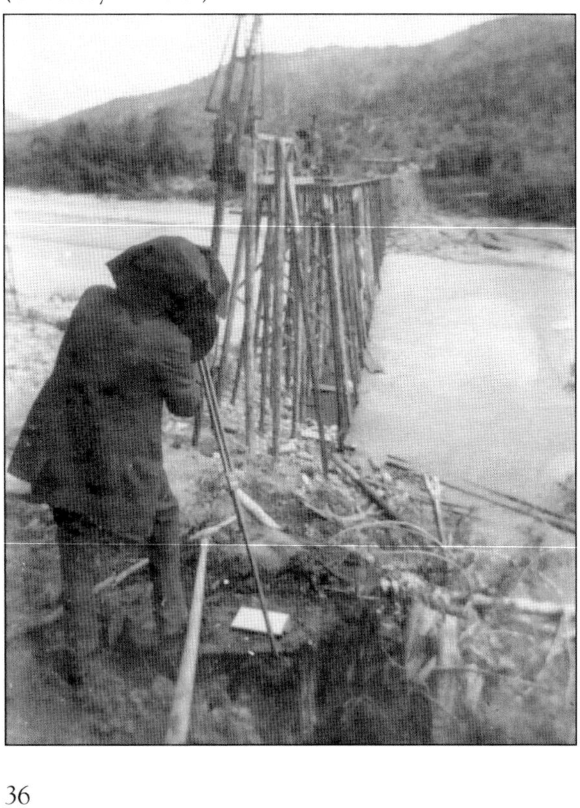

A longer bridge was required at the confluence of the south and main forks of the Eel River. After crews reached the confluence in 1910, bridge construction took most of that year. In April 1910, six tons of structural steel arrived in Eureka so that crews could begin construction. Here, a photographer captures the initial bridgework. (Courtesy of HRIA.)

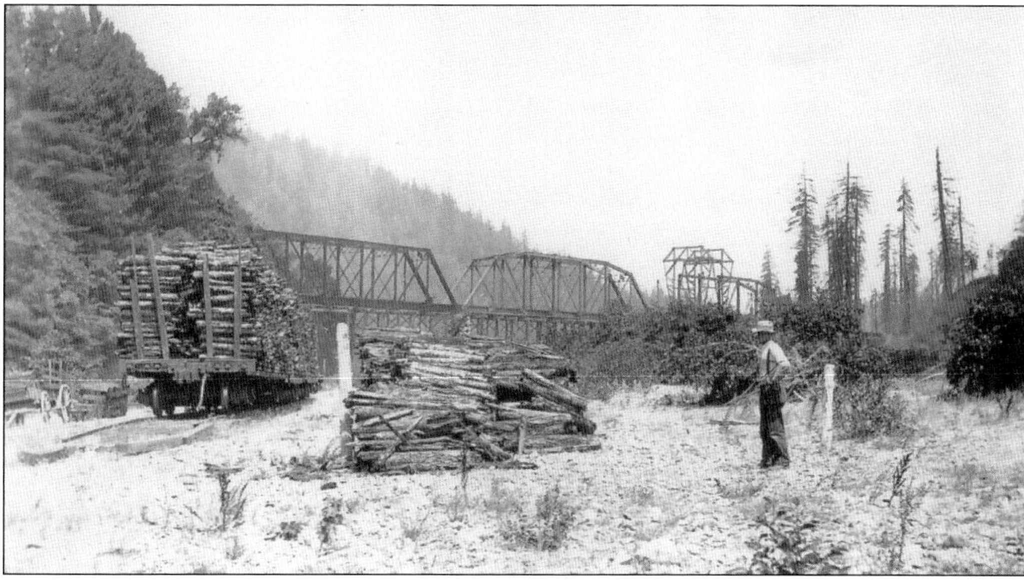

As at Laribee Creek, concrete piers provided stability for the Eel River bridge. In August 1910, workers erected four piers, taking advantage of the low water that allowed workers access along the river bar. This photograph shows a railroad spur built onto the river bar to haul tanbark, which was harvested in late summer. The bark of the tan oak tree was peeled and shipped to tanneries, where the tannins were leached out of the bark. (Courtesy of NWPRRHS.)

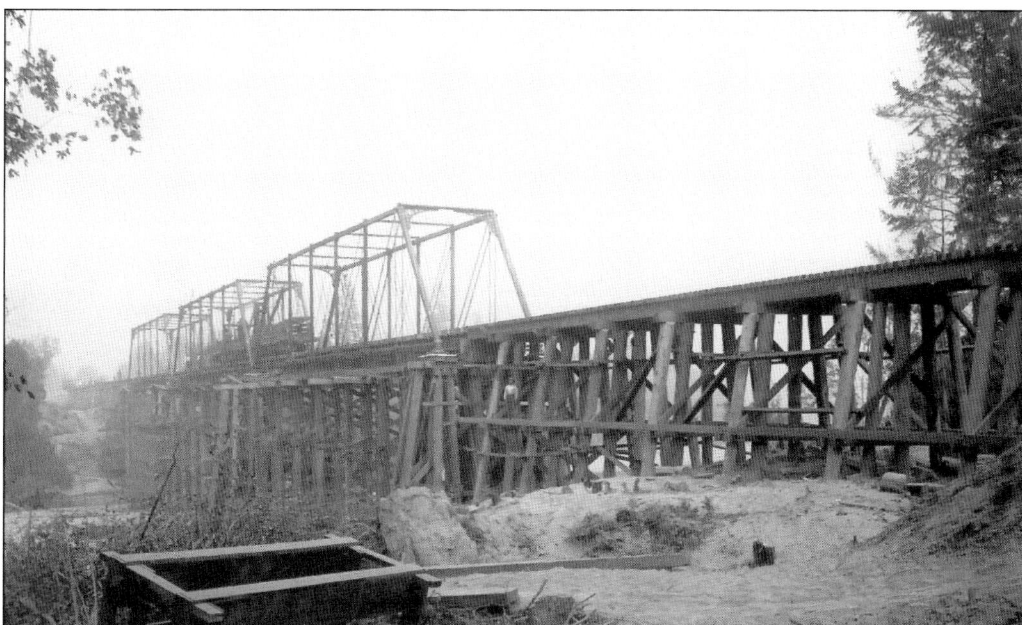

The new Eel River bridge allowed timber companies access to many miles of redwood lands. A town—South Fork—sprang into existence near the bridge. The new community eventually usurped Dyerville's importance to the region, and the local post office moved to South Fork in 1933. South Fork was a loading depot for many of the mills in the area as well as a shipping point for both tanbark and locally produced railroad ties.

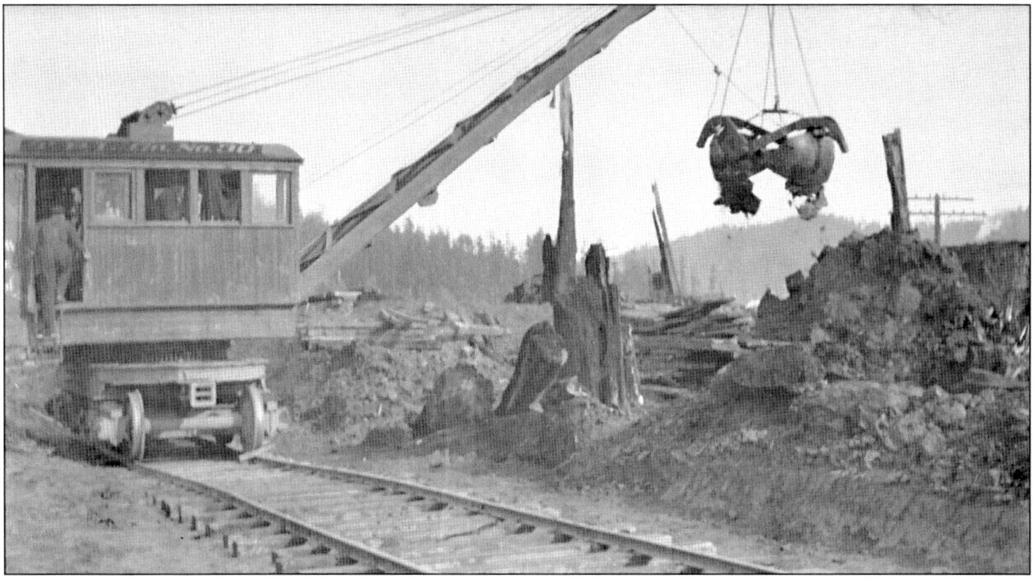

Construction also continued north from Longvale. Since these workers did not have to bore so many tunnels, the northward work moved more quickly. Additionally, steam shovels and other tools could be transported along rail lines instead of being shipped to Eureka on steamers. In 1910, there were several railroad camps in northern Mendocino County. The November 18 issue of the *Ukiah Republican Press* included an account of a trip to these railroad camps. The writer explained, "A person who has never been along this route or who has never seen a great amount of railroad construction work can not realize the vast amount of labor and engineering skill necessary to build a railroad through the mountainous country which this survey passes."

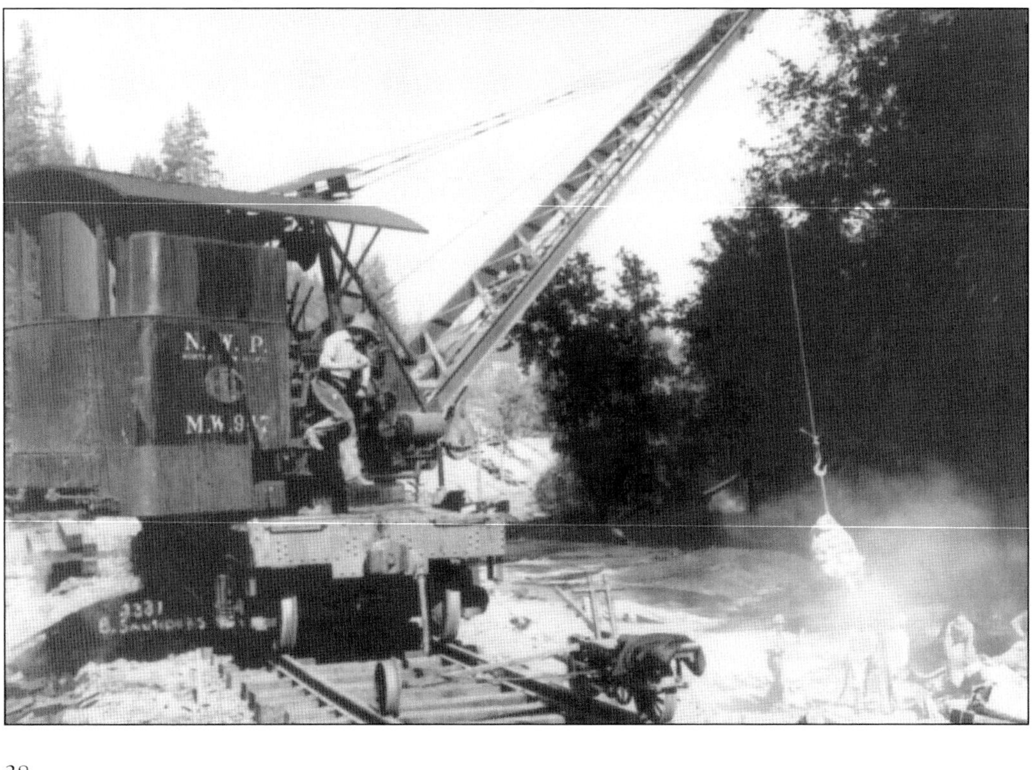

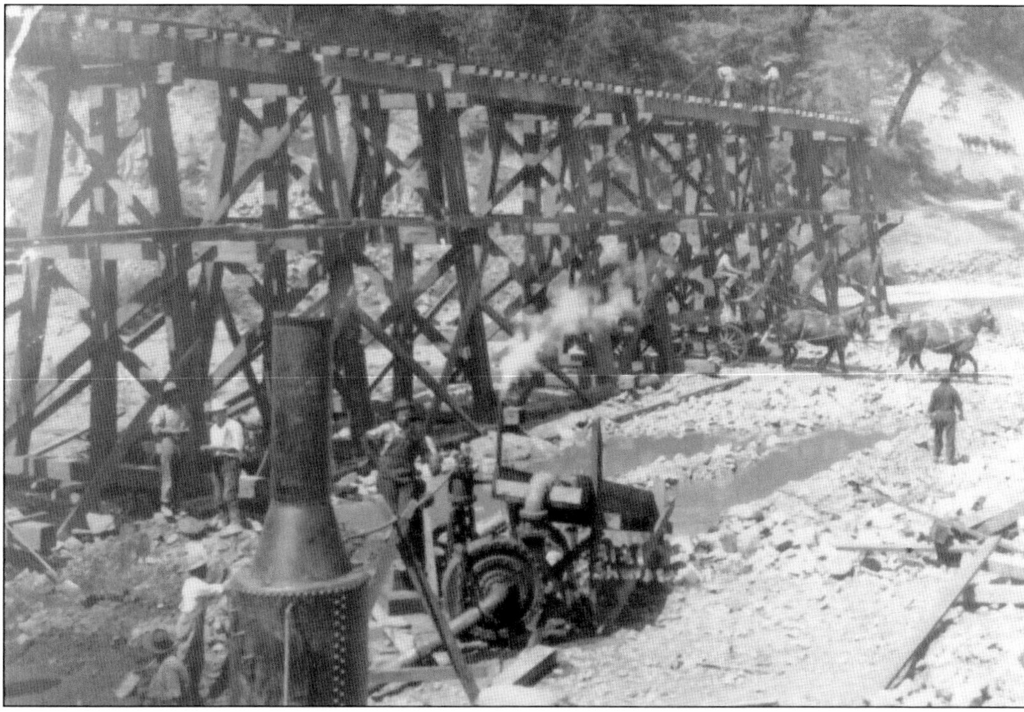

As the route extended north from Willits, it paralleled Outlet Creek as it turned toward Round Valley, with the line following the creek north and east to the Eel River. This is the bridge that crossed Longvale Creek as the line continued to what became known as Dos Rios. The line to Longvale, 13 miles north of Willits, opened for limited traffic on August 1, 1911.

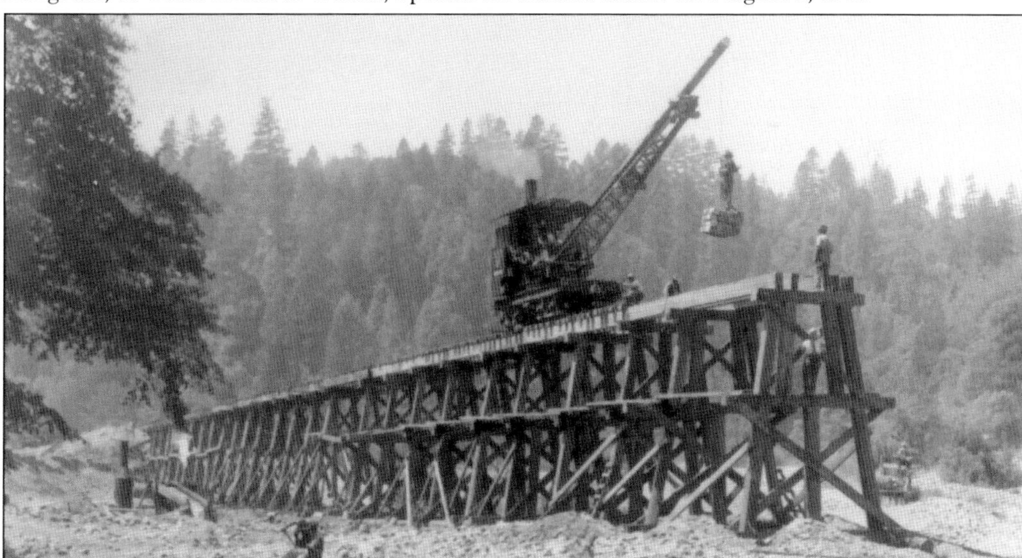

In November 1910, W.O. White, the editor of the *Ukiah Republican Press*, visited the railroad camps. At one camp, he learned that "engineers figure . . . the angle, depth, width, or height of each curve and cut, the cost of the removal of each shovelful of dirt, the size and cost of every timber used, and the cost of removing every rock, no matter the size, and how to do it in the most economical way."

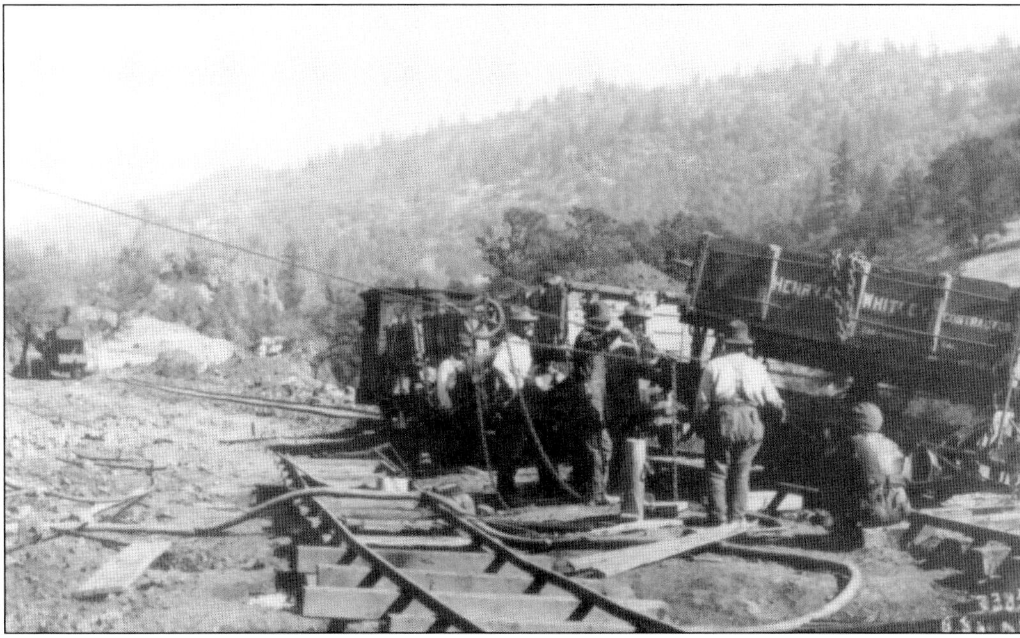

In his November 1910 reports, W.O. White, editor of the *Ukiah Republican Press*, also noted that "the Chief Engineer is a very busy man, . . . [and after an] interview with him you will come to the conclusion that what that man does not know about the different formations of the earth and rock and the sizes and strengths of different kinds of timber is not worth knowing."

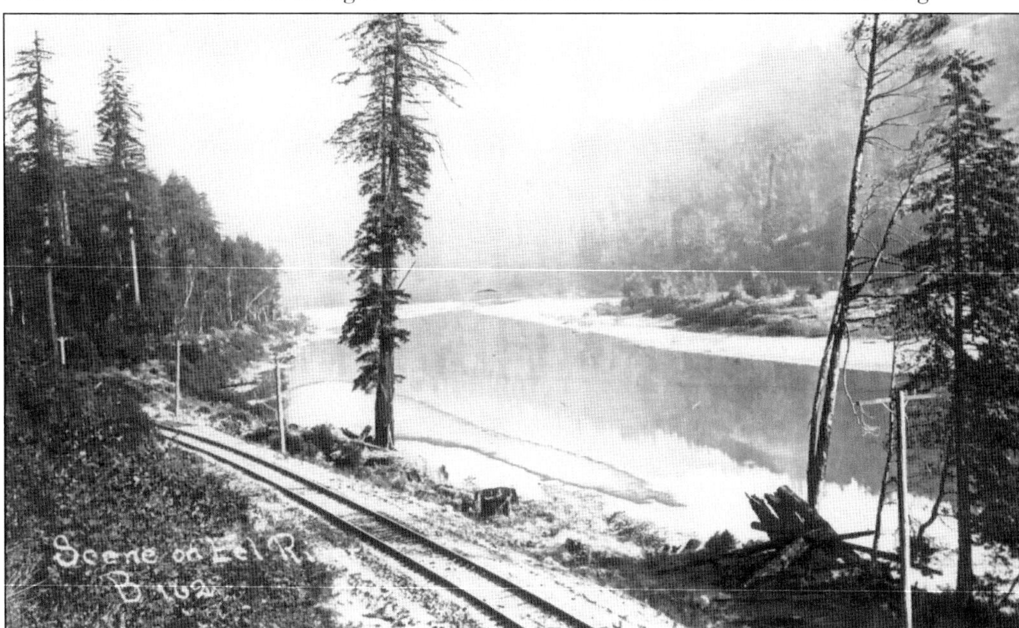

To the north, work progressed much more slowly. In June 1911, NWP president A.H. Payson told the *Humboldt Times*: "There is no use trying to keep it a secret. The progress made on construction of the extension is highly unsatisfactory to us. The work is not going as it should . . . no further contracts are to be let to small contractors . . . the work will be rushed along with all possible haste."

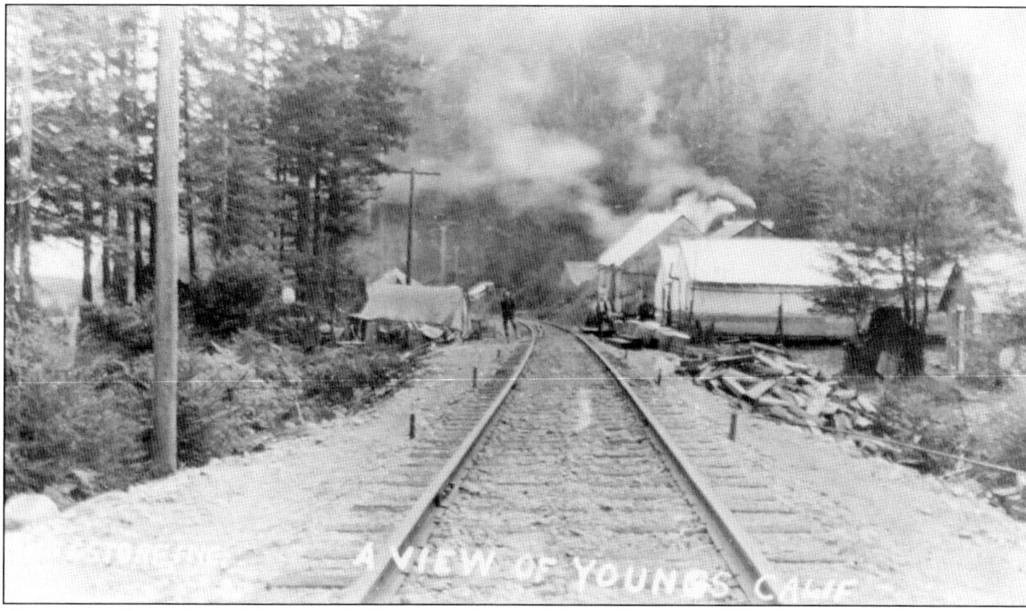

One issue for contractors in Humboldt County was difficulty in hiring workers. Contractors competed with lumber companies for laborers. New communities along the railroad were devoted to both railroad construction and the logging industry. One such town, Youngs, was located five miles south of Dyerville on the Eel River. Youngs, which received a post office in 1912, was named after entrepreneur George Young from Pepperwood. (Courtesy of HSU.)

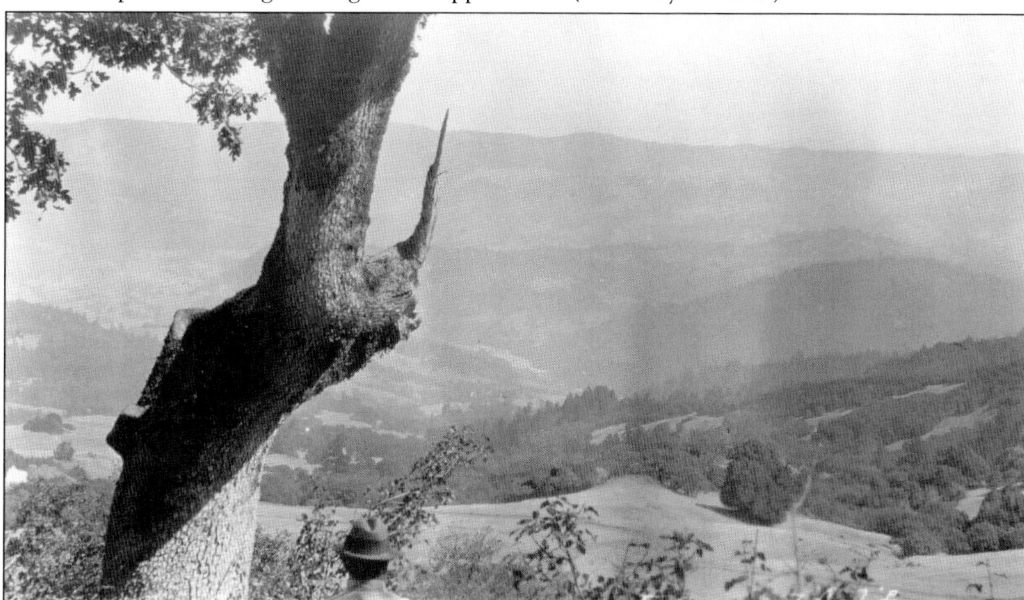

New problems arose as contractors followed the Eel River south. Unable to purchase a right-of-way from area ranchers, NWP officials compromised with permission to build. In 1912, as construction neared Fort Seward, in remote southeastern Humboldt County, mountainous country slowed construction and meant that all supplies had to be hauled in by rail. The steep terrain is revealed in this photograph from the collection of Joseph F. "Joe" Lockhart, who became an NWP surveyor in 1913.

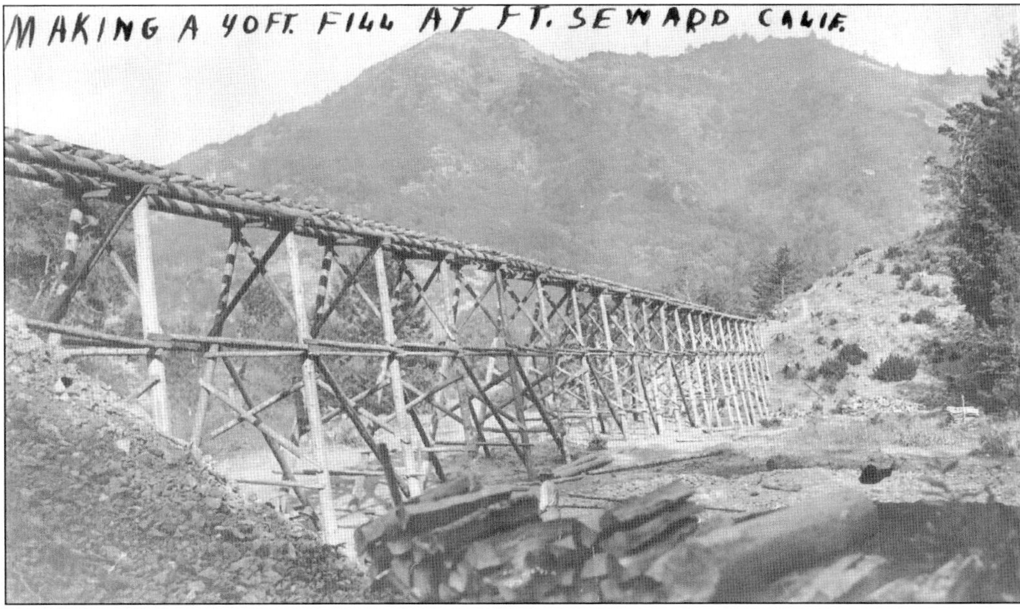

Bridges had to be built in order for the construction crews to cross creeks and precipitous ravines. Moreover, unlike with earlier work on the line, lumber for the bridges and ties had to be hauled to the worksite. Fort Seward has a hot, dry climate that is not conducive to the growth of redwoods. This is one of the large bridges built in the region.

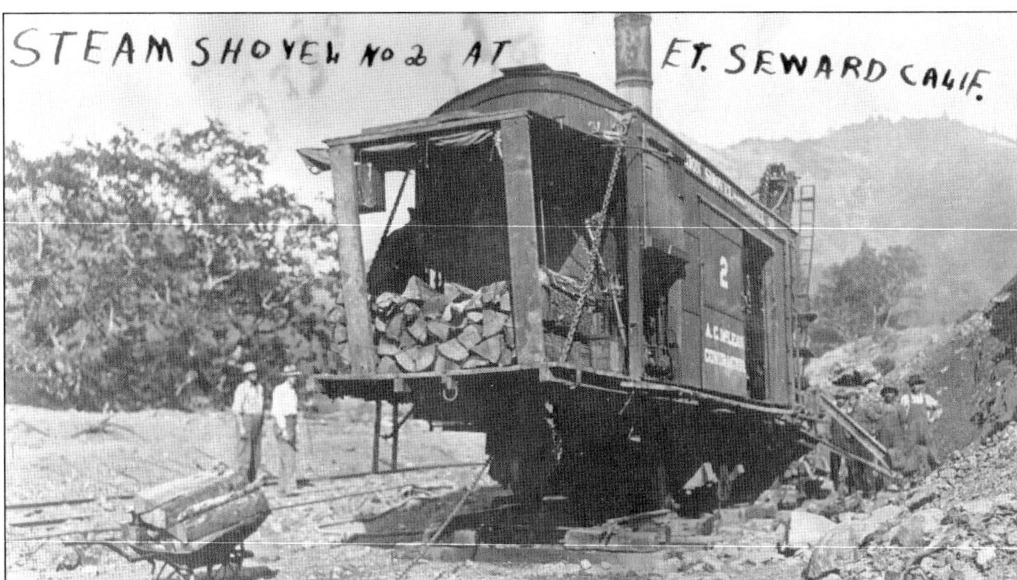

Weather impacted construction, as demonstrated in an April 1913 report in the *Ukiah Dispatch Democrat*: "Along the entire route from Dyerville to Fort Seward slides have been carried in by storms, the last rain alone destroying the work of two months. Track is carried out, slides have covered the roadbed in other places, the entire route is broken up and impassable." Work crews faced the daunting, dispiriting task of rebuilding lines that they had just completed.

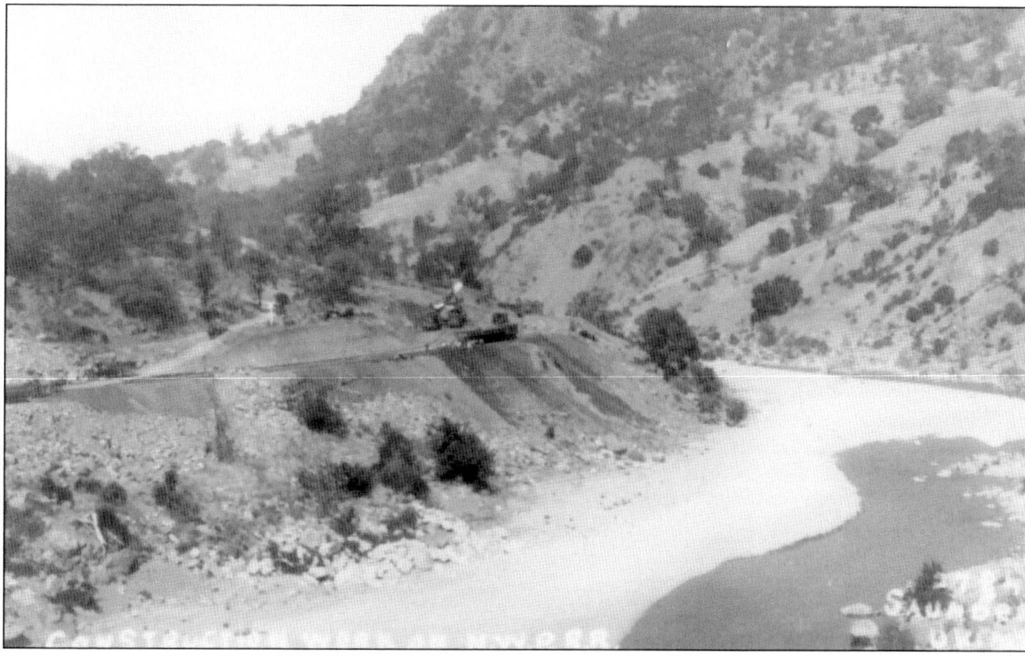

Beginning in 1911, the Utah Construction Company, which had been used extensively by the Southern Pacific lines, was responsible for construction on the Willits end of the extension. Since the company employed over 1,000 men, it was able to build farther than the contractors in the north. This postcard shows construction on the line near Dos Rios.

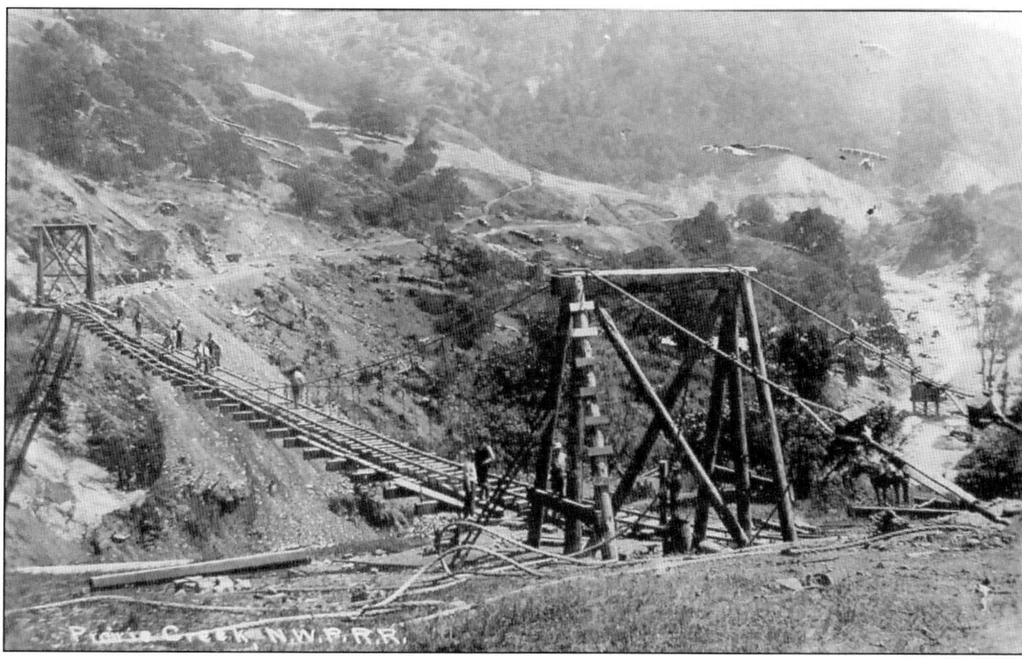

By 1913, the gap in the rail line between Willits and Eureka had been halved to 50 miles. Within this gap was some of the most challenging work. For example, two and half miles south of Alderpoint, the largest bridge across the Eel River required 12 concrete piers rising 36 feet from the low water of the river in summer. (Courtesy of NWPRRHS.)

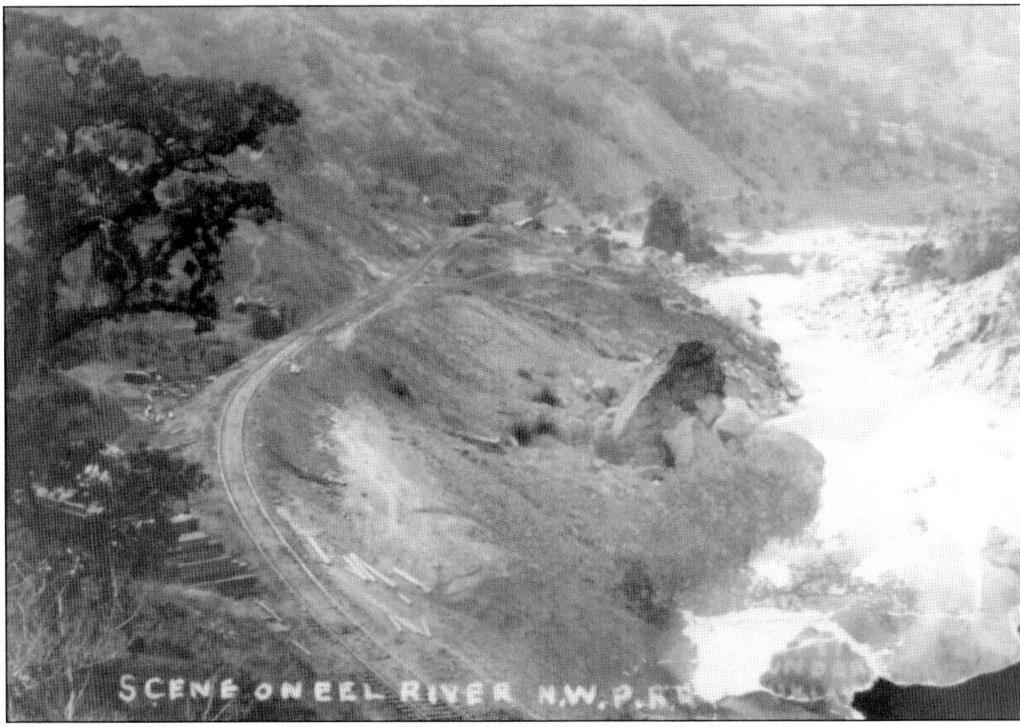

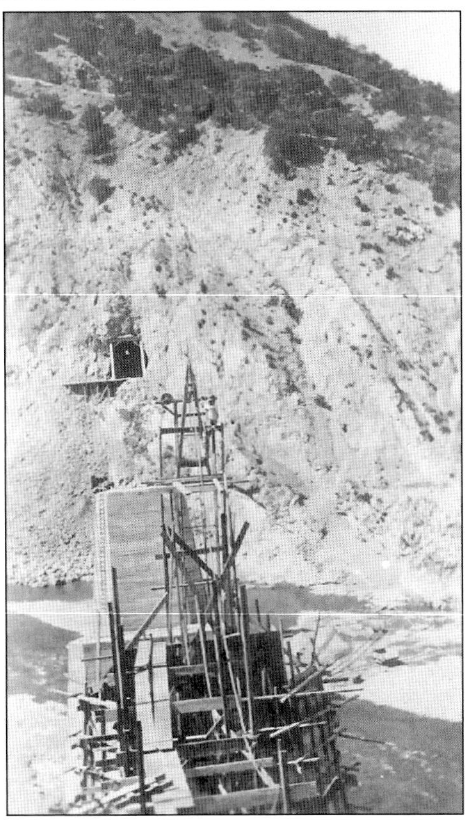

The experienced Utah Construction Company pushed the line north as day and night shifts worked to lay track and build roadbed. They also hired trucks to haul cement to various worksites so that, as Ukiah newspapers reported, "culvert and bridge construction might proceed during the winter."

The most challenging engineering feat under the jurisdiction of the Utah Construction Company was found at Island Mountain. A large oxbow bend in the river required the company to build a bridge across the river and then bore a tunnel into the mountain. Work on the bridge and tunnel began in 1911 and took three years to complete. (Courtesy of NWPRRHS.)

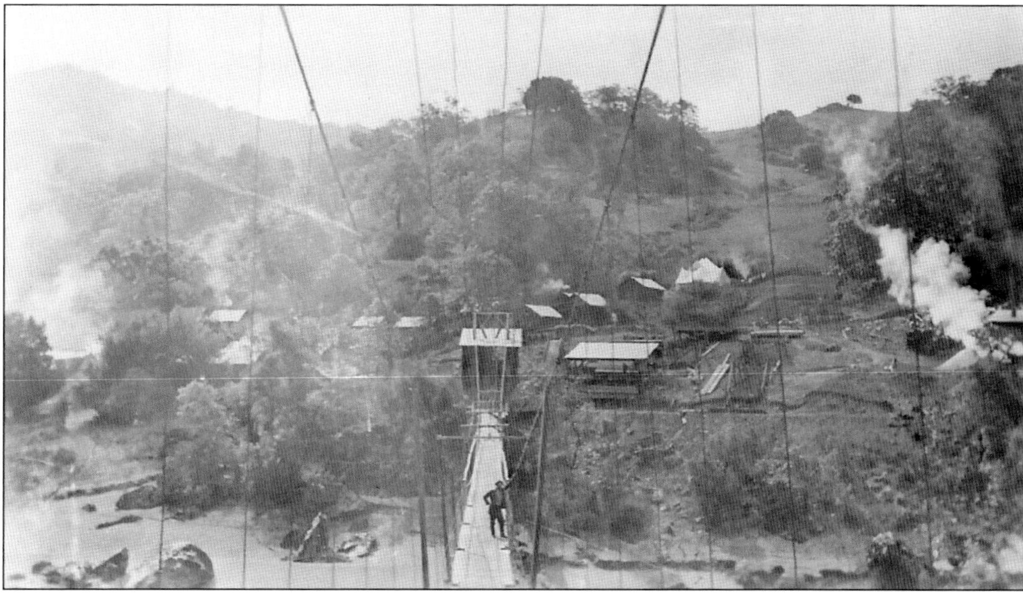

The Utah Construction Company hired Willits businessman Fred Smythe's two trucks to haul materials and supplies to a workers' camp located south of the bridge at Island Mountain during the summer. By April 1912, the tunnel had been bored to a length of 800 feet. Upon completion, it was 4,313 feet long and was the longest tunnel on the line. (Courtesy of NWPRRHS.)

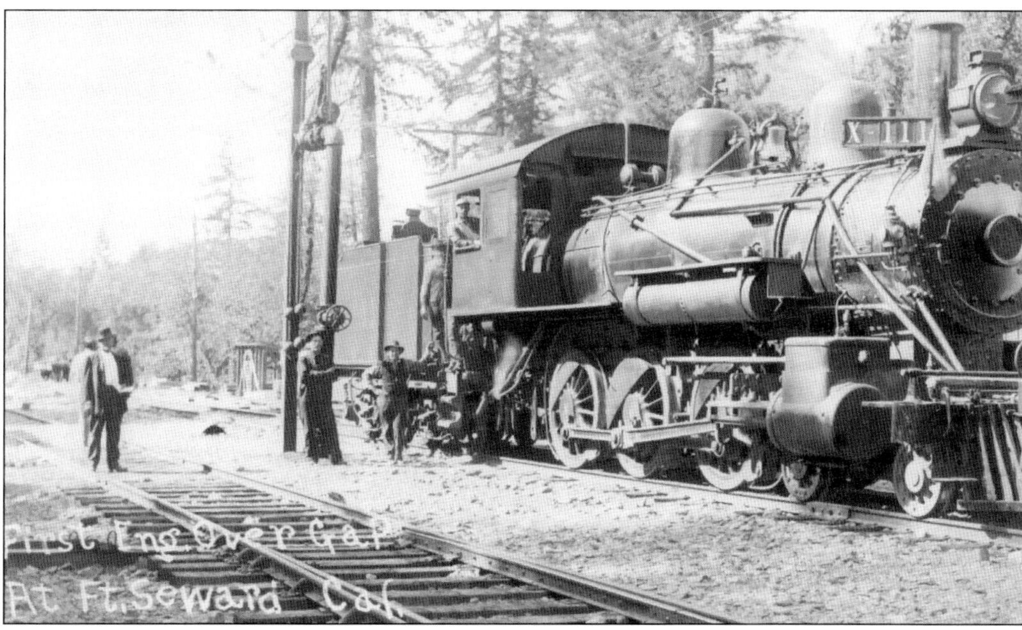

In October 1914, the gap between Willits and Eureka was closed. Engine No. 111 received the distinction of being the first engine to bridge the gap by rail. The engine and her crew are pictured here at Fort Seward. Engine No. 111 was purchased by the NWP in 1908 and served the line until it was retired in 1949.

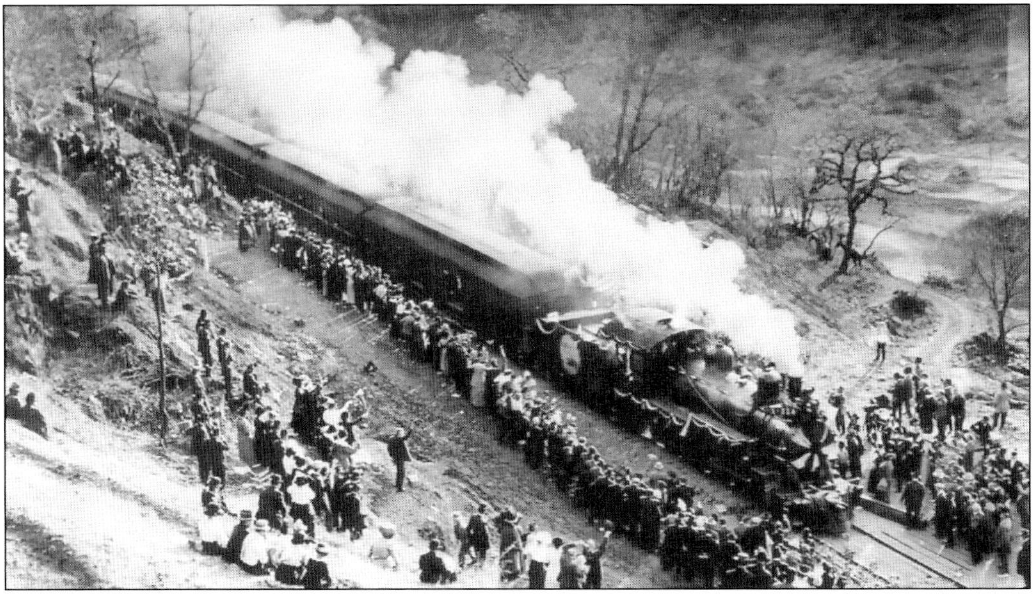

With the gap closed, the ceremonial driving of a golden spike was planned at Cain Rock, where construction crews finally met. Engine No. 114, decorated with bunting and pictures commemorating the day, pulled a train filled with NWP dignitaries and other celebrants north from San Francisco to Cain Rock on October 23, 1914. Railroad workers spruced up the dedication site with greenery and built a stage for the speakers. (Courtesy of NWPRRHS.)

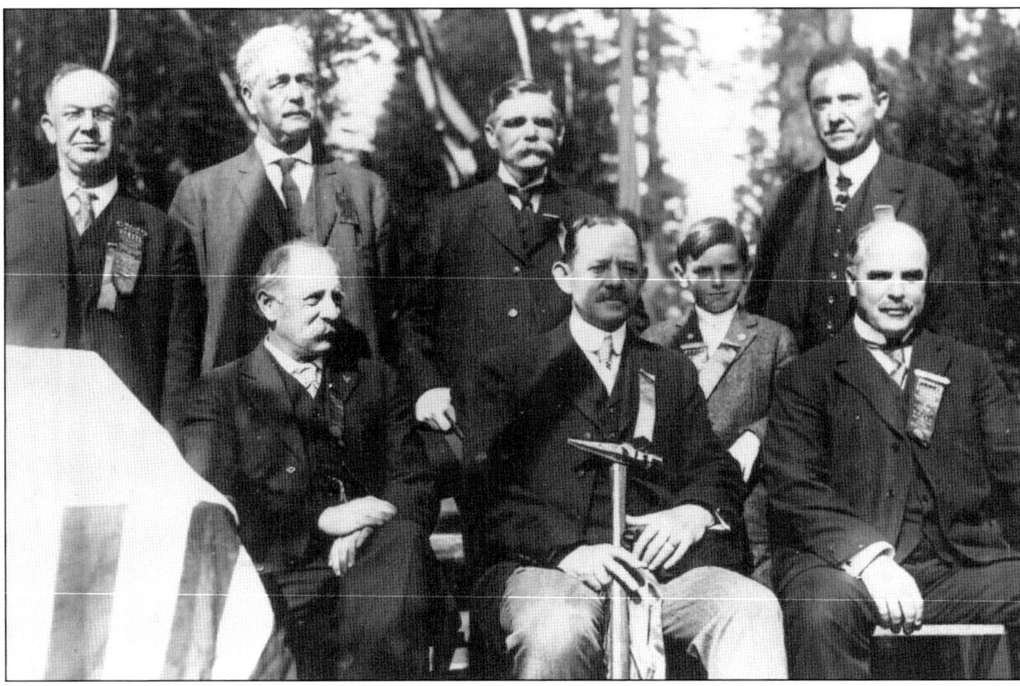

NWP president and general manager Warren S. Palmer, who is holding the silver hammer used to drive the golden spike, was only one of the dignitaries who gave a speech. Others included Mayor James Rolph of San Francisco, Mayor W.S. Clark of Eureka, officials from the Southern Pacific and the Santa Fe, and former California governor James Gillett. (Courtesy of NWPRRHS.)

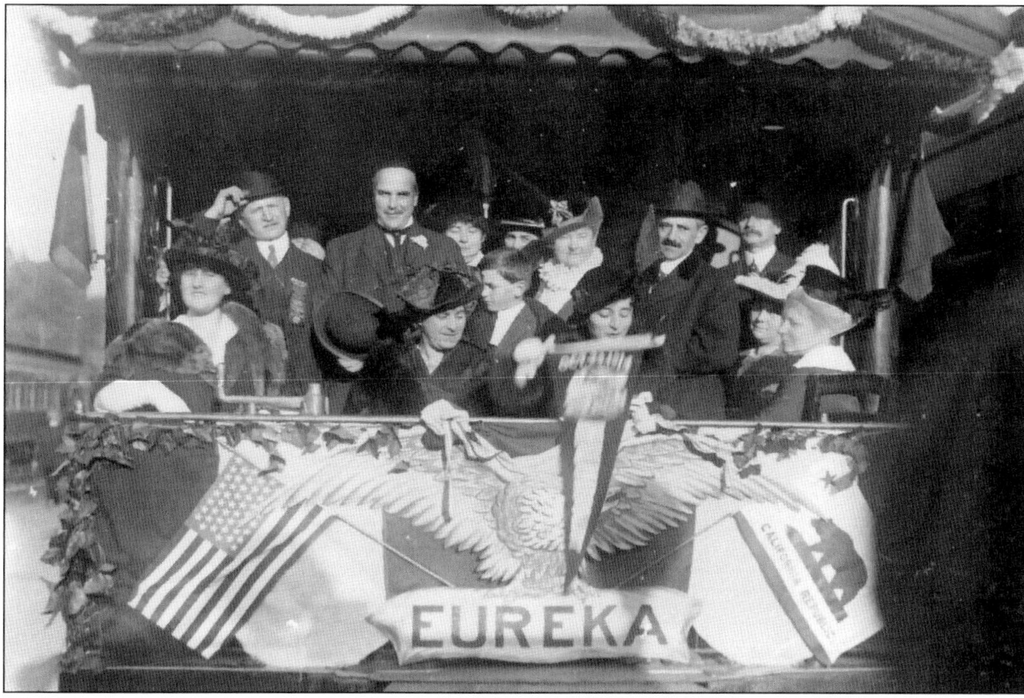

The train from San Francisco was met by two that came from Eureka filled with observers from towns near Humboldt Bay. Local residents, who had begun to settle in the region when access was provided by the railroad, and longtime ranchers also came to observe the event. One local family, the Pattons, recalls that Maybelle Patton was very despondent that she could not attend, as she was pregnant with her daughter Elva. Others flocked to the site to hear the speeches and take in the spectacle. Yager Creek resident Bertha Hinckley was in attendance and captured the event on her special postcard camera; one of her images is shown on page 78. Never before or since did so many gather at the remote location along the river. Onlookers sported banners, ribbons, or flyers indicating that the railroad was bringing prosperity to the region. (Both courtesy of NWPRRHS.)

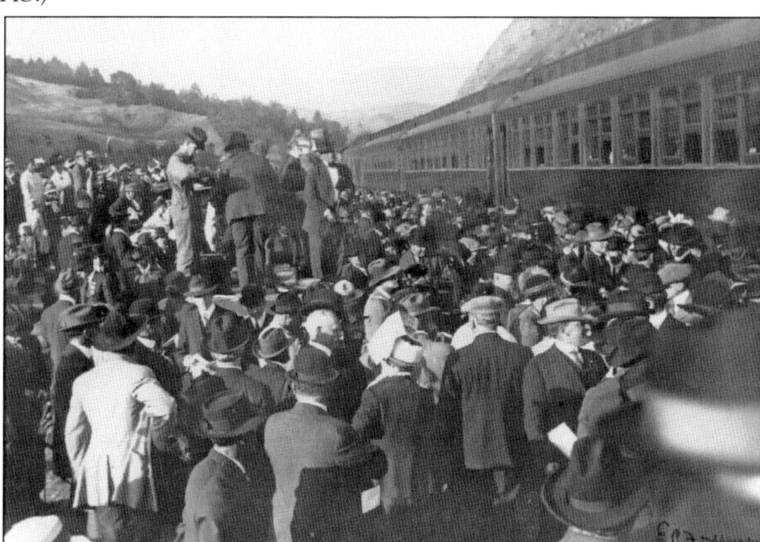

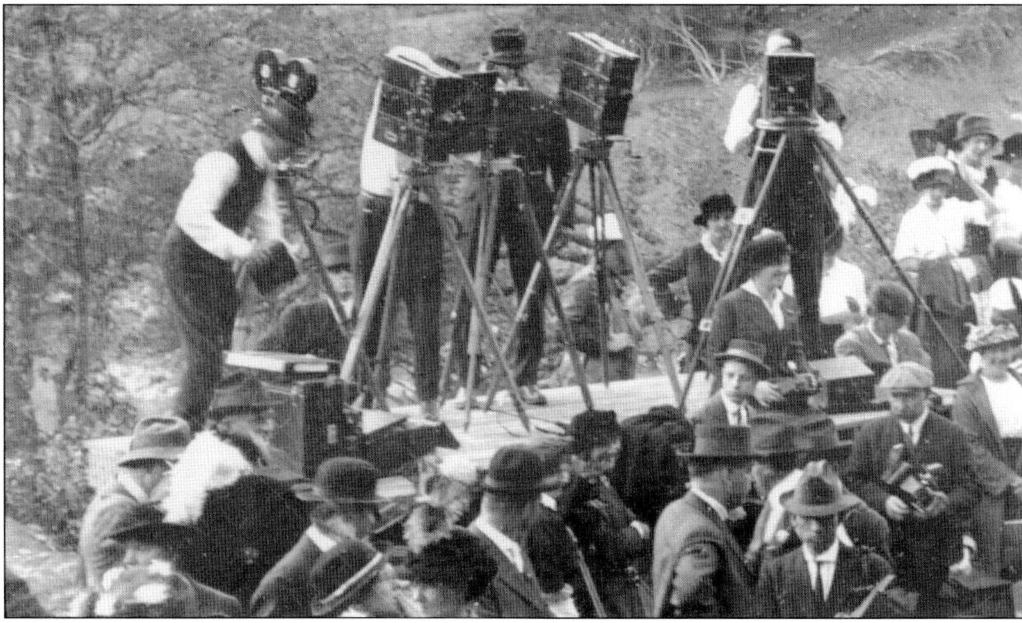

Completion of the railroad and the ceremony at Cain Rock were memorialized on film. Moving picture cameras, a newly developed technology, accompanied travelers from San Francisco and filmed the speeches at Cain Rock. They also captured the rising of white smoke that marked the completion of construction in the "time honored fashion" of the "costliest railroad in America," according to Ukiah Chamber of Commerce president J.W. Eversole. (Courtesy of HSU.)

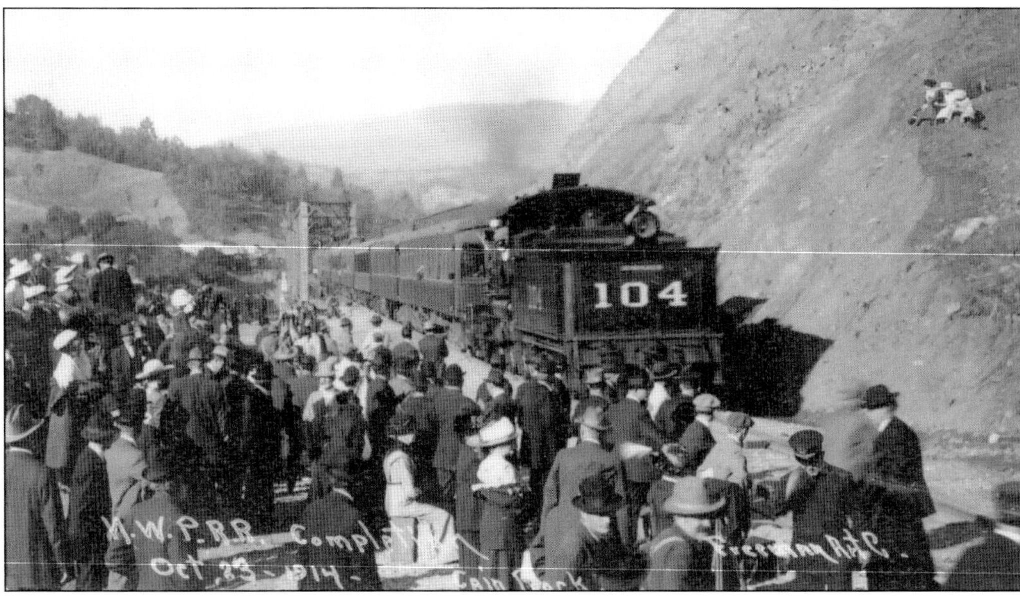

J.W. Eversole reported on events at Cain Rock for readers of the *Ukiah Republican Press*. Traveling north with 350 well-wishers from the San Francisco Bay Area, he arrived at Cain Rock at 3:50 p.m. Impressed by the number of people at the celebration, he described the spike-driving for the readers of the *Press*, stating that NWP president and general manager Warren S. Palmer drove the golden spike, and Palmer's "handsome daughter christened the completed railroad with California champagne."

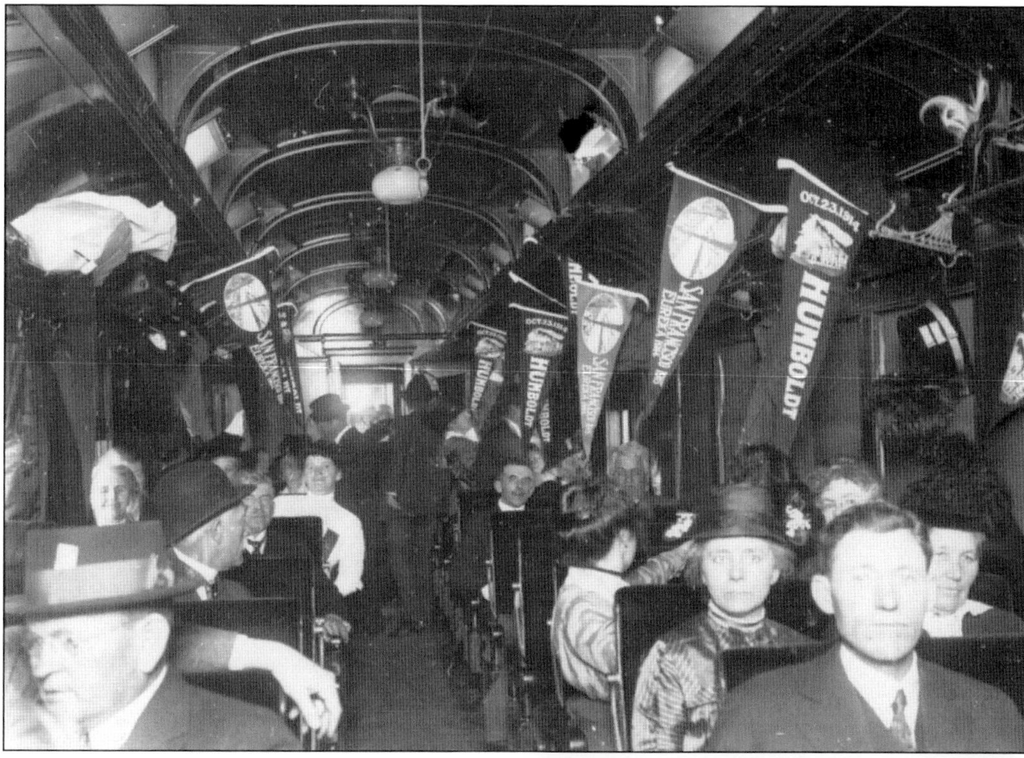

Following the benediction, the large crowd climbed aboard the three trains to travel to Eureka. The trains were quite full and decorated with banners and other memorabilia commemorating the day. Passengers were eager to arrive in Eureka and continue their celebrations. (Courtesy of HSU.)

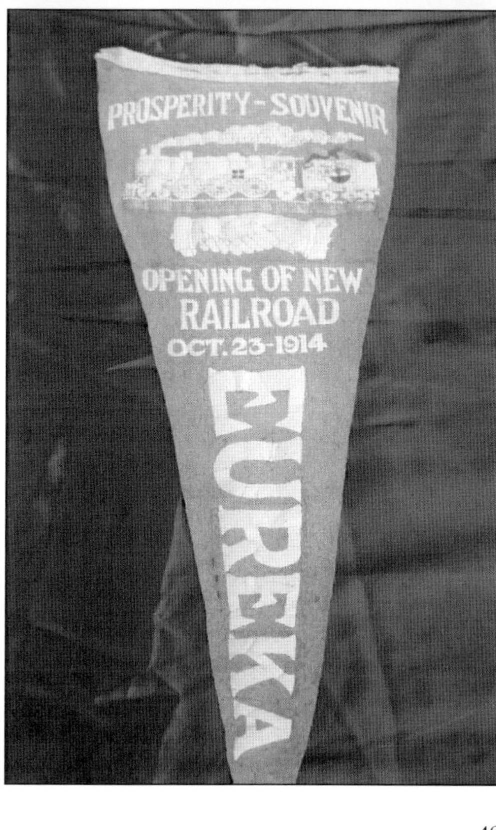

This souvenir flag is in the collection of the Fortuna Depot Museum. Optimism regarding the prosperity seemingly ensured by the opening of the railroad is shown in the handshake and details of the train image. Many flags mentioned both Eureka and San Francisco, as the former was no longer isolated from the rest of the state.

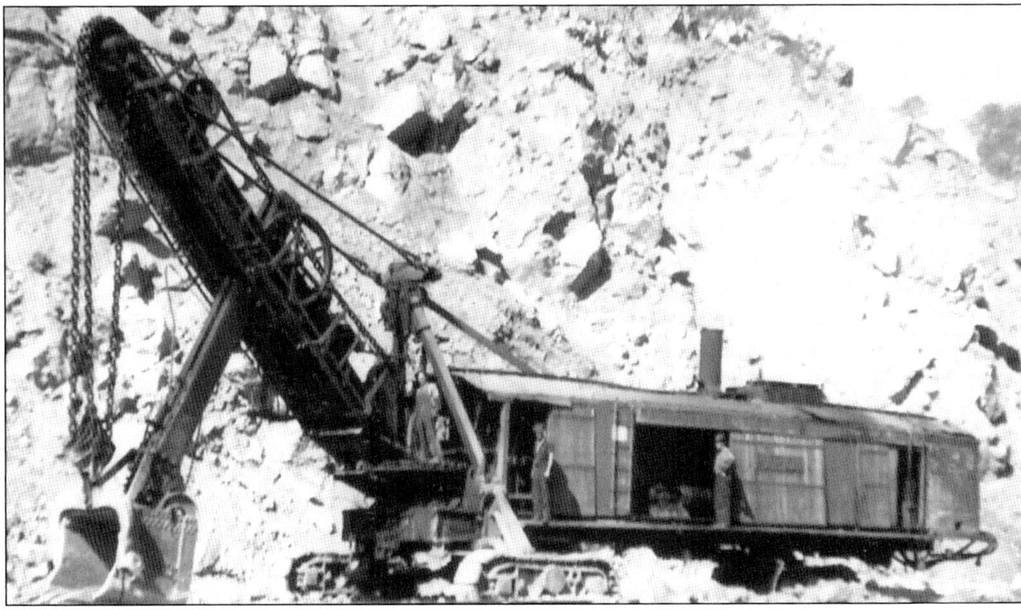

The golden-spike trains did not arrive as expected, since a landslide covered the tracks near McCann. A rancher who lived across the river at the time, Albert Whitlow, was told that some former construction crew employees, not wanting to be unemployed, dynamited the hill. Whatever the cause, another track had to be laid before the celebration trains could go on to Eureka. (Courtesy of NWPRRHS.)

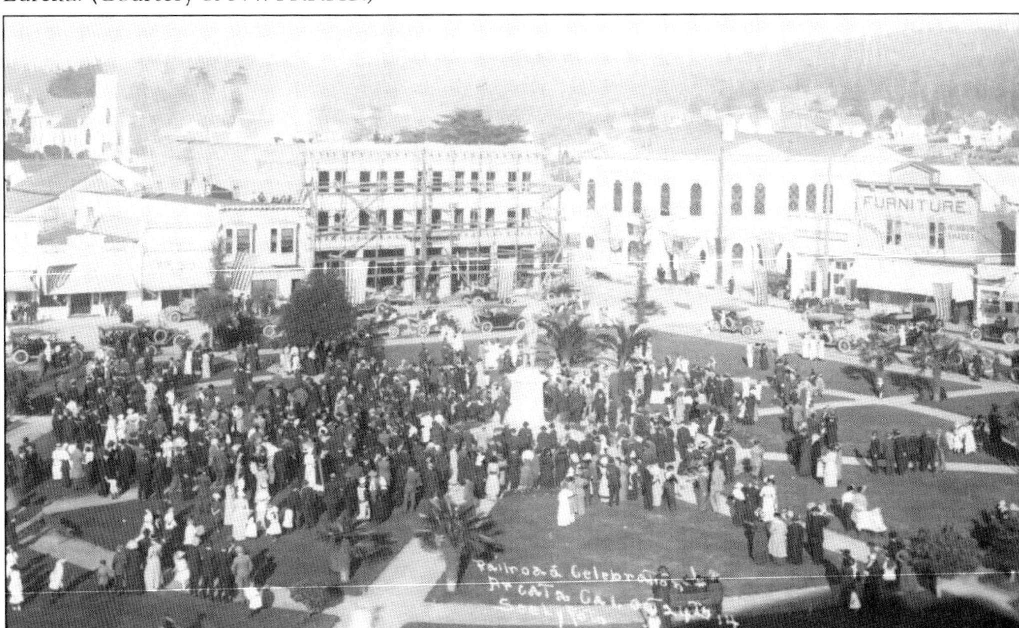

In Eureka and Arcata, parades and celebrations delayed by the slide were rescheduled for the following day. In today's time of instant communication and rapid travel, it is hard to understand the difference the railroad meant, but in the early 20th century, the idea of getting daily news and being able to travel to San Francisco in a matter of hours instead of days was electrifying for the citizens of Humboldt County. (Courtesy of HSU.)

Three

Faces of the NWP

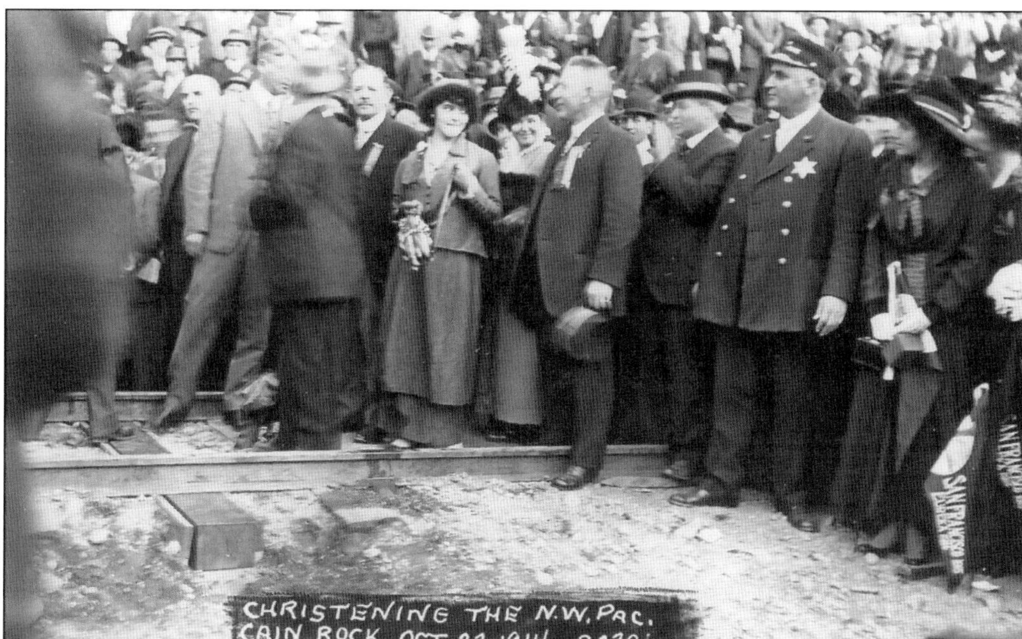

Alice Palmer, the 17-year-old daughter of NWP's president and general manager, Warren S. Palmer, became the poster girl for the Cain Rock celebrations by holding the golden spike her father struck. She stands on the rail in the center of this photograph. On July 4, 1918, she christened another transportation venture, Navy torpedo destroyer boat *Burns*. Alice and her father were native-born San Franciscans. Warren Palmer, son of transplanted New Englanders, graduated from the University of California in 1875. (Courtesy of NWPRRHS.)

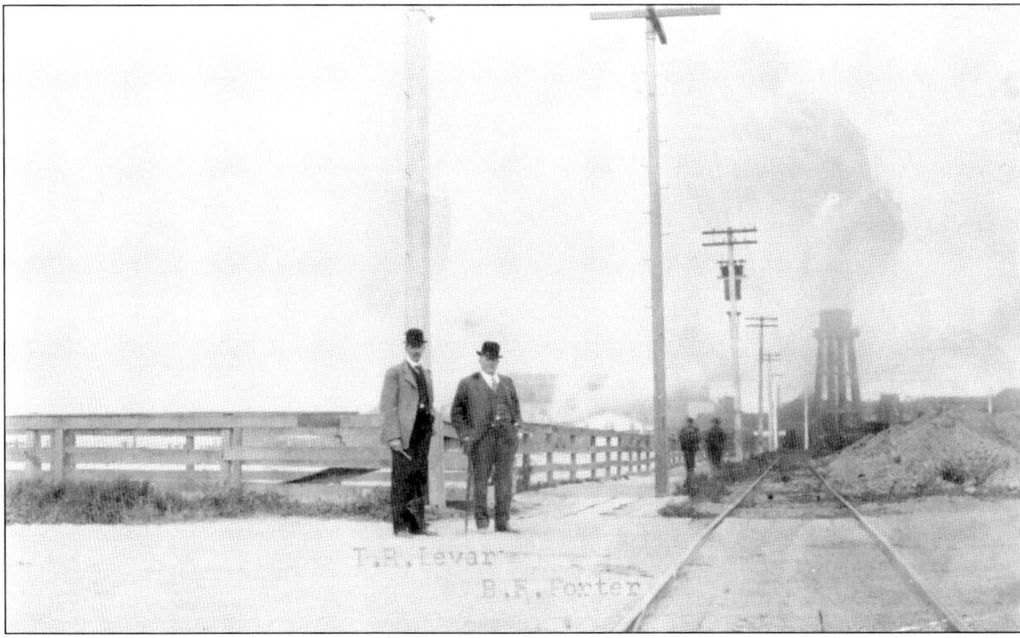

Canadian-born Thompson R. Lever, left, and Benjamin Faneuil Porter from Alabama were Eureka-based officers of the San Francisco & Northwestern Railroad and, later, the NWP. In February 1907, the journal *Railway Age* reported Porter's appointment as "assistant general manager, in charge of operated lines north of Shively Tunnel, with office at Eureka." The two men lived on the same block of E Street in Eureka. (Courtesy of HSU.)

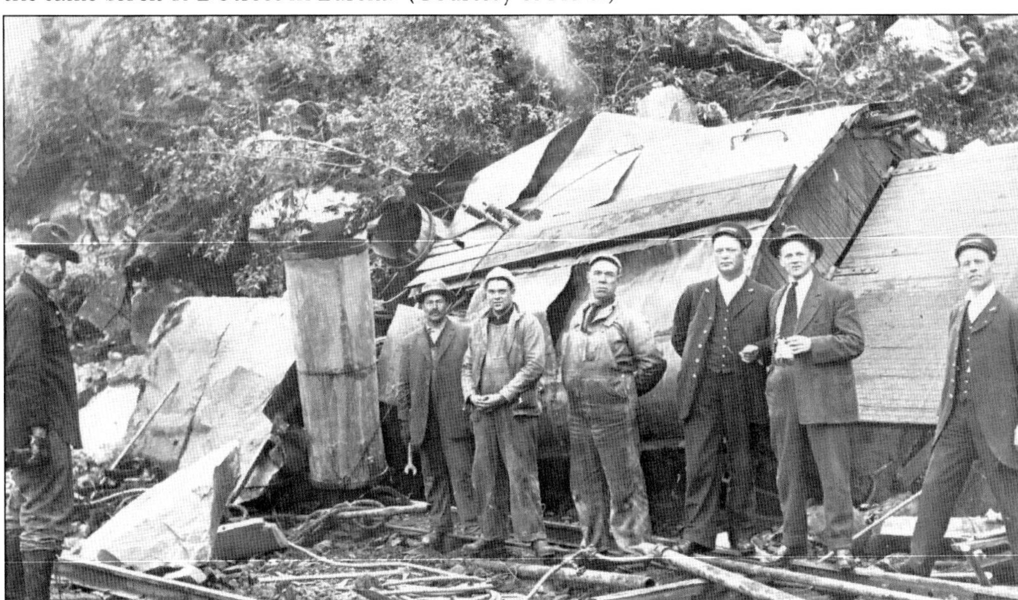

This wreck took place at the east end of Tunnel No. 36 just south of McCann. The unidentified men illustrate the wide range of work associated with a railroad. At right, two uniformed conductors flank a suit-clad man who presumably works on the clerical or management side. In the center are, perhaps, an engineer, fireman, and brakeman. At left, another man stares at the photographer, possibly impatient with the interruption of his work.

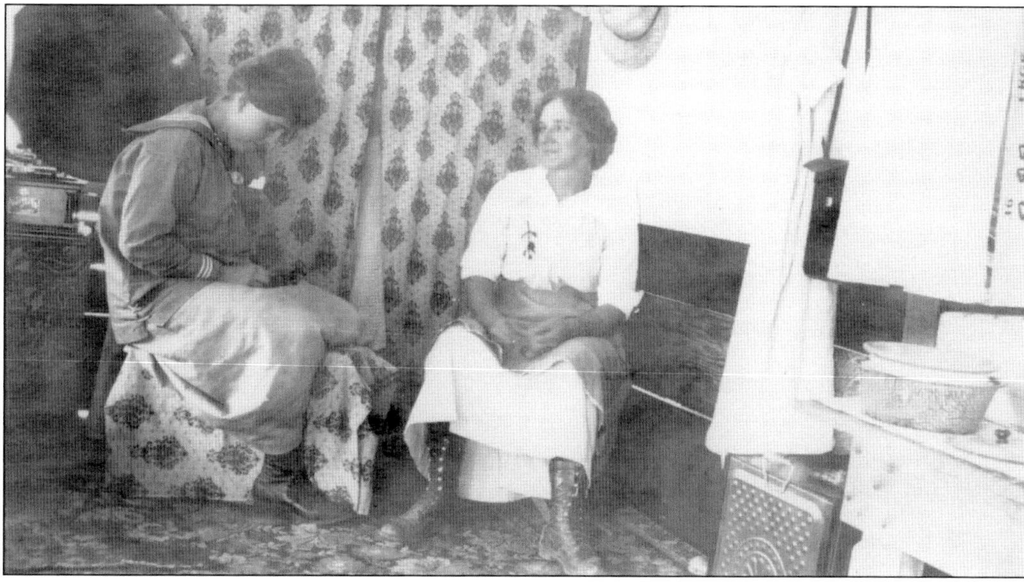

The children of the Roberts, Schorlig, and Dolson families grew up in Arcata in the early 1900s. Atlant Roberts (left) married Rush Dolson, and Lula Shorlig (right) married Rush's brother Dave. Dave Dolson became a brakeman for NWP. Rush Dolson took this photograph while visiting Dave and Lula in their tent cabin provided as NWP employee housing at Island Mountain in 1915. (Courtesy of HSU.)

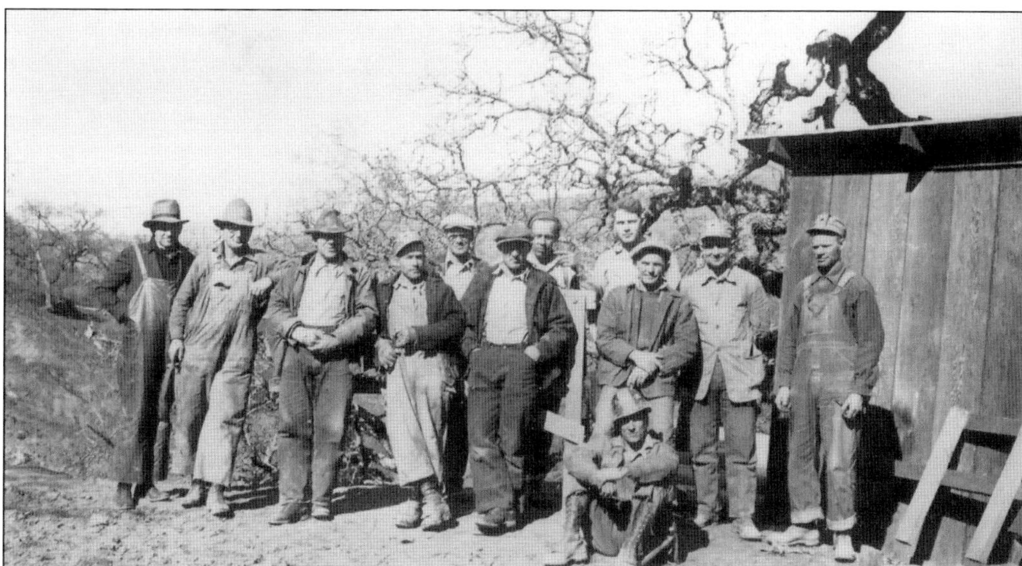

The life of Joseph F. "Joe" Lockhart, who photographed this NWP work crew, was intricately intertwined with the Northwestern Pacific. His father, Joseph A. Lockhart, was a brakeman for the NWP. In 1913, at age 17, Joseph F. began working with the company on a survey team during construction. Joseph F. Lockhart met his future wife, Vera Wilson, on a train ride. A Willits schoolteacher, Vera frequently commuted by NWP between Willits and her hometown of Fortuna.

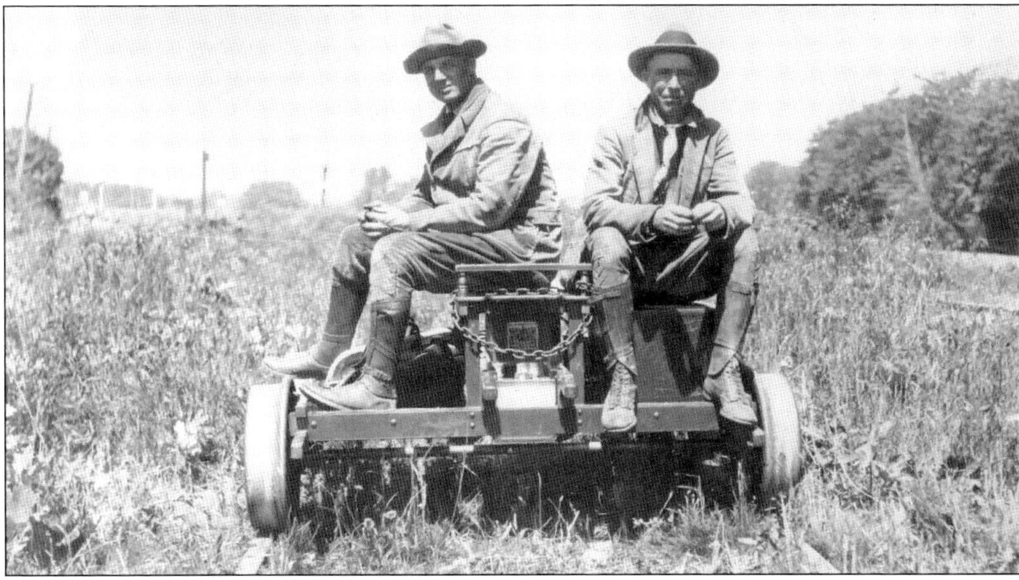

Joe Lockhart's photograph collection contributed many images used in this book. Lockhart (right) served the NWP for 41 years, progressing from transit man to rodman, instrument man, assistant engineer, acting road master, road master, and, finally, division engineer. As division engineer, he had responsibility for all tracks and bridges between San Rafael and Eureka—a distance of over 270 miles. At left is Laurence Upshur, who was a rodman for NWP in 1926.

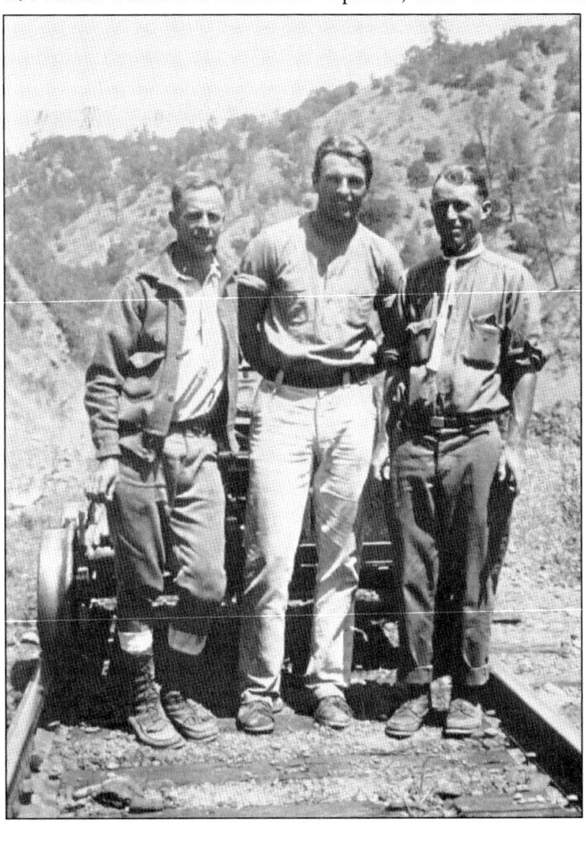

Joe Lockhart (right) is pictured here with Frank Wadak (left) and Darrell Glendon Shively. Wadak, a civil engineer and surveyor born in Wisconsin, worked as an instrument man for NWP. His mother was Wisconsin-born, with German and Bohemian ancestry, and his father was a saloonkeeper from Vienna. Surveyor Shively was a grandson of the pioneer who was the namesake for the town of Shively, and his father was a mail carrier whose route ran from Eureka to Bridgeville.

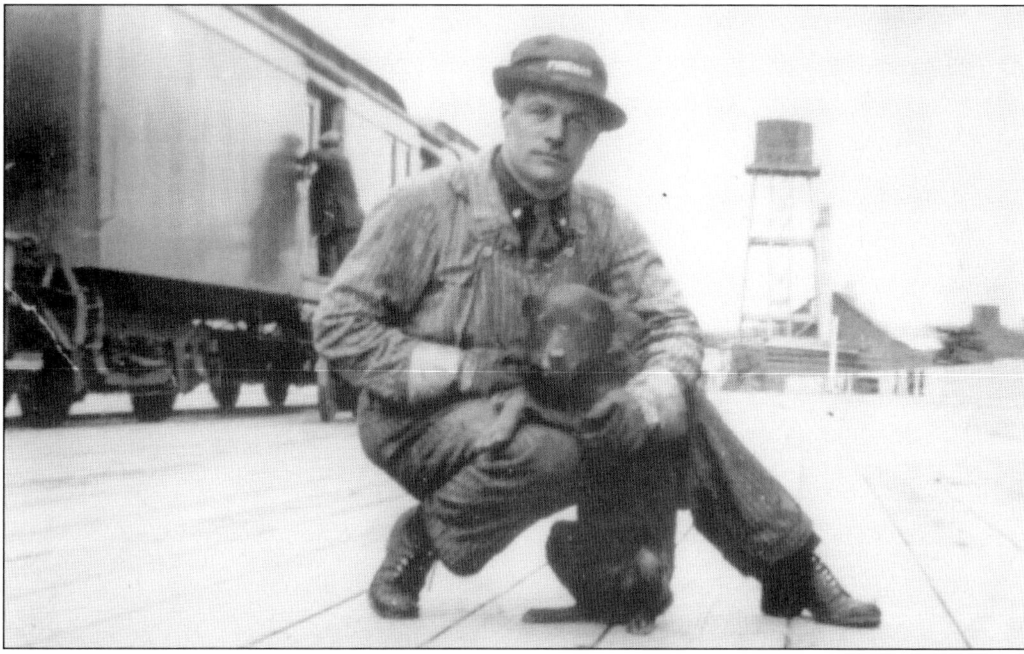

Boomer Jack, shown with fireman Charles Shirley Luther in Eureka around 1918, became the unofficial NWP mascot. The free-spirited dog rode the rails and followed railroad employees home, staying for hours or days before hitching a ride on another train. His name came from the "boomers," or freelance railroad workers. After Boomer Jack wandered as far away as South Carolina, he was sent home thanks to the NWP badge on his collar. (Courtesy of Lincoln Killian.)

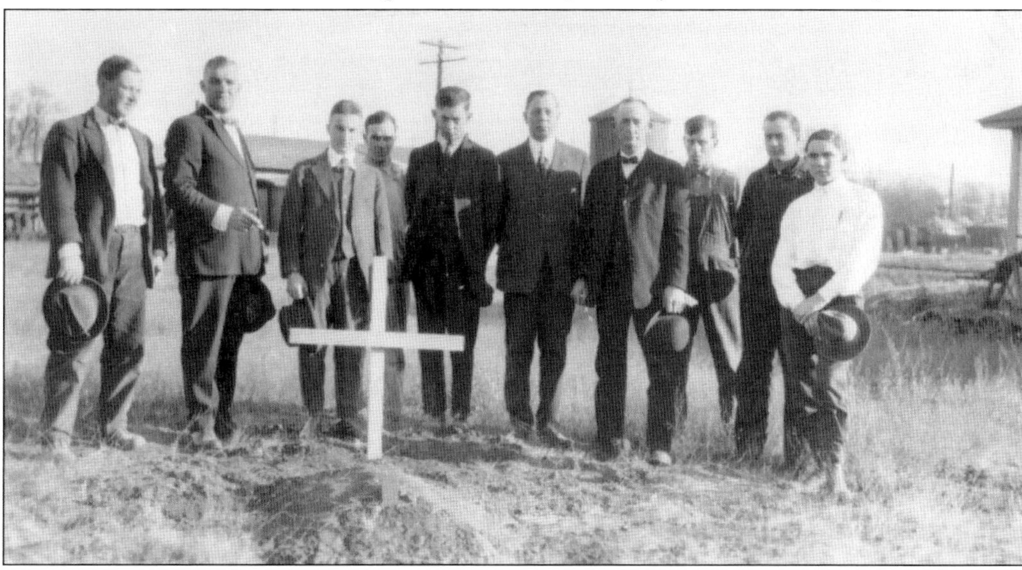

Boomer Jack was buried at the Willits train yard in 1926. Two of these NWP employees photographed at his grave are identified on the back of the picture as roundhouse foreman Fred Nelson (fourth from right) and section crew foreman Marlon Fauerbaugh (third from right). These notations are probably erroneous identifications of, respectively, Charles Nelson, listed in Willits in the 1920 census as "train master-railroad," and Henry Fauerbach of Scotia, listed in the 1940 census as a laborer-maintainer on the railroad. (Courtesy of HSU.)

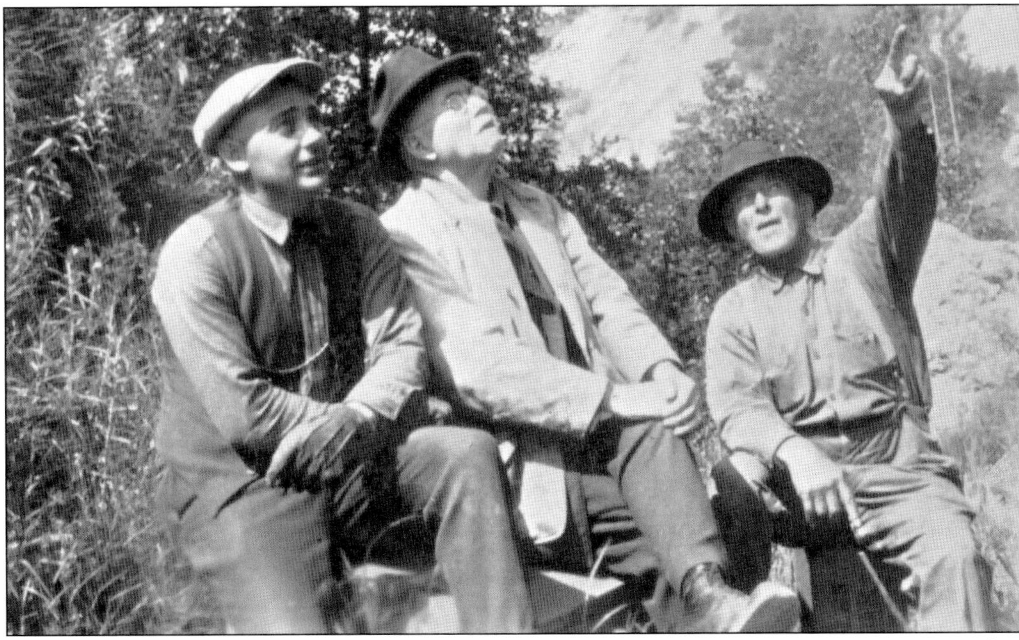

These men eyeing a landslide at Scotia Bluffs are identified on Joe Lockhart's photograph as "Goodwin, G.C. Douglas and Owens." G.C. Douglas was a Eureka-based NWP road master during the early years of construction between Willits and Eureka. Goodwin is probably Eureka native John O. Goodwin, listed in the 1920 census as a railroad accountant and in 1930 as NWP's assistant road master at Island Mountain.

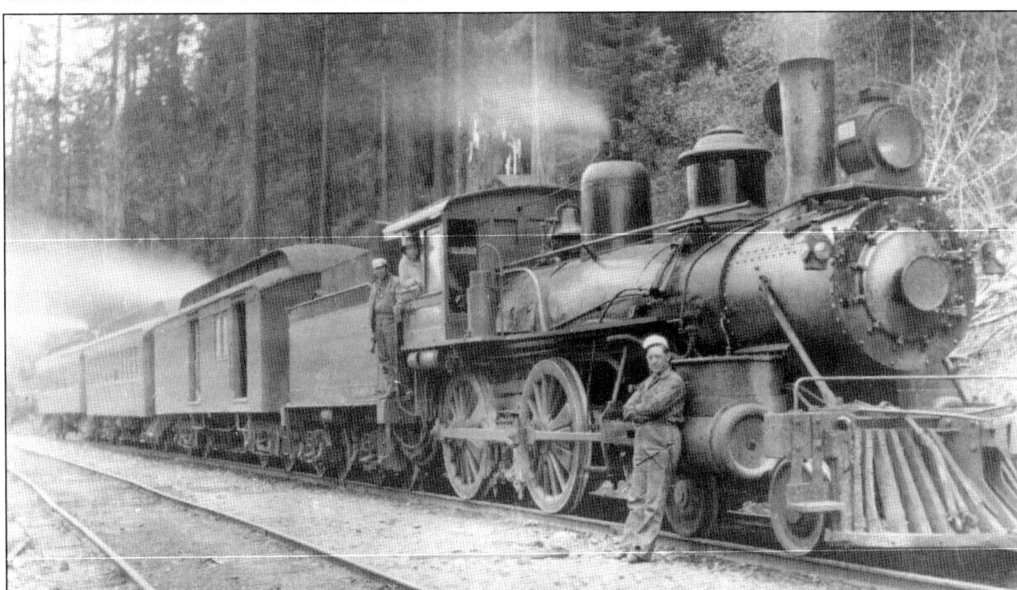

This photograph is annotated as follows: "Passenger train at McCann – Eddie the engineer." Eddie, shown standing beside his locomotive, was Ed Weatherby, who was initiated into the Eureka chapter of the Brotherhood of Locomotive Engineers in 1919. Weatherby, along with two crewmates, lost his life on August 6, 1937, in what newspapers called "the first fatal train wreck in the history of the Eureka division of the Northwestern Pacific Railroad." (Courtesy of HSU.)

Brakeman George Still died with Ed Weatherby and fireman Carl Bartlett in the wreck on August 6, 1937. Engine No. 182 crashed through the bridge east of Pepperwood that had burned in a smoldering fire believed to be caused by sparks from the brakes of the previous night's passenger train. An article carried in Ukiah and Eureka newspapers reported that "Weatherby had seen trouble ahead when he rounded a curve in the track and applied his brake, but on too-short notice to stop the train."

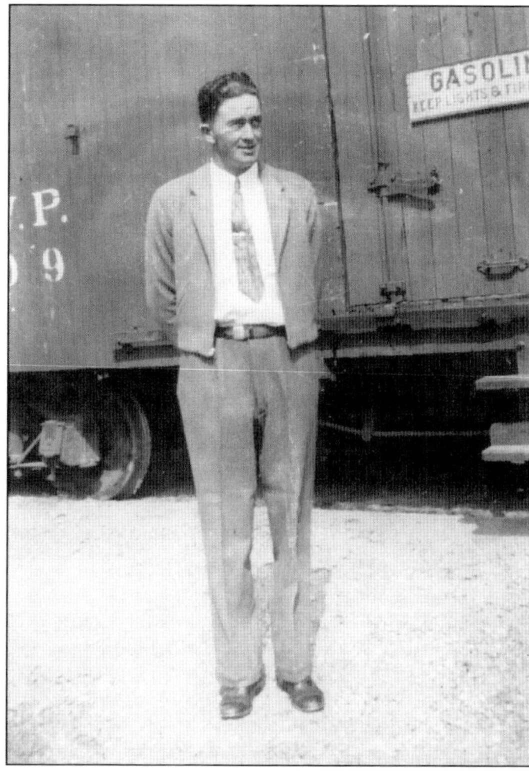

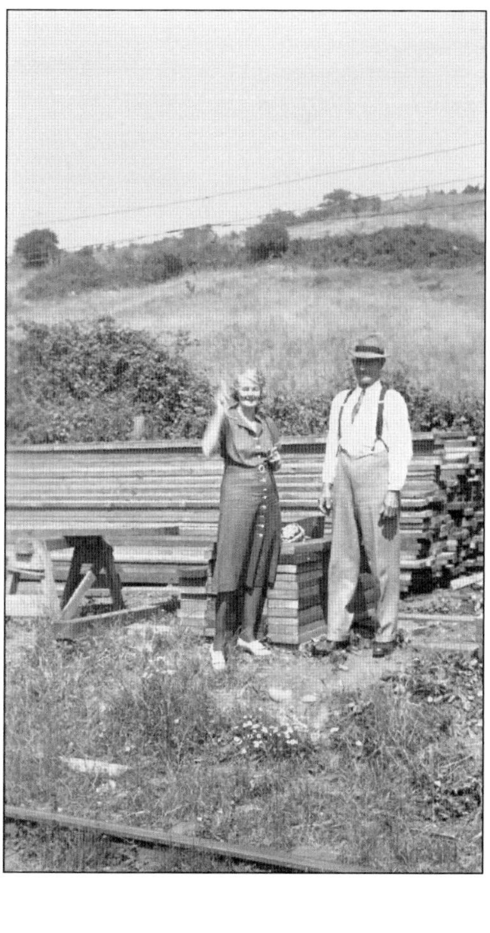

Brakeman Still's parents, Edna and Clifford Still, are pictured "at this end Loleta Tunnel." The photograph also notes that Clifford was a bridge gang foreman. According to the *Humboldt Times* obituary, George Still "was transferred here only a short time ago from the Sausalito division to Eureka, following which he was promoted from student brakeman to a permanent journeyman's rating . . . his father, Clifford Still, and a brother are also railroadmen, residing at Field's Landing."

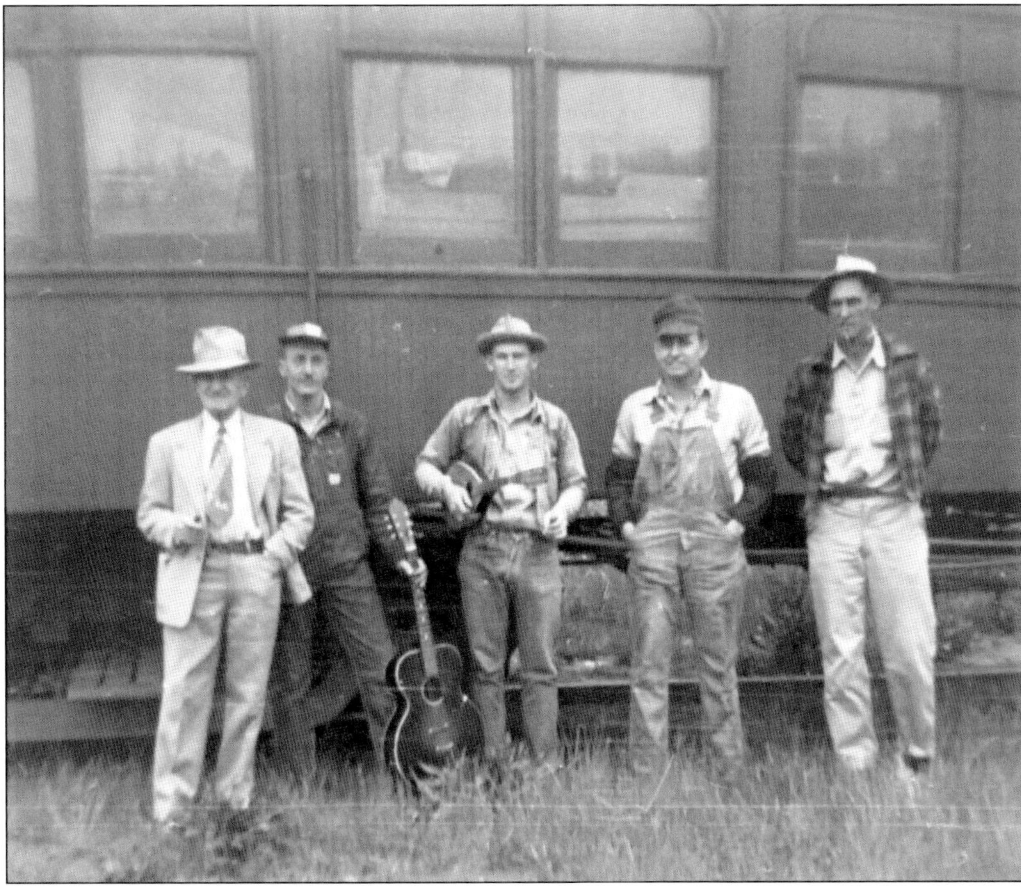

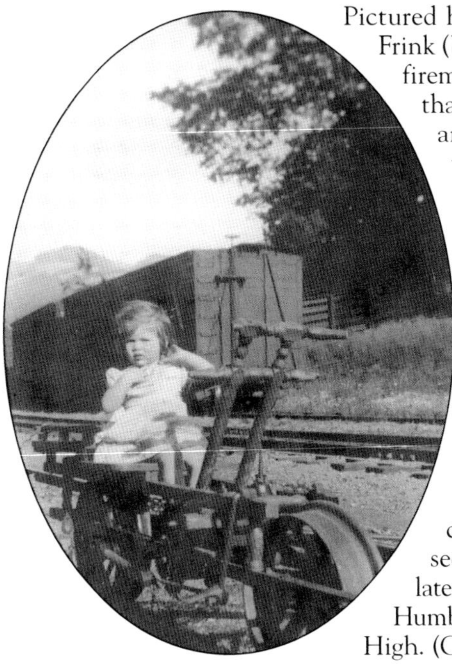

Pictured here are, from left to right, W.E. Graham and R.E. Frink (brakemen), W. West (engineer), E. Campbell (engineer-fireman), and ? Kruse. NWP employee seniority lists show that Edgar Campbell became an engineer on April 3, 1949, and Wade West made engineer on March 12, 1951. West was previously a truck driver, as was his father. Navy veteran Campbell also followed family tradition in his profession; his father was a railroad telegrapher.

Marguerita Moody is pictured in Alderpoint on a three-wheeled speeder. Her father worked on the Alderpoint railroad maintenance crew. After Marguerita was born at home in a small NWP-owned cabin, she and her mother rode the train to Fortuna to see Dr. Comfort when she was a day old. The railroad later provided Marguerita— along with fellow southeastern Humboldt students—with weekly transportation to Fortuna High. (Courtesy of Marguerita Nichols.)

Elva Patton Moody took this picture of her husband, Harry Moody, and their daughter Marguerita beside the tracks at Alderpoint around 1939. Harry's family homesteaded a ranch southeast of Alderpoint in 1913; Harry began working at an early age. He rode his horse to Kekawaka, where he sold jugs of milk to railroad employees. During the Great Depression, he was employed by the NWP. (Courtesy of Marguerita Nichols.)

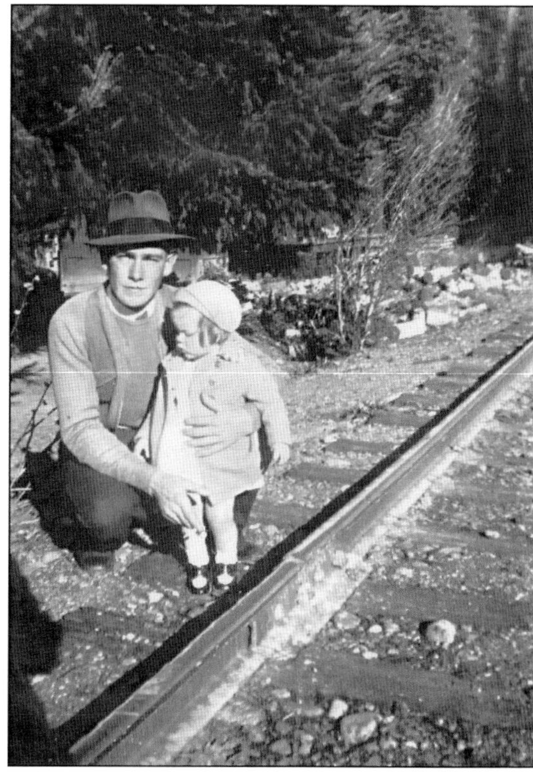

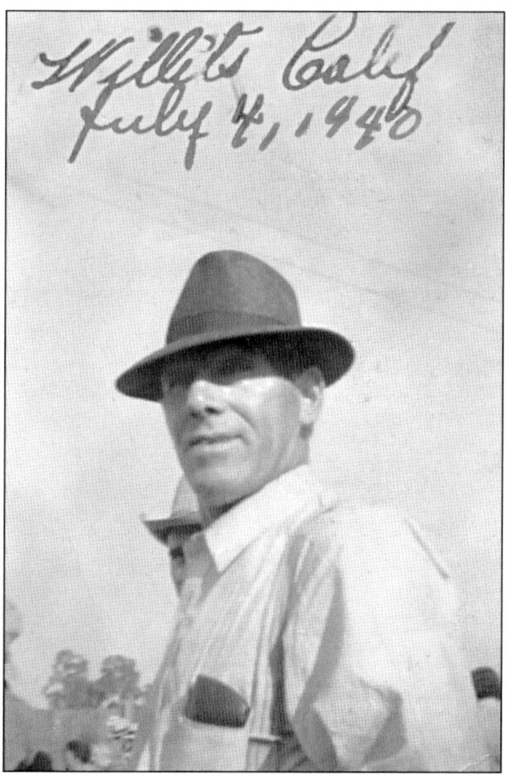

Maine-born Howard Moody, NWP section worker at Alderpoint, died in July 1941 at age 55 at the railroad hospital in San Francisco. He was fatally injured while operating a railroad handcar. Howard Moody left behind a widow, 10 children, and 12 grandchildren. After Howard's death, his son Harry quit the NWP and moved to the nearby family ranch. Moody family members still reside there in the early 21st century. (Courtesy of Marguerita Nichols.)

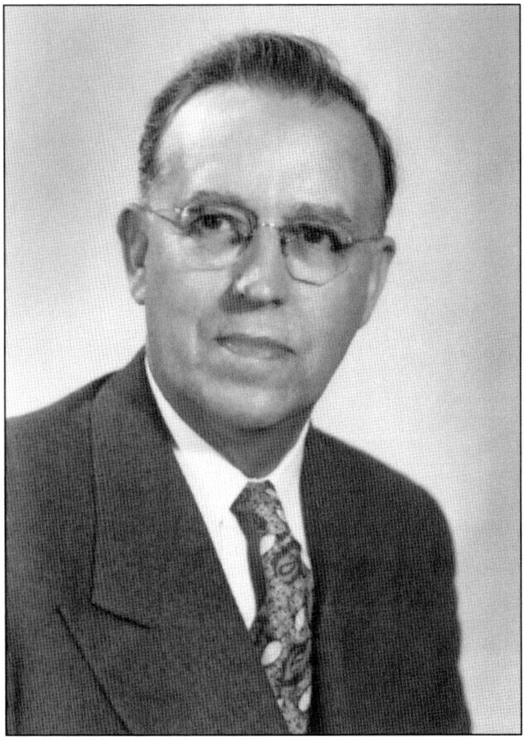

After moving from Canada to California with his family in 1890 at age four, Clinton Veale began working for the Southern Pacific (SP) in 1907. He rose through the ranks in the Southern Pacific and the NWP, becoming NWP vice president and general manager in 1941. In 1942, he wrote to division engineer Joe Lockhart commending his work but advising, "I am afraid some of this is being done at the expense of your health."

Officials of the SP and NWP met in Eureka in 1953 to make plans to complete the switch from steam to diesel locomotives. They dined with area civic and business leaders at the elite Ingomar Club housed in the mansion built in 1885 for lumber baron William Carson, a founder of the Eel River & Eureka Railroad (ER&ERR). At far left is Eureka-based trainmaster L.E. Dubose, and SP assistant vice president W.G. Peoples is second from left.

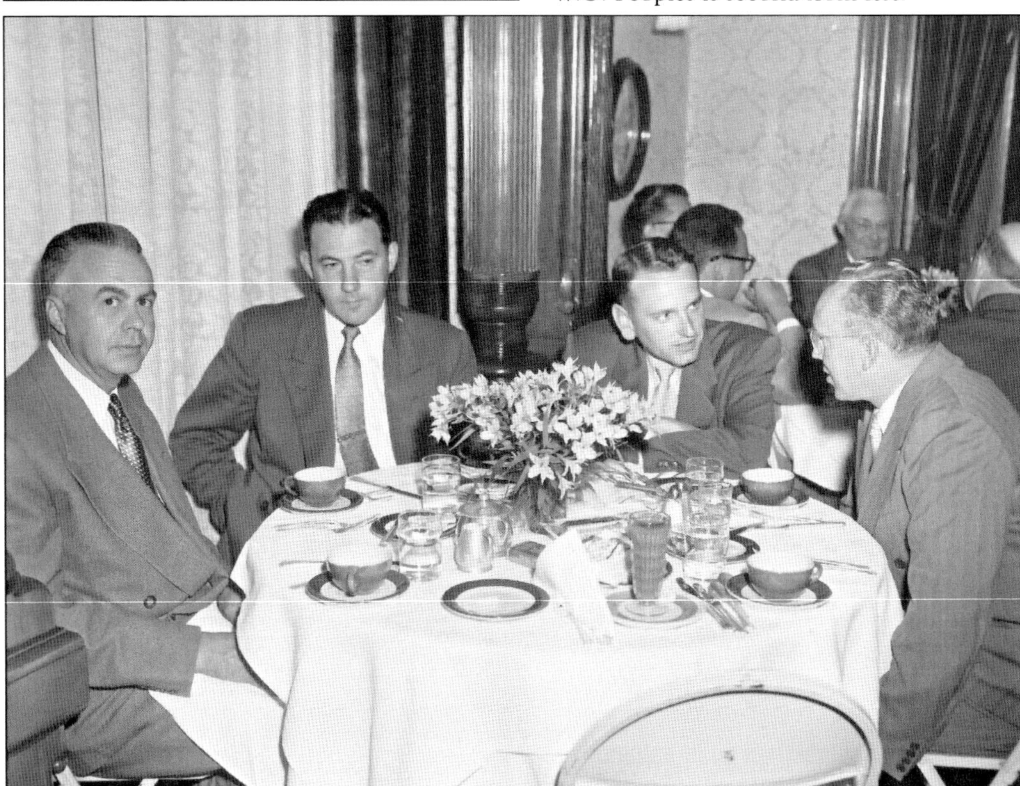

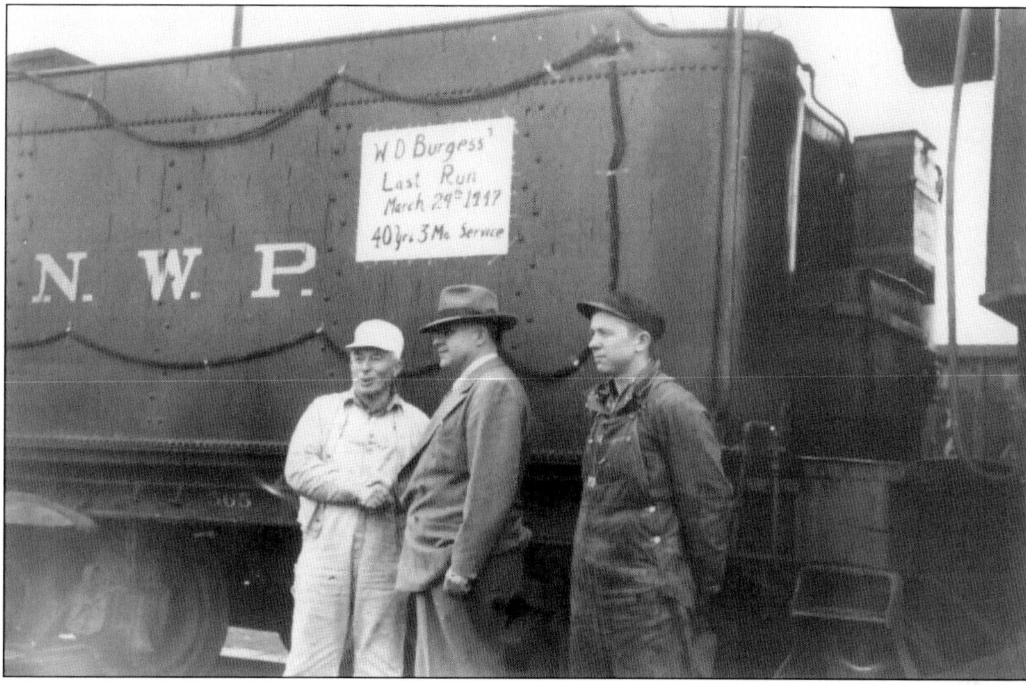

Wallace Burgess (left) grew up in Mattole Township in southern Humboldt and became a locomotive engineer for the NWP on April 23, 1908. In the 1942 NWP employee seniority list, Burgess is listed as the third-longest-serving engineer for the northern division. This image, taken on March 29, 1947, commemorates Burgess's "last run" and is from the collection of Guy B. Rhodes, who, in the 1950s, was an NWP mechanical department foreman based in Eureka.

This image shows the "last trip" of Henry W. Allen, who was made engineer on May 4, 1914. In the 1942 employee listing, Allen is named as the local chairman of the Eureka chapter of the Brotherhood of Locomotive Engineers. The 1910 US census lists him as a locomotive fireman living in Hydesville with his wife and baby daughter, with their nearest neighbor being a brakeman of a logging train.

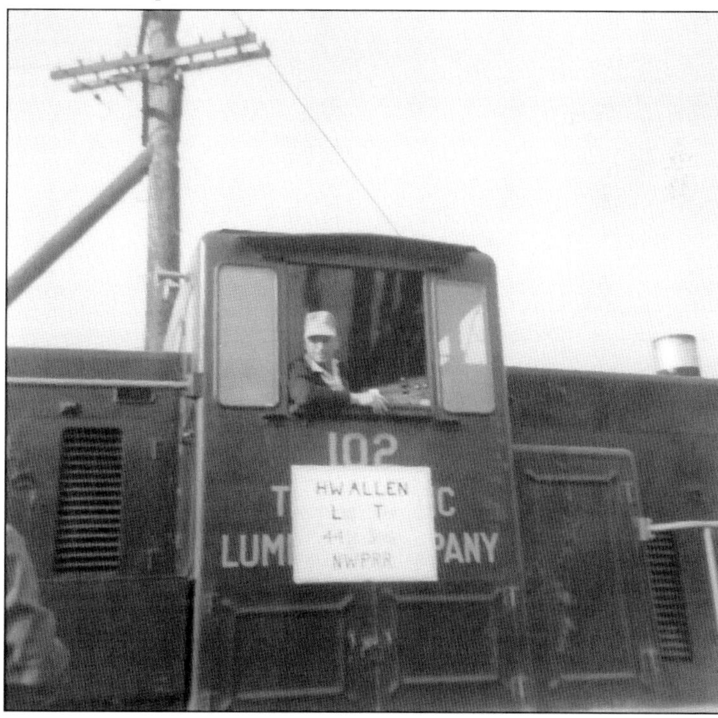

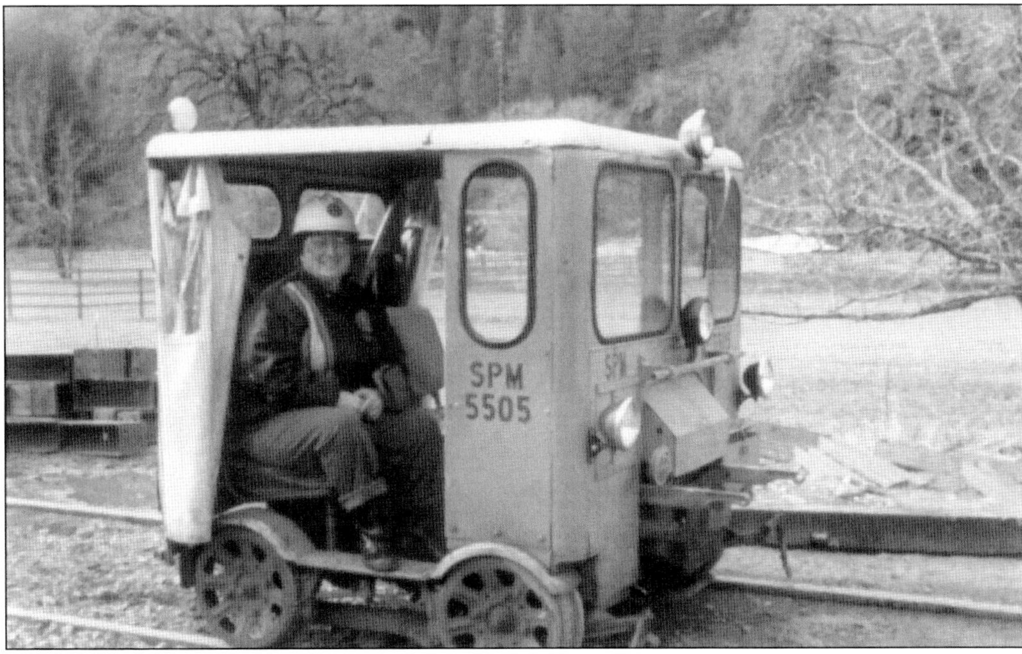

Francee White worked for the NWP from July 1970 through March 1985. She served for 10 years as secretary to district superintendent H.B. "Hi" Fowler, for three years as extra board clerk, and for two years as maintenance of way clerk. Her photograph albums, which she donated to the Fortuna Depot Museum in 2000, extensively document the final years of NWP's northern division.

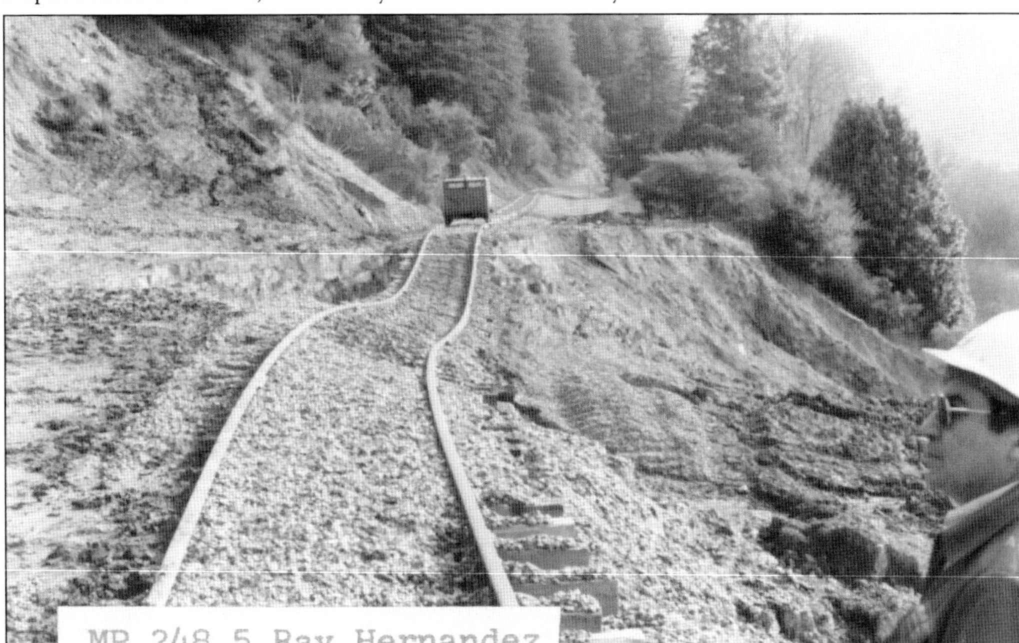

This and the remaining images in this chapter are from the Francee White collection. Here, NWP employee Ray Hernandez is inspecting a slide a few miles north of Shively. Hernandez needed to learn the depth, width, and contents of a slide before crews could begin to efficiently remove the material.

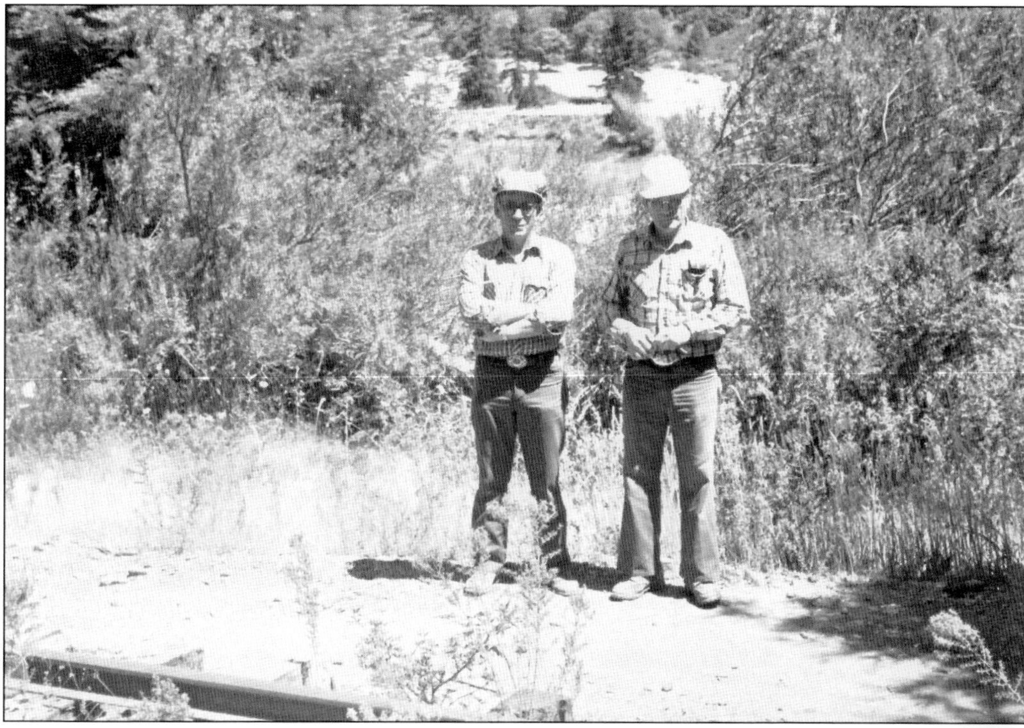

This photograph, taken by George Jesenko in July 1984, shows Ernie Wilson (left) and Walt Spain at McCann, milepost 232.5. Wilson became an NWP section and extra gang laborer in 1955, burro crane operator and crane engineer in 1956, and shovel engineer in 1959. Spain became an extra gang laborer in 1968, tractor crawler operator in 1969, and powder man (worker in charge of explosives) in 1971.

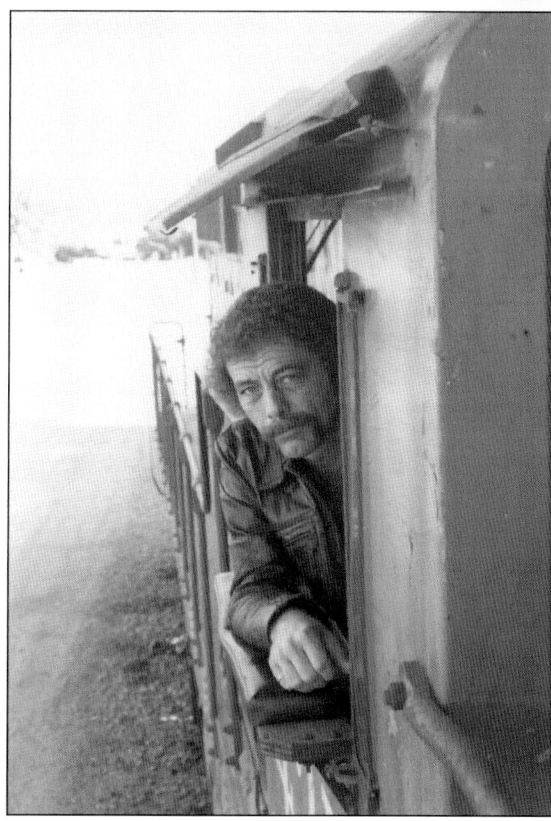

Engineer Fred L. Danforth is pictured at the Willits train yard around October 1983. The engine is Southern Pacific No. 4310. Danforth became a reserve engineer in September 1974 and was made a full engineer on May 8, 1975. After Southern Pacific sold the northern end of the NWP line to Bryan Whipple, Danforth worked as an engineer for Whipple's short-lived Eureka Southern Railroad.

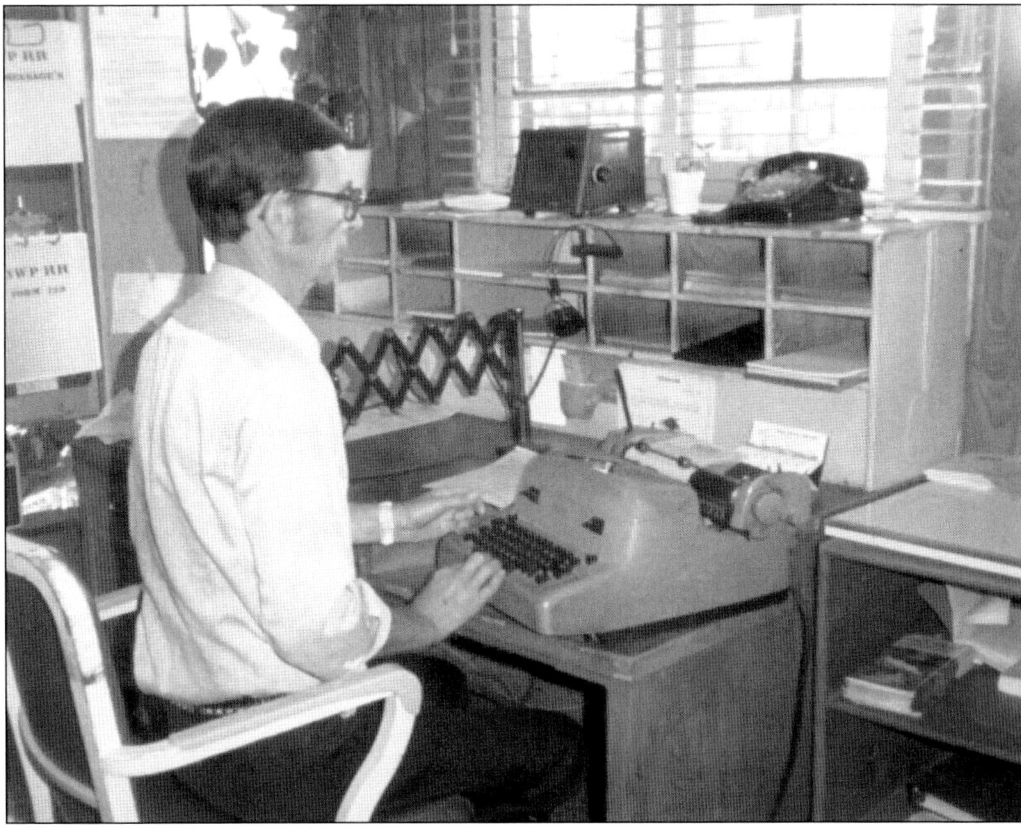

This photograph is labeled in Francee White's album as "Eddie Parks, Agent, Willits Depot, doing his job. October 1984." At the beginning of his career, Richard E. "Ed" Parks Jr. worked as a clerk in the Eureka yard. He retired from the Northwestern Pacific after 36 years of service.

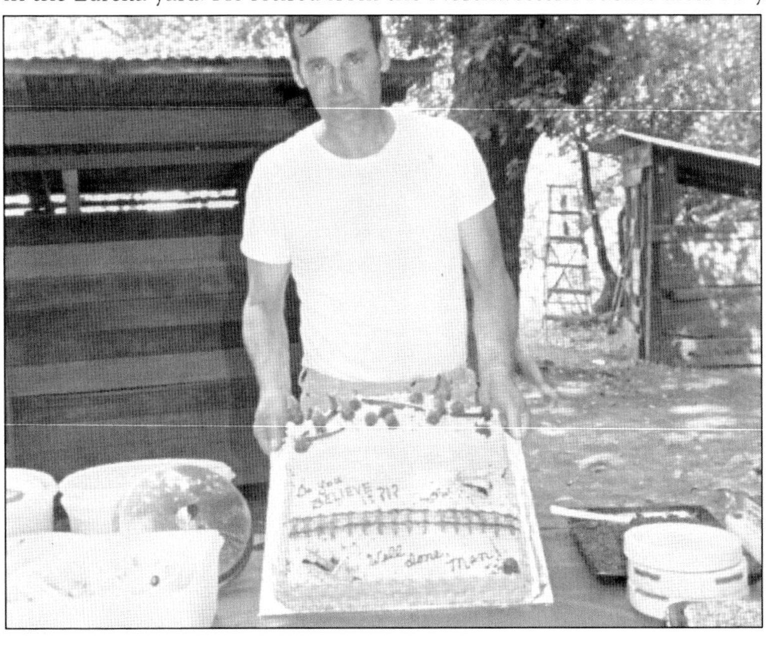

George Jesenko grew up in Dos Rios along the NWP line. After becoming an NWP section laborer in 1955, he was made tie handler operator in the roadway machine department in 1962. This image shows Jesenko at a picnic held at Dos Rios in July 1984 to celebrate completion of bank correction and track realignment at Berger Creek Hump. The month after this picnic, NWP ran its last train on the northern end.

Four

Along the Railroad

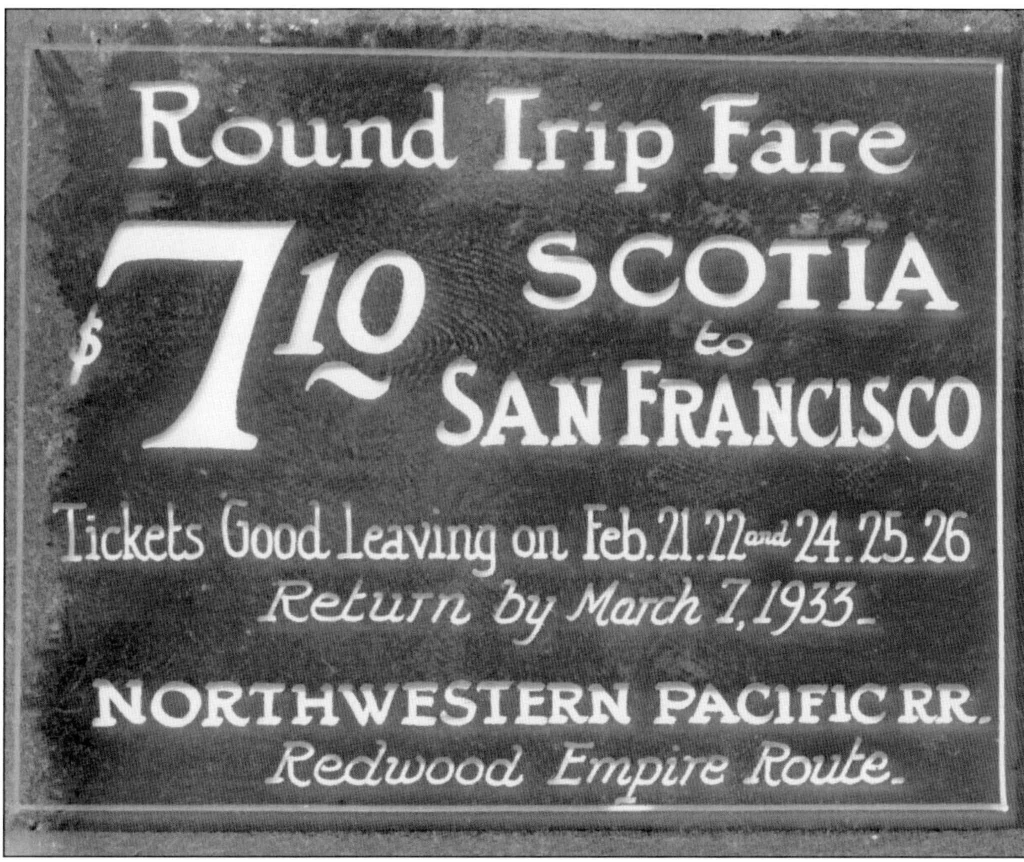

This 1933 lantern slide advertising a $7.10 Scotia-to-San Francisco round-trip fare was likely shown before movies at the Pacific Lumber Company's Winema Theater. The ease and speed of transportation made possible by the railroad were luxuries that can only be dreamed of in 21st-century Humboldt and northern Mendocino Counties. This chapter documents the sights seen by railroad passengers as they traveled from Trinidad to Willits.

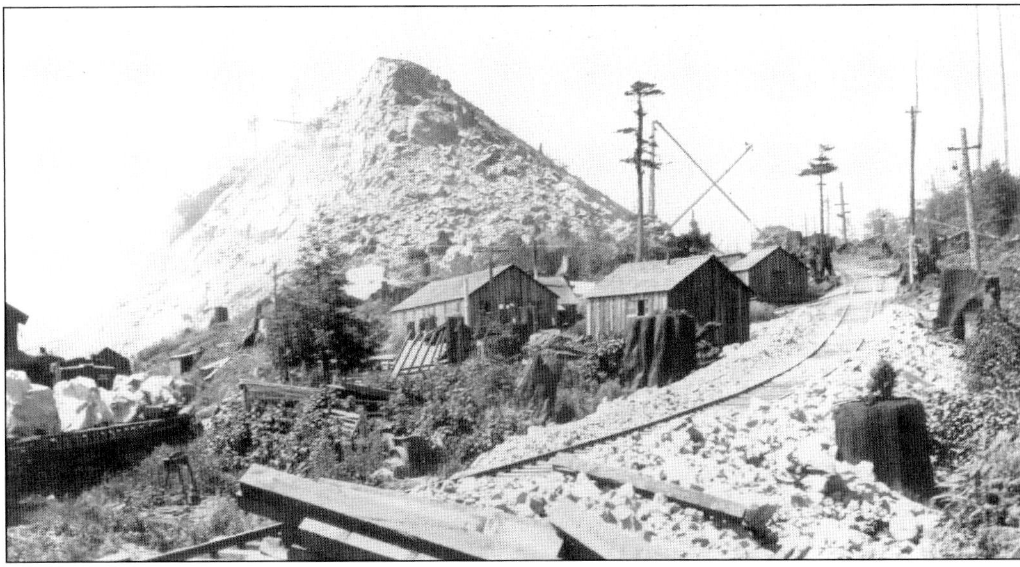

The northernmost terminus of the line was the seaside village of Trinidad. A portion of the yard is shown in this 1926 photograph from Joe Lockhart's collection. During the 1914 golden-spike celebrations, a second spike was driven at Trinidad to symbolize the line's future northward expansion to Crescent City. These plans remained under discussion until 1924, when railroad executives made an inspection journey by train to Trinidad and then by automobile north to Orick, after which the executives decided that the rough terrain and a lack of funds would prevent the extension of the line.

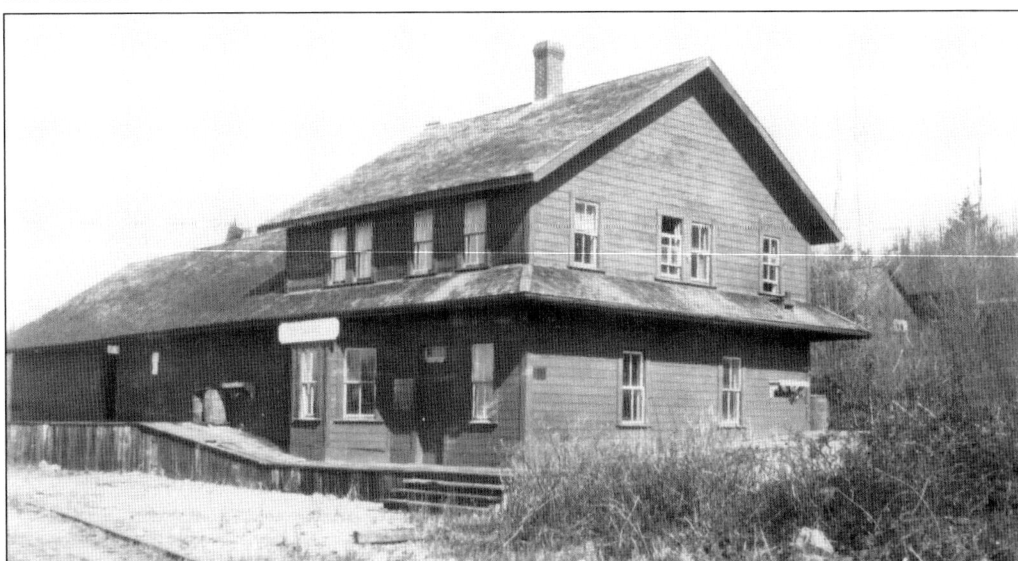

The railroad from San Francisco to Portland never materialized, and NWP's northern terminus remained in Trinidad. The Oregon & Eureka Railroad built this depot a half mile east of town in June 1907. The *Arcata Union* reported the following on June 22: "Beginning today, the long cherished hope of Trinidad residents . . . of being connected with the outside world by rail, will be realized, as passenger trains will now make this station their terminal instead of Luffenholtz." (Courtesy of NWPRRHS.)

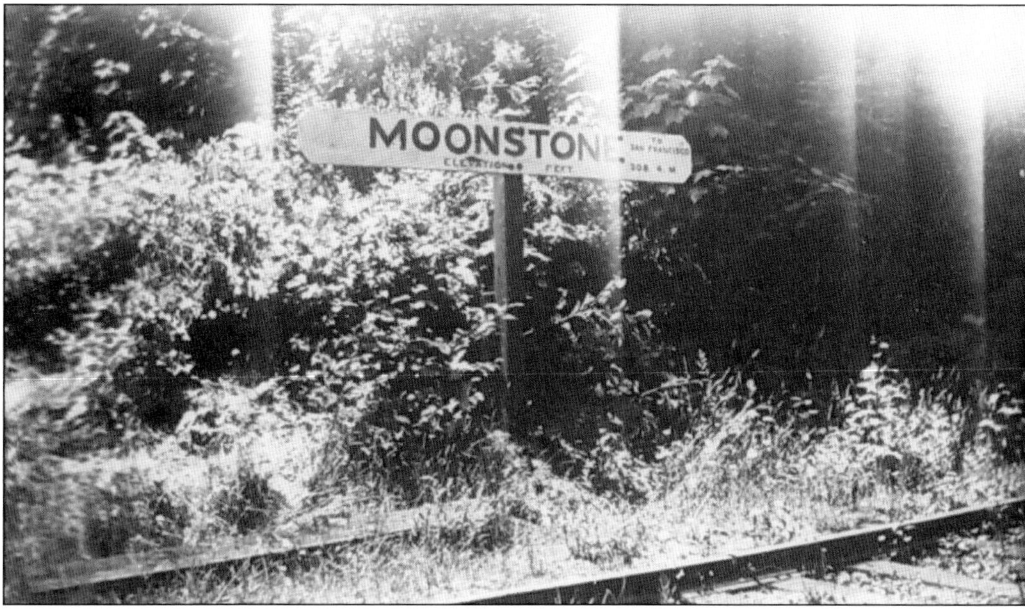

Some stops along the line boasted extensive depots, warehouses, and sidings; some only had small shelters or freight sheds. Some stops—such as Moonstone, located four miles south of Trinidad—were marked by nothing more than one of the railroad's regulation-design station signs. (Courtesy of HSU.)

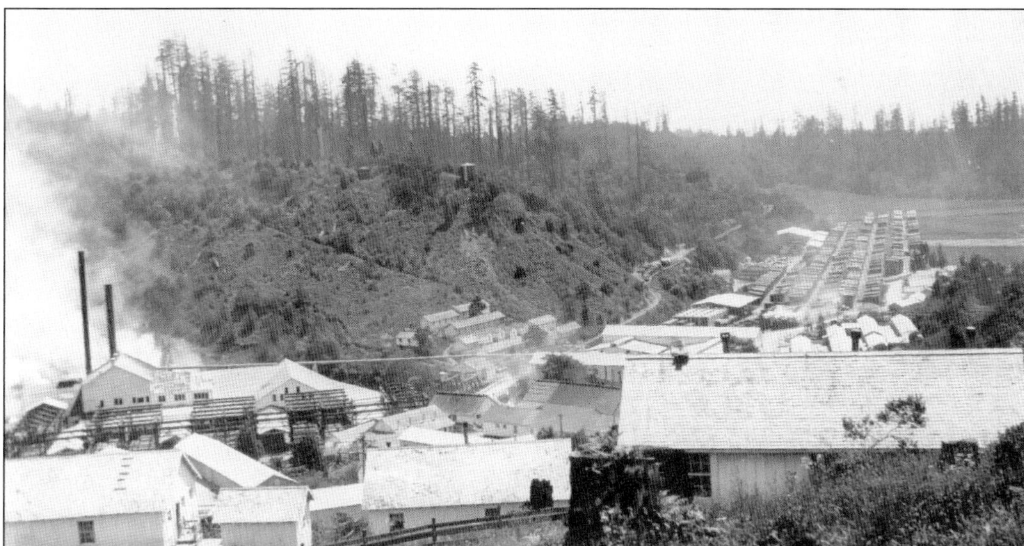

Little River Redwood Company commenced operations in 1908 and hosted a railroad stop from 1911 to 1933. Crannell (initially named Bullwinkel after an area landowner) was at its height when this photograph, from the Joe Lockhart collection, was taken in the 1920s. The Little River Redwood Company merged with Hammond Lumber Company in 1931. After the merger, Hammond dismantled this sawmill and moved the Crannell mill workers to Hammond's company town, Samoa.

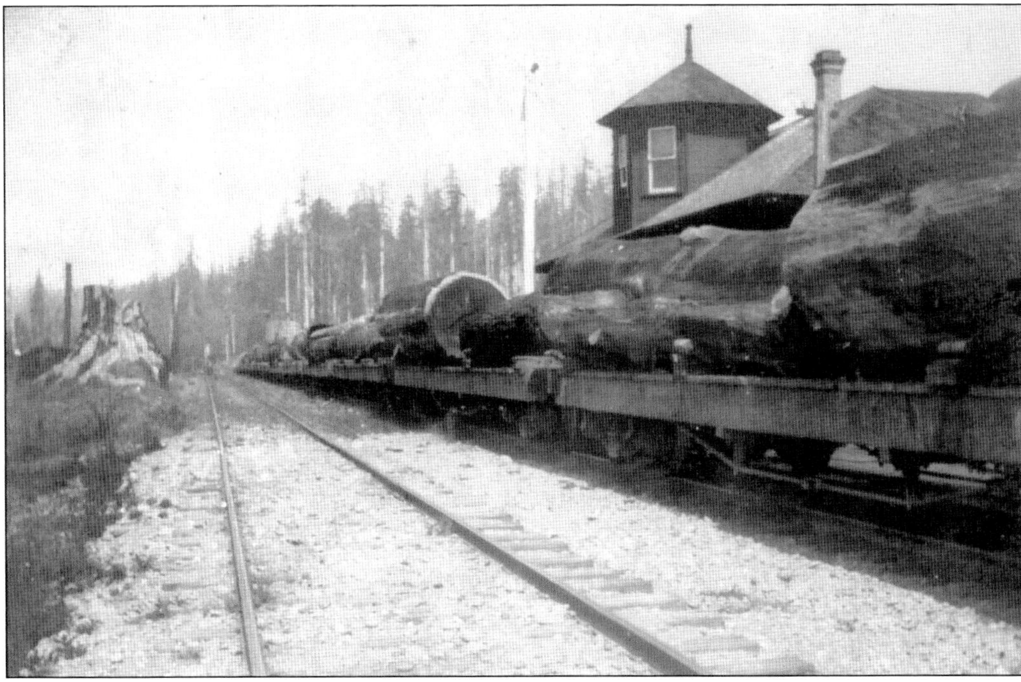

Another of Joe Lockhart's images shows the Fieldbrook depot just visible behind a logging train. Fieldbrook is located at milepost 17.8 on the Trinidad Branch line that has Eureka as the starting point and Trinidad at milepost 28.2. The Fieldbrook post office was open from 1902 to 1932.

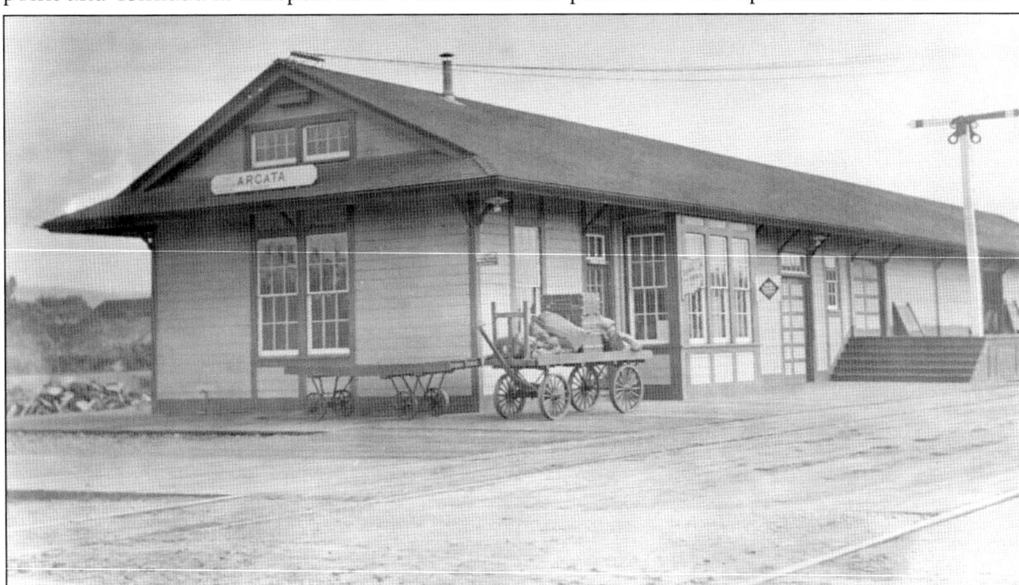

In the 1890s, the Arcata & Mad River Railroad constructed Arcata's depot according to Southern Pacific's standardized design for "One Story Combination Depot Number 23." In 1971, despite objections from the Arcata City Council, NWP closed the depot; NWP demolished it in 1972 as computerization replaced manned stations. The *Times-Standard* quoted an anonymous NWP employee as saying: "Men mean nothing (at rail headquarters) in San Francisco. All they see is the dollar and the decimal point." (Courtesy of HSU.)

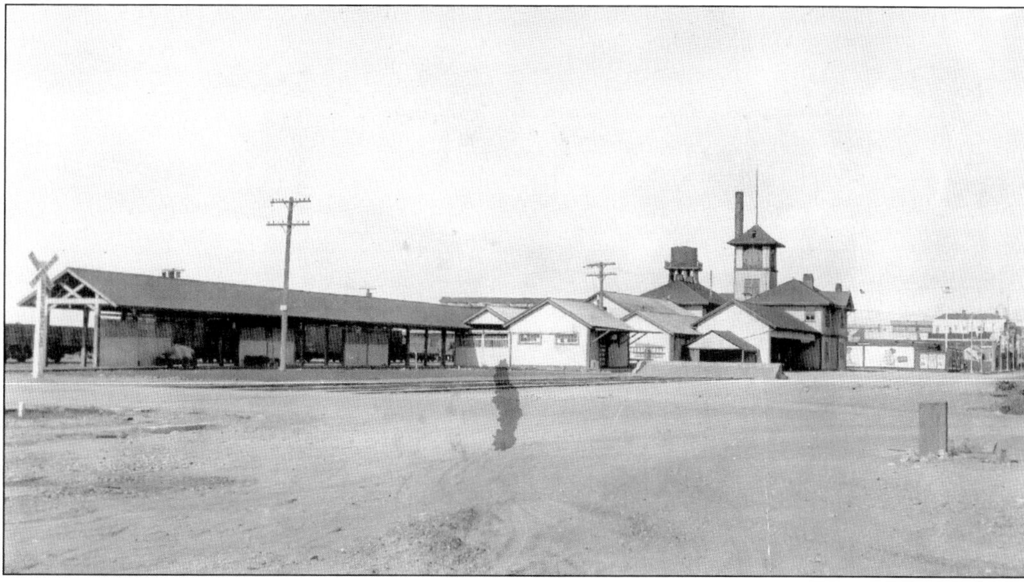

When construction began in August 1900 on Eureka's distinctive towered depot, the *Humboldt Times* reported the following: "The upper floor will be the private offices and meeting rooms of the directors and officials of the road, while the ground floor will be given over to the daily business of the corporation . . . ticket offices, baggage rooms, closets [presumably meaning restrooms] and waiting rooms." After it was completed in March 1901, the building replaced the one-story Eel River & Eureka Railroad (ER&ERR) depot that had been constructed in the 1880s.

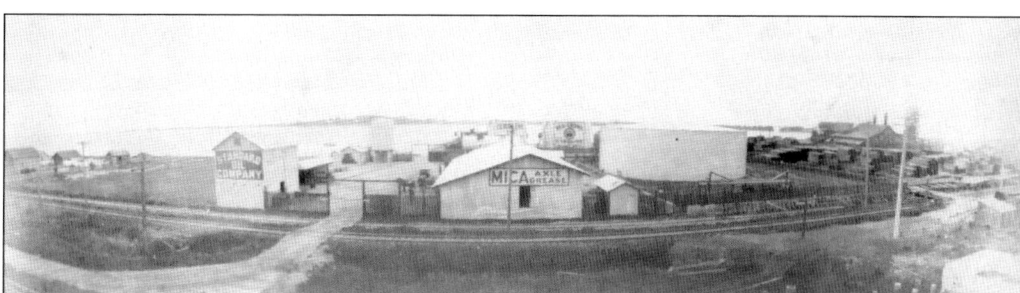

The Eureka station, located at milepost 284.1, became NWP's northern district headquarters. The rail yard eventually included a turntable, an eight-stall roundhouse, oil storage tanks, railroad car barns, repair buildings, and warehouses. Among the spur rail lines, sidings, and flag stops between the Eureka yard and South Bay were the Holmes Eureka Lumber Company plant (visible at right) and the Standard Oil docks at milepost 281.8.

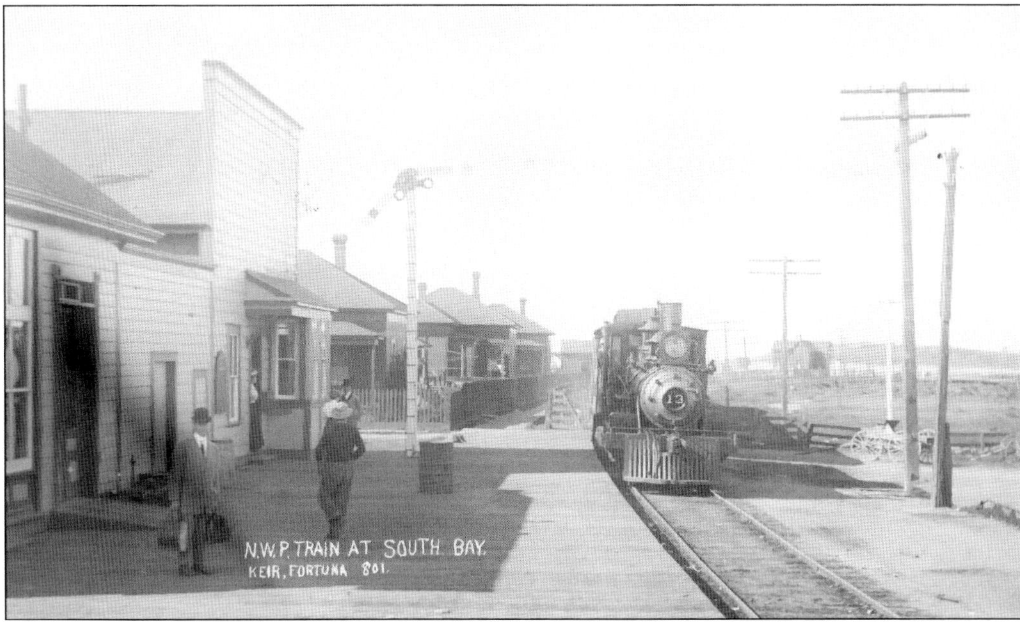

South Bay, shown in this 1911 postcard, was the railroad station for Fields Landing at milepost 277.8. Disagreements between John Vance, co-owner of the ER&ERR, and landowner Waterman Field led to the establishment of the station and post office at South Bay rather than in Fields Landing. In the mid-20th century, the South Bay Hotel (shown on page 17) was moved to a new location beside Highway 101 in Fields Landing.

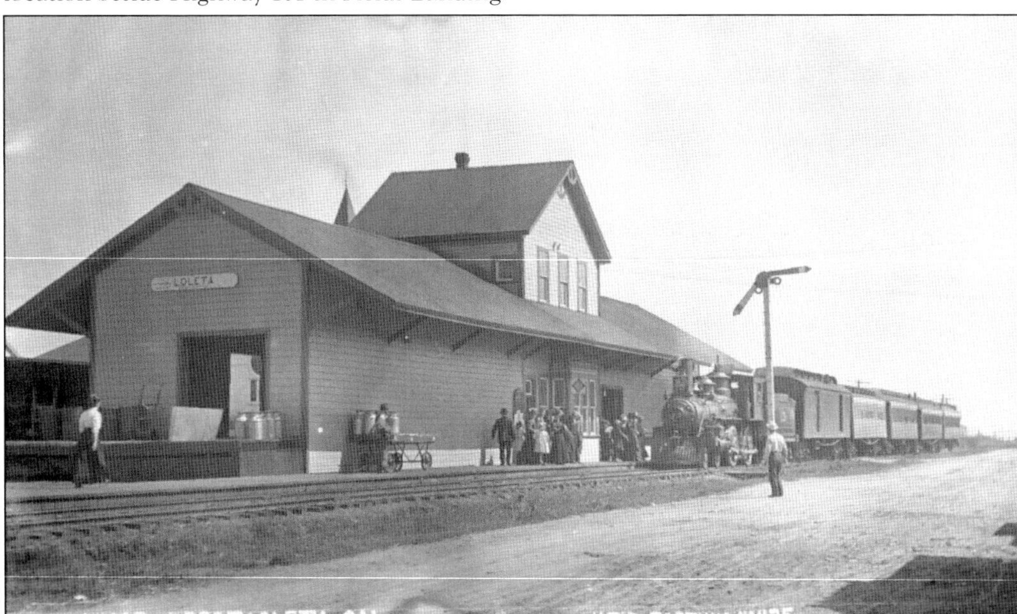

The 1898 ER&ERR depot in Loleta used a design similar to that of Southern Pacific's standardized two-story combination depots. The ticket office, with the telegraph operator's bay window, was at the center, with the stationmaster's residence above. The freight room is visible in the left foreground, and on the other side of the office is the passengers' waiting room. The milk cans on the freight loading dock are indicative of Loleta's dairy industry. (Courtesy of HSU.)

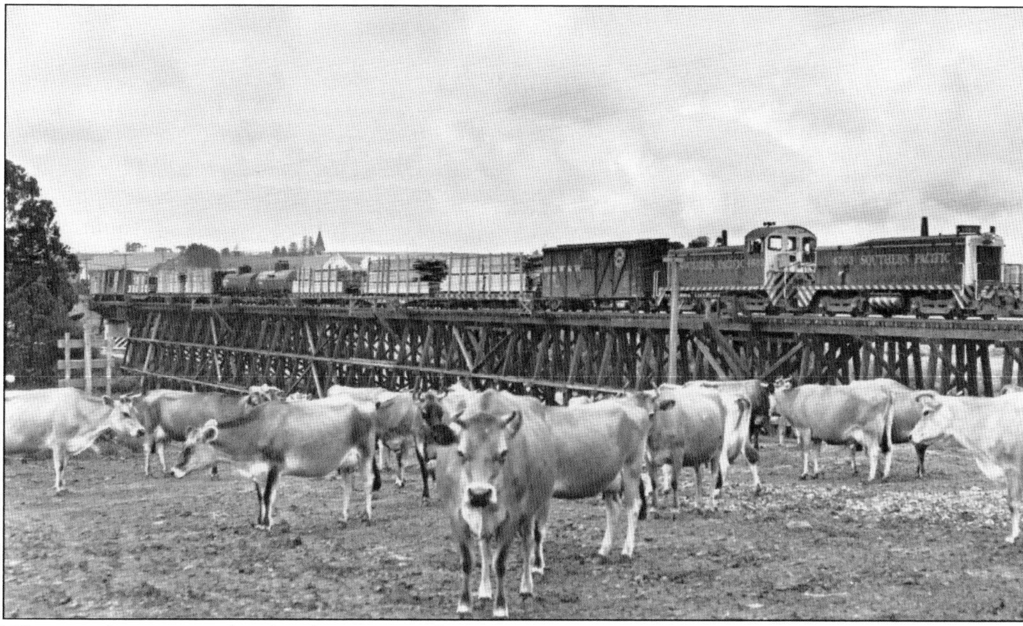

The trestle just south of Loleta crossed above the original Redwood Highway. The railroad overpass was notorious among emergency responders due to the number of reckless motorists who crashed into the trestle at the bend in the road. This 1950s image may have been intended to be somewhat tongue-in-cheek with the paired "cow and calf" engines visible beyond one of the many herds of cattle in Loleta.

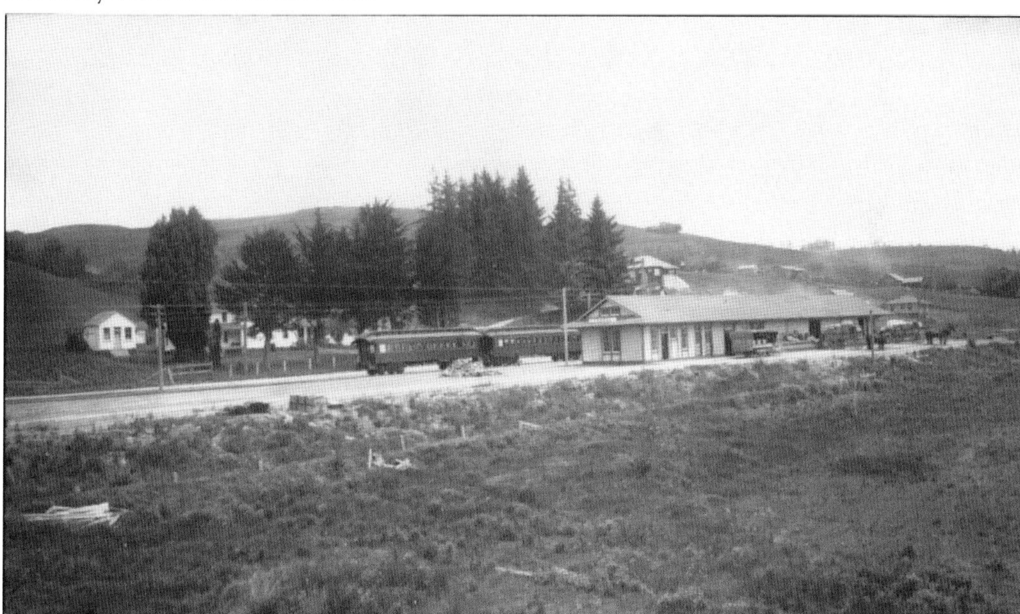

The Fernbridge depot, like the one at Arcata, followed the design of Southern Pacific's "One Story Combination Depot Number 23." At the time of this photograph, the station was called Ferndale Junction. This photograph was taken before the construction of Fernbridge, which was the longest concrete bridge in the world when it was completed in November 1911. The field shown in the foreground became the site of the bridge. (Courtesy of HSU.)

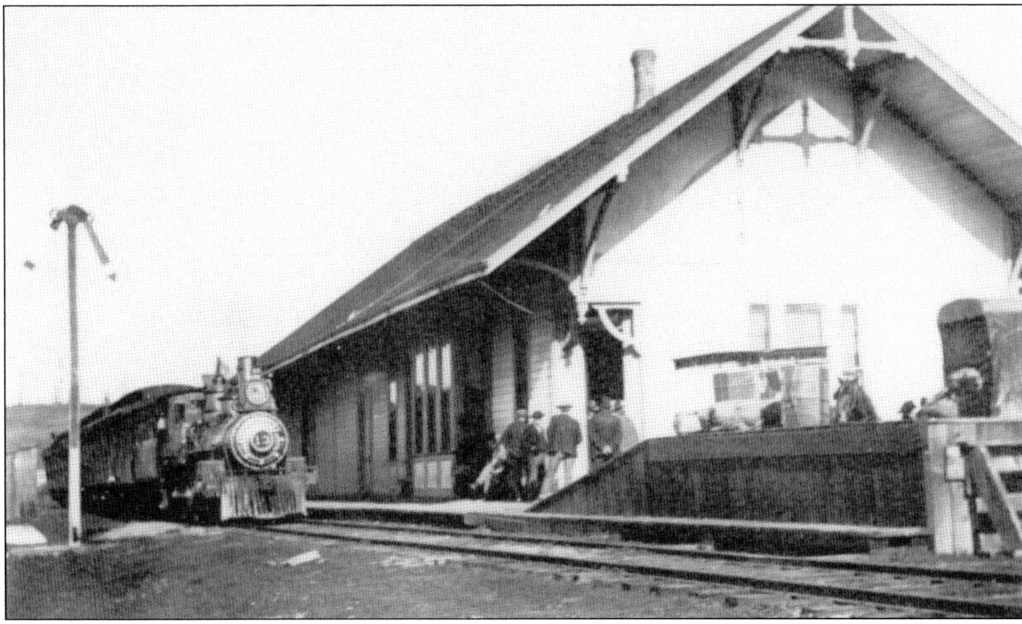

In March 1889, the *Humboldt Times* reported that, "The Eel River & Eureka Railroad is laying the foundation of a depot at Fortuna. It is said this will be one of the most substantial buildings the company will have on the line, as Fortuna is the most important station." A tall, one-story building with a passenger waiting room, office, and attached freight building, the Fortuna depot features large, round attic vents and a notable amount of decorative woodwork.

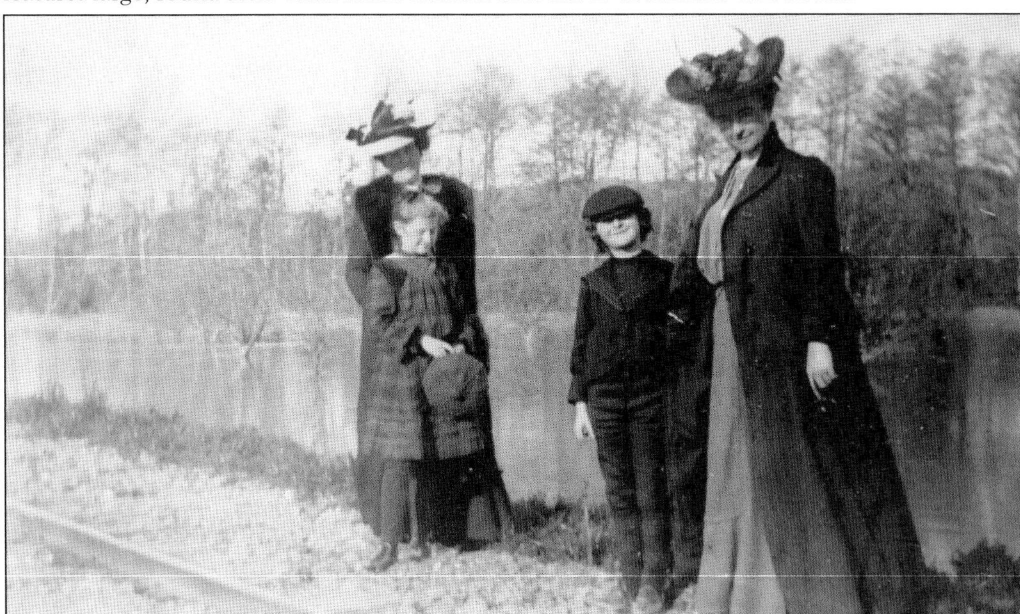

This image, captured by Fortuna photographer Frank Spesert, is labeled "Terminus of S.F.&N.W.R.R. near Rohnerville, Feb. 16, 1904." In 1904, the Santa Fe Railroad purchased the ER&ERR and began operating it as the San Francisco & Northwestern Railroad. Rohnerville's depot was three quarters of a mile from Rohnerville, below Campton Heights Bluff, near the present-day junction of South Fortuna Boulevard and the Highway 101 freeway overpass.

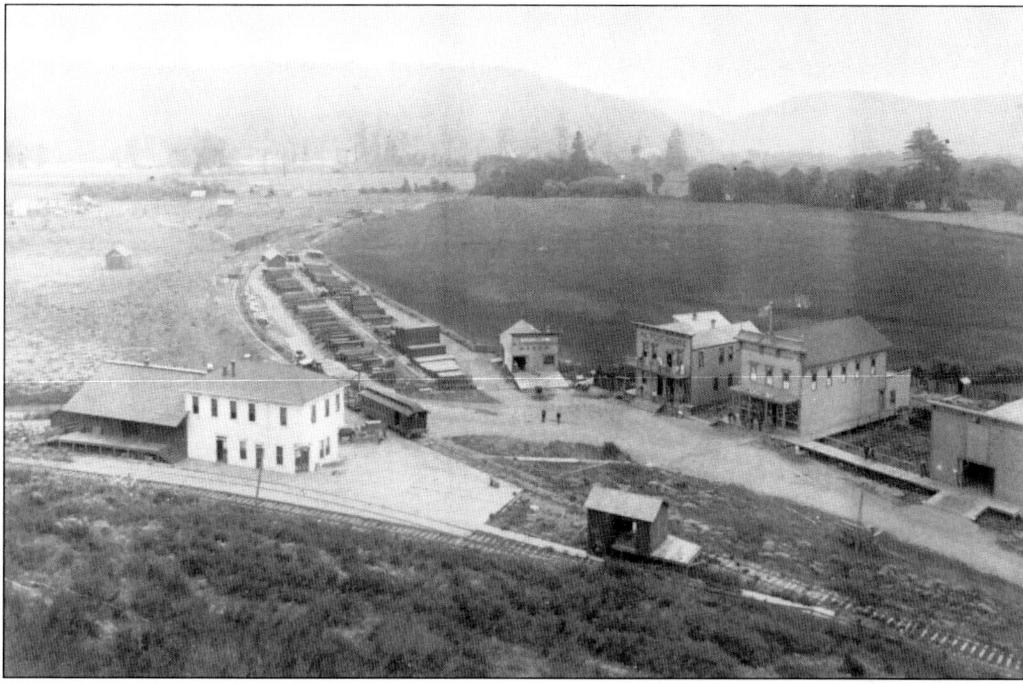

Alton, located at NWP milepost 262.7 and laid out in 1887, was at the junction of the main ER&ERR line with the Pacific Lumber Company's railroad. The Carlotta Branch Line from Alton eventually also connected lines of companies such as Holmes Eureka and Hammond Lumber. Alton was also an important livestock shipping point. The depot, at left, included upstairs living quarters for the stationmaster.

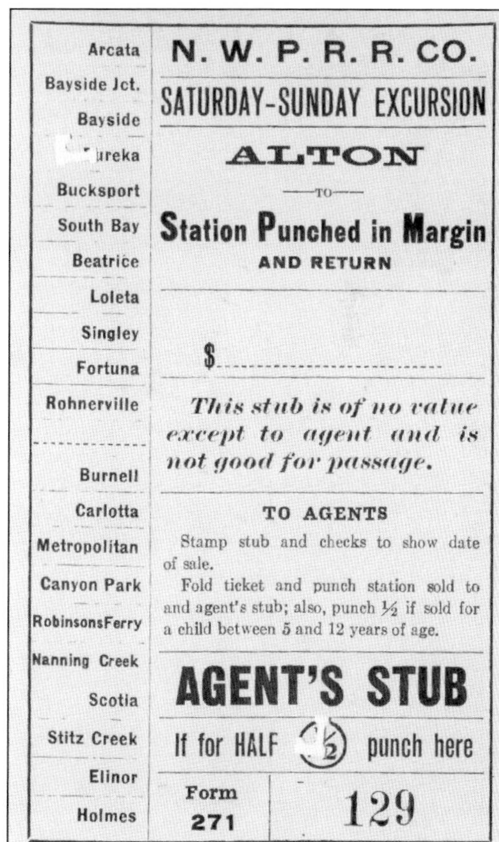

Arcata
Bayside Jct.
Bayside
Eureka
Bucksport
South Bay
Beatrice
Loleta
Singley
Fortuna
Rohnerville
Burnell
Carlotta
Metropolitan
Canyon Park
RobinsonsFerry
Nanning Creek
Scotia
Stitz Creek
Elinor
Holmes

N. W. P. R. R. CO.

SATURDAY-SUNDAY EXCURSION

ALTON

—TO—

Station Punched in Margin

AND RETURN

$..............................

This stub is of no value except to agent and is not good for passage.

TO AGENTS

Stamp stub and checks to show date of sale.

Fold ticket and punch station sold to and agent's stub; also, punch ½ if sold for a child between 5 and 12 years of age.

AGENT'S STUB

If for HALF ½ punch here

Form 271

129

This Saturday–Sunday excursion ticket, which is now in the Fortuna Depot Museum collection, was used for a child's round trip from Alton to Eureka on June 11, 1910. It provides a glimpse at the extent of NWP's northern division when the company was about halfway done with its efforts to close the gap between Willits and Humboldt Bay.

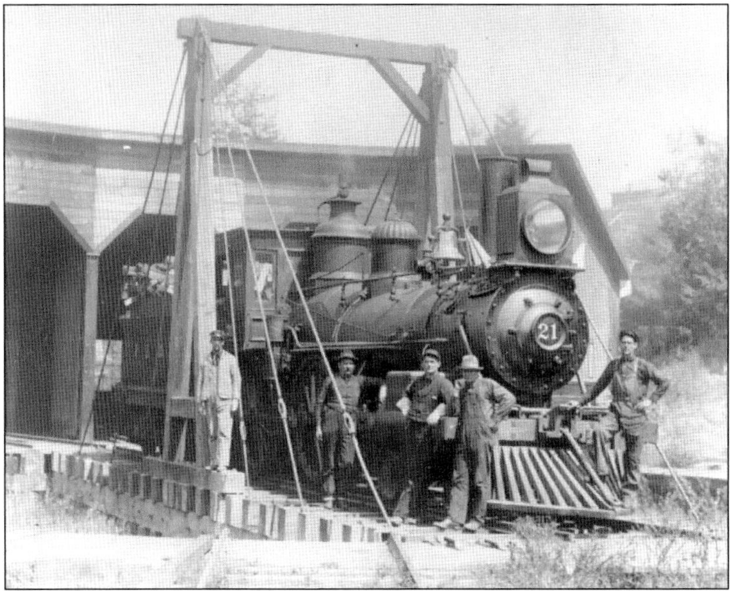

This 1905 image shows the first roundhouse and turntable at Scotia. These structures were essential to the Pacific Lumber Company (T.P.L. Co.) operations. The company maintained its own fleet of locomotives, which required housing and repairs. In addition to this roundhouse and its replacement, Scotia has had three depots. The first was in a building shared with the town hall. A second, built in 1908, was destroyed in the 1964 flood.

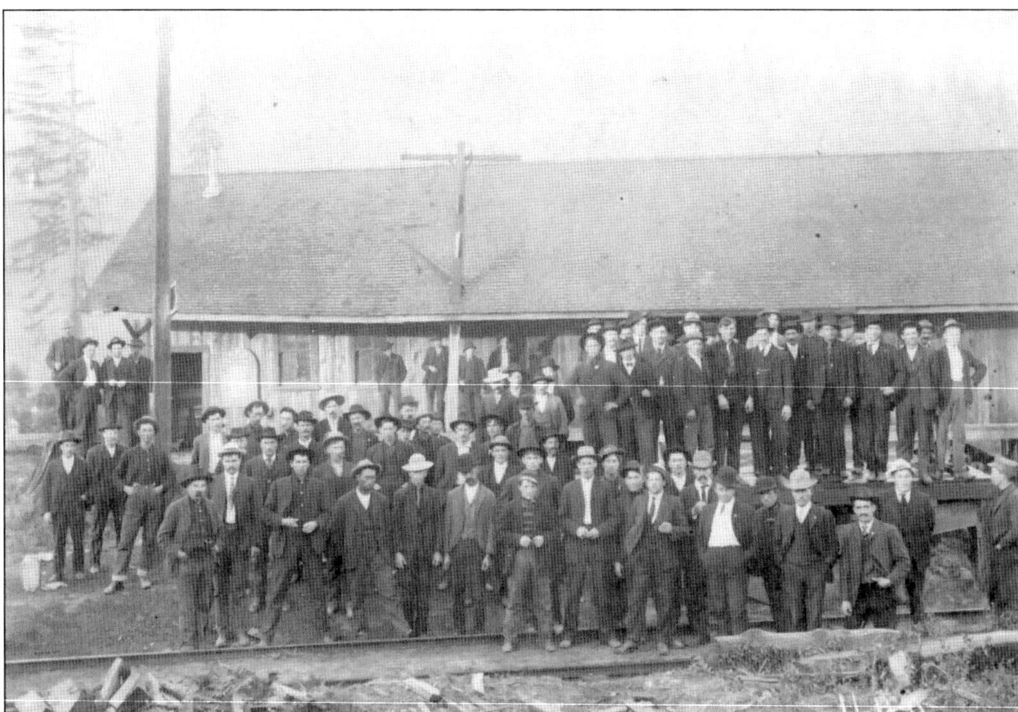

Loggers who posed at the Elinor depot on October 4, 1906, were en route to Fortuna to protest the hiring of Chinese workers at a nearby salmon cannery. The hiring move violated Humboldt's unwritten ban against people of Asian descent, which was in place from 1885 until the mid-20th century. The railroad station and post office, first known as the Pacific Lumber Company's Camp Five, were named "Elinor" in May 1906 for either the stationmaster's wife or the wife of NWP assistant manager B.F. Porter.

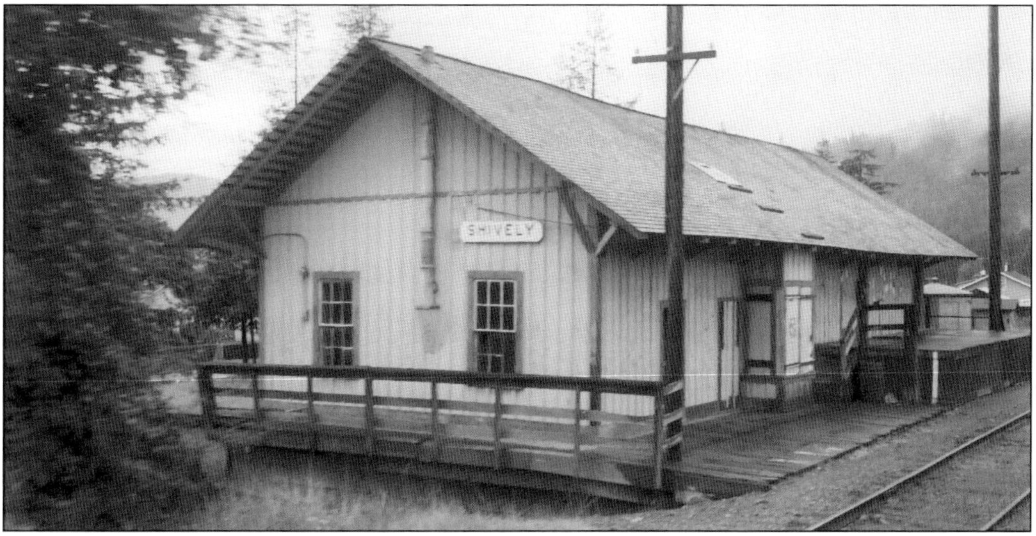

In April 1910, assistant manager B.F. Porter selected the site for Shively's Southern Pacific–style freight station. County surveyor Conners and second district supervisor Williams laid out the half-mile road connecting the station to the town. The *Humboldt Beacon* reported, "For years Shively has wanted a railroad depot . . . to go to Elinor several miles distant meant much time spent in travel . . . crossing the Eel River four times in making the round trip." (Courtesy of NWPRRHS.)

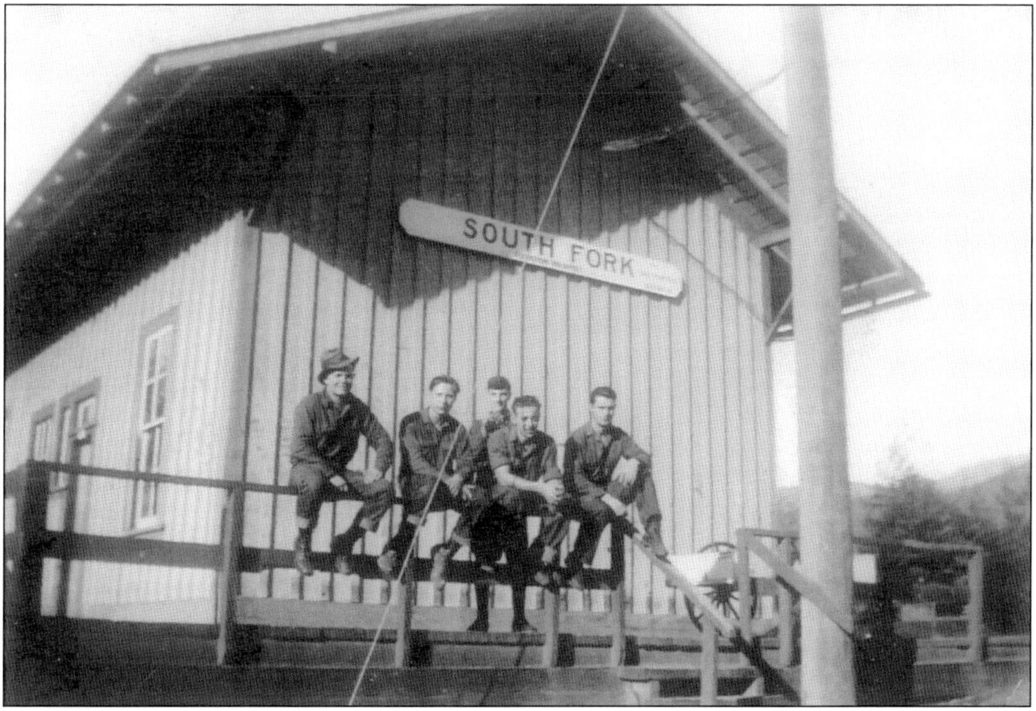

As at Shively, South Fork had a standardized SP freight depot. Built in 1914, it was destroyed by fire in 1955. These young men are likely members of the Civilian Conservation Corps, which had a camp at nearby Dyerville during the Great Depression. The corps provided employment for single men ages 18 to 25. They were paid a monthly salary of $30 with the stipulation that $25 be sent home.

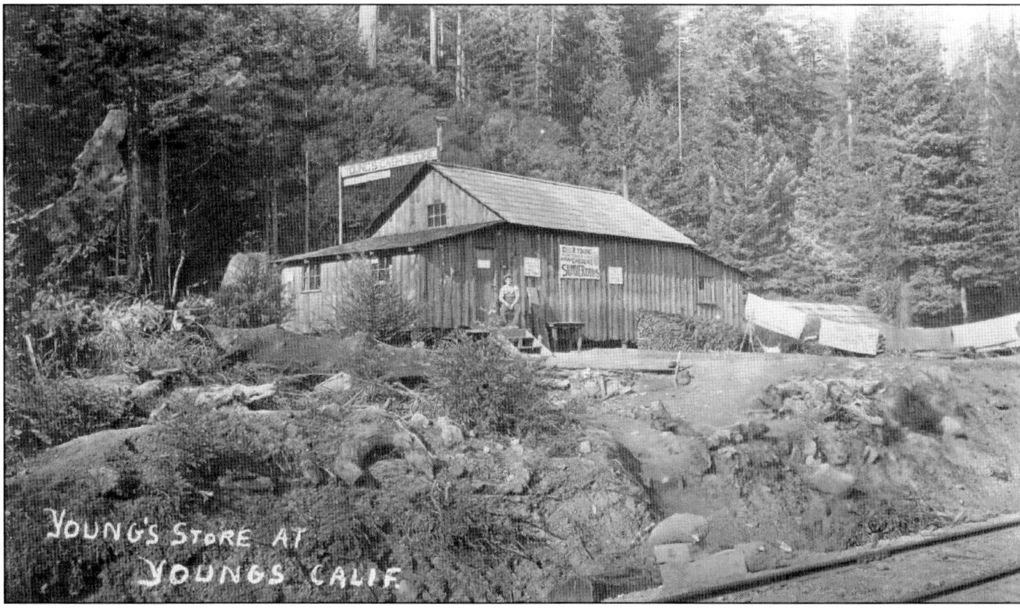

This is George Young's Cash Store, the center of the community of Youngs that briefly flourished during the push to "close the gap" in the NWP line. The fruit boxes and sacks of potatoes visible next to the tracks in the foreground have either arrived as stock for Young's store or contain local farmers' produce waiting to be shipped via the railroad.

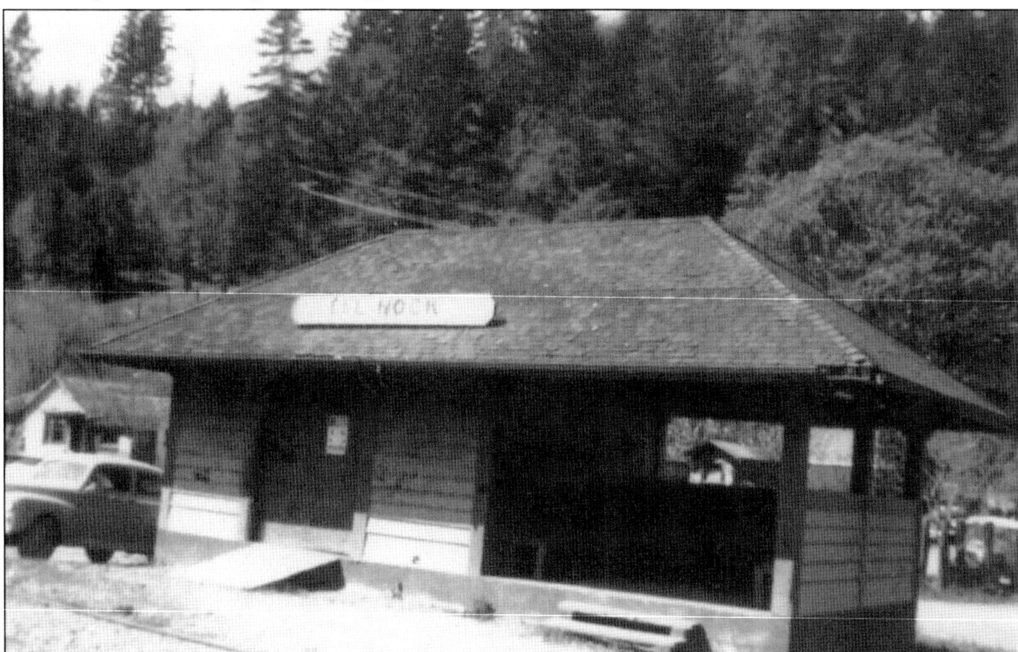

Eel Rock's small depot, with its freight storeroom and a covered passenger waiting area, is pictured here in 1954. Ted Gruhn, who traveled by NWP from Eureka to join the Navy in September 1941, recalled the neighborly interactions between train crews and rural residents; he said that trains often stopped for locals making short trips who paid for rides with "fresh corn on the cob, fruit, blackberries, or once in a while a pie."

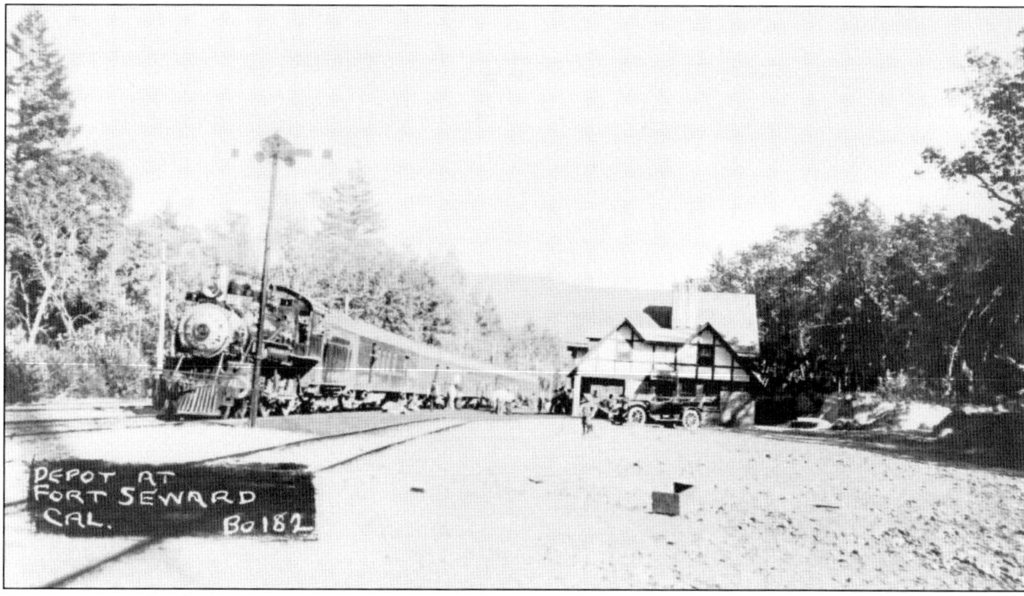

Fort's Seward's depot shares some design elements with Southern Pacific's standardized two-story depots, but the Tudor-style half-timbering gives the building its own distinctive flair. The NWP maintained a cookhouse here for employees that was run by the J.V. Moan Commissary Company. NWP brakeman Leslie "Blinky" Hallstone recalled that Moan contracted "to feed all the maintenance of way gangs and . . . run all the cookhouses in the Eel River Canyon" at South Fork, Fort Seward, and Island Mountain.

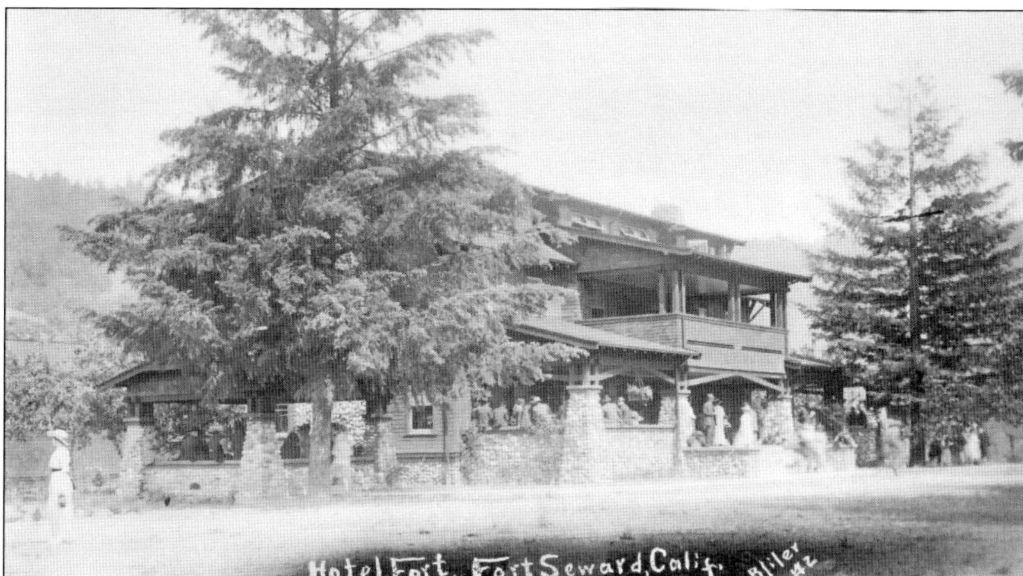

The Fort Seward Hotel, built between 1912 and 1914, was destroyed by fire in 1956. In a 1915 listing of Humboldt County's "Hotels which Cater to the Tourist, Sportsman and Fisherman," Fort Seward was singled out for its "deer, bear, and excellent fishing; excellent climate, fresh fruits and vegetables, magnificent scenery." The "fine hotel and cottages" were praised as a quail-hunting resort. Additionally, the tourism guide declared that Humboldt County has "the greatest fishing in all America."

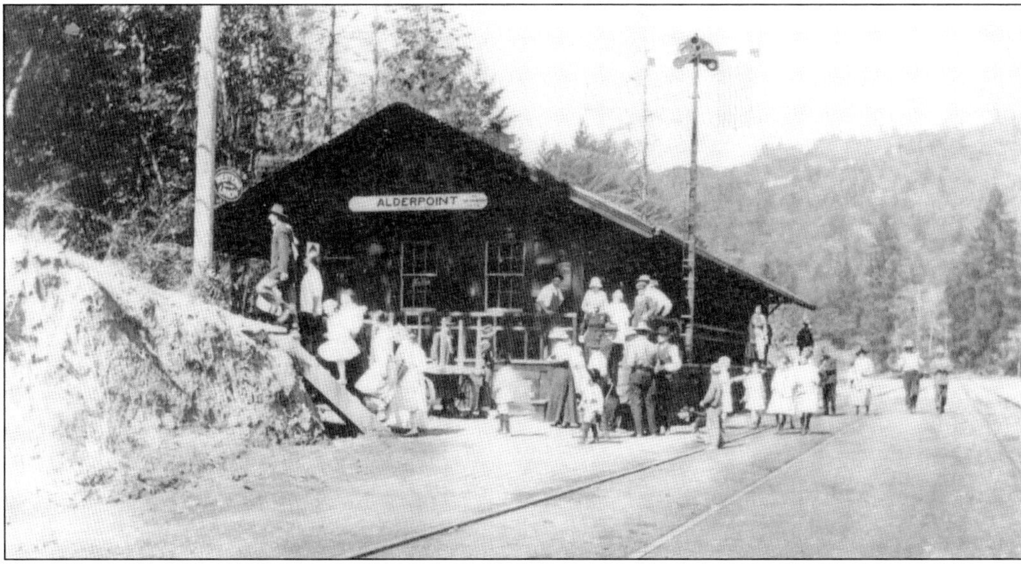

This postcard of the Alderpoint depot was mailed in October 1917. After serving as a stagecoach stop in the 1870s, Alderpoint saw rapid development during the period of NWP construction, with a hotel and post office opened in 1911. The community suffered a corresponding decline with the railroad's closure in 1984.

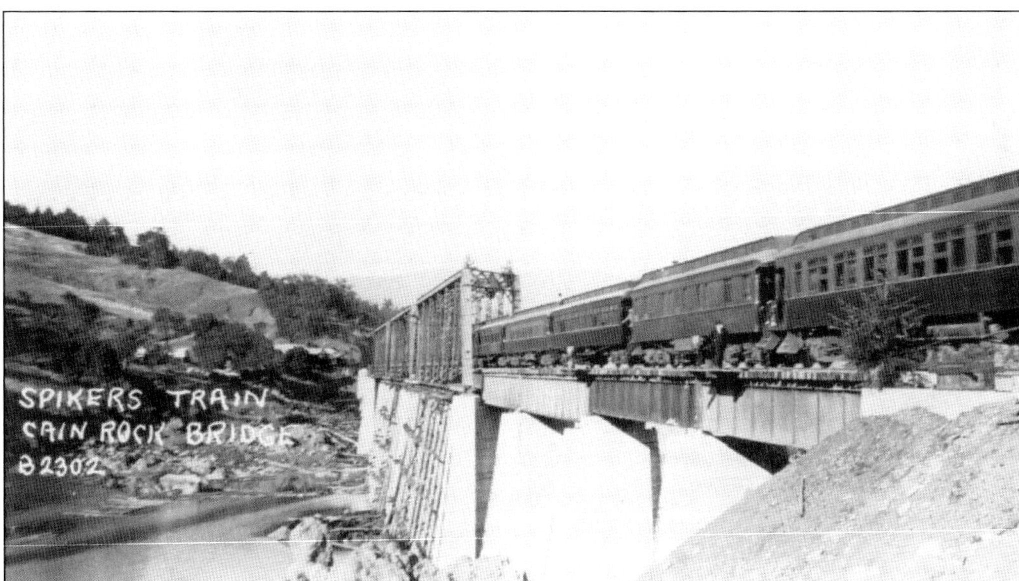

This October 23, 1914, photograph of the "spikers train" crossing the Cain Rock Bridge was captured by Bertha Hinckley on her turn-of-the-century postcard camera. Hinckley was among thousands who attended the Cain Rock golden-spike celebration. Cain Rock Bridge, the final link in closing the gap, was constructed in summer 1914 by work crews consisting of local recruits and men sent by San Francisco employment agencies.

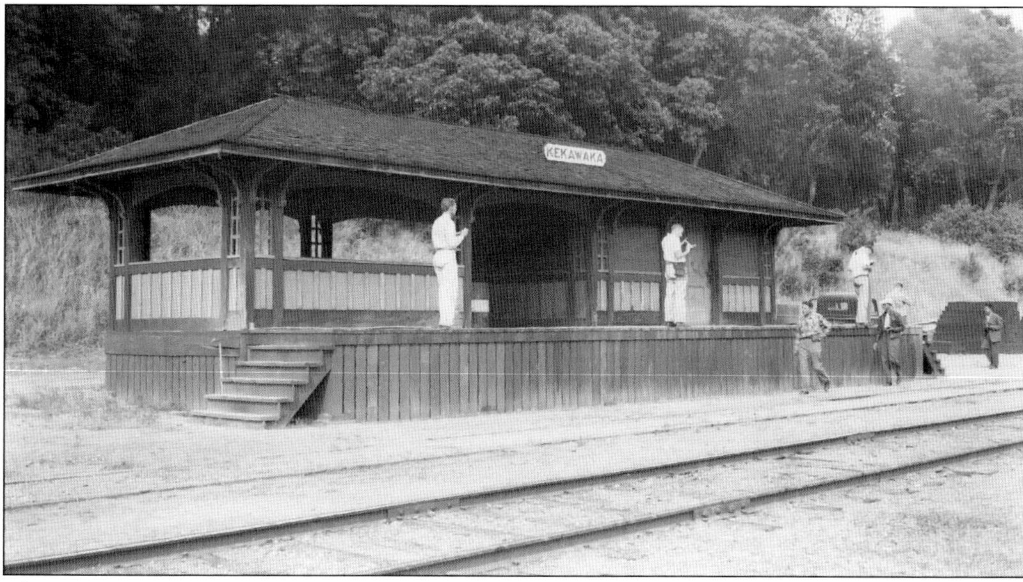

This 1940s image from the collection of the Northwestern Pacific Railroad Historical Society is identified as showing railfans photographing a train as it approaches the Kekawaka station. The name Kekawaka has been traced to the Eel River Athabaskan Lassik dialect. The stretch of the NWP line including Kekawaka and Island Mountain is the sole portion of the railroad that passes through Trinity County. (Courtesy of NWPRRHS.)

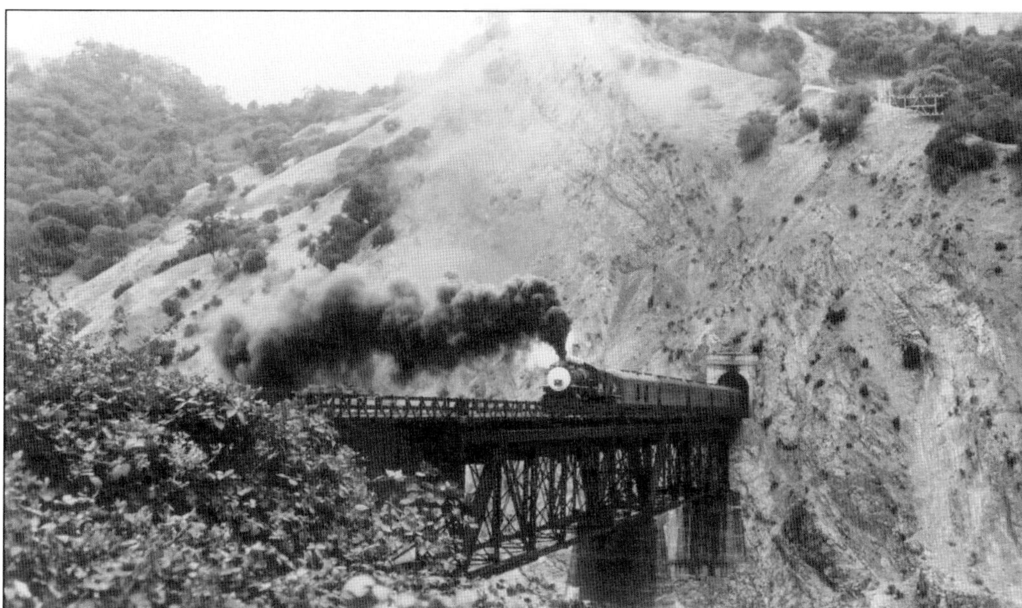

Island Mountain Tunnel is NWP's Tunnel No. 27, located at milepost 194.8 at its west portal. At 4,313.8 feet long, it is over twice as long as the second-longest tunnel on the line. Infamous for a 1978 fire that played a major role in the closure of NWP's northern division, the tunnel was also a major hurdle during construction; 17 men were killed in an explosion during initial blasting for the Island Mountain Tunnel. (Courtesy of NWPRRHS.)

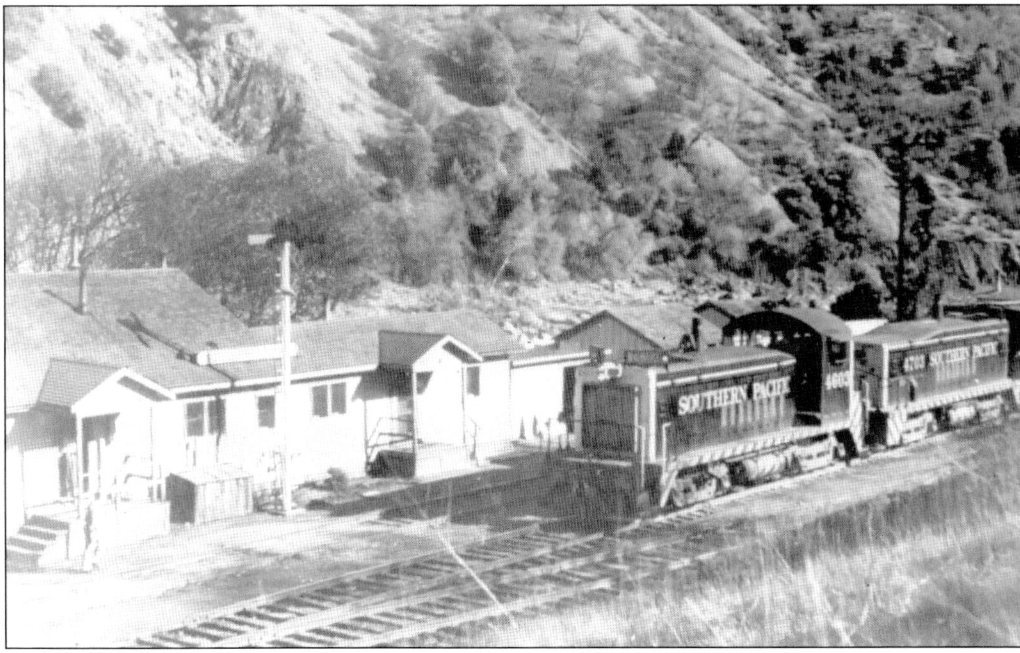

Island Mountain station, shown in this image from the Joe Lockhart collection, was among the many NWP buildings washed down river in the 1964 flood, which also destroyed Island Mountain Bridge. Island Mountain, the base for an NWP maintenance crew, had worker housing (also lost in the flood) made from old boxcars and passenger cars.

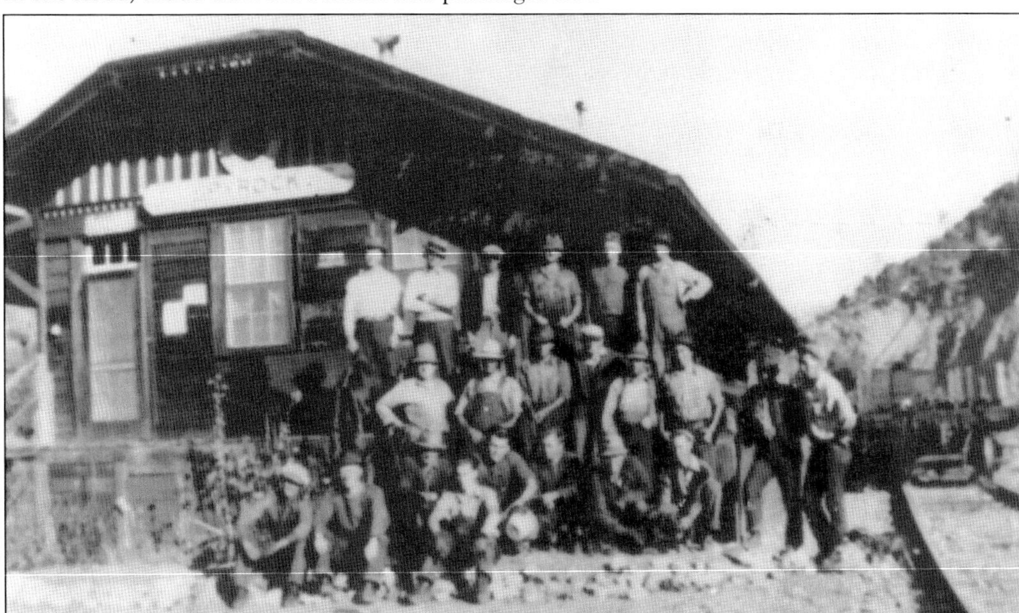

This 1940 image from the Francee White collection shows Spyrock Station in Mendocino County at milepost 180, with a notation stating, "Claude Hoaglen on extreme right." According to a "Milepost Minder" guide given to passengers on the North Coast Daylight excursion train in the 1980s, "the rock is seen across the river . . . It's possible to drive here, but not advisable, especially during 'harvest season,'"—a reference to illegal marijuana cultivation on the north coast.

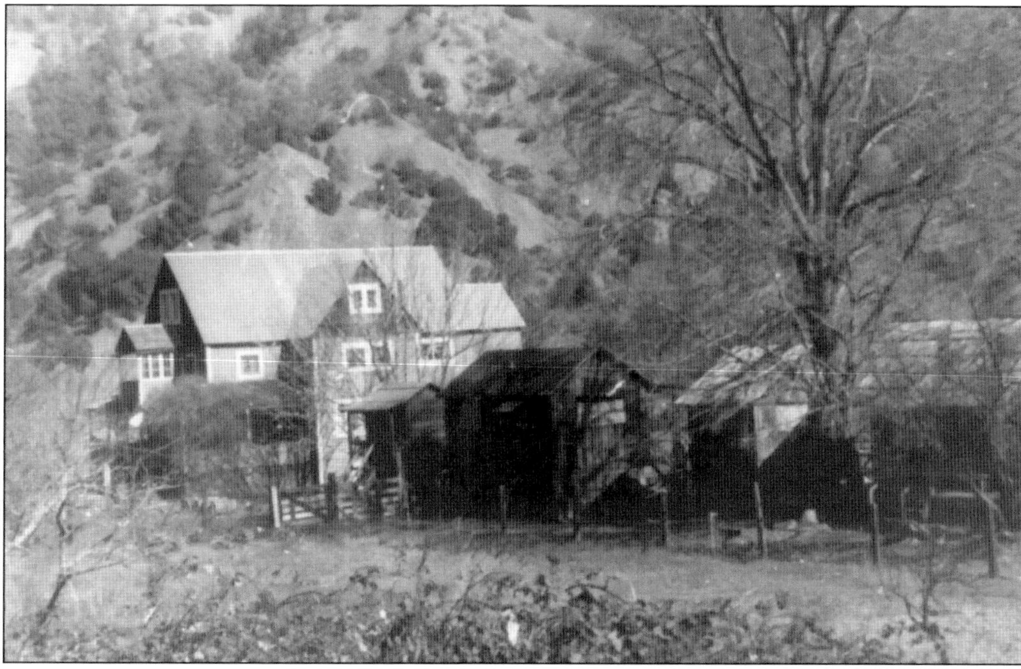

Francee White noted on this photograph: "Deer Lodge M.P. 169 washed away in 1955 flood." In 1924, the NWP's publication *Headlight* praised resort hotels along this section of line as follows: "The surrounding mountains are beautifully wooded and have well traveled trails . . . saddle horses may be procured at reasonable rates . . . the people who patronize these resorts are 'repeaters,' after the first time, they go again and keep going."

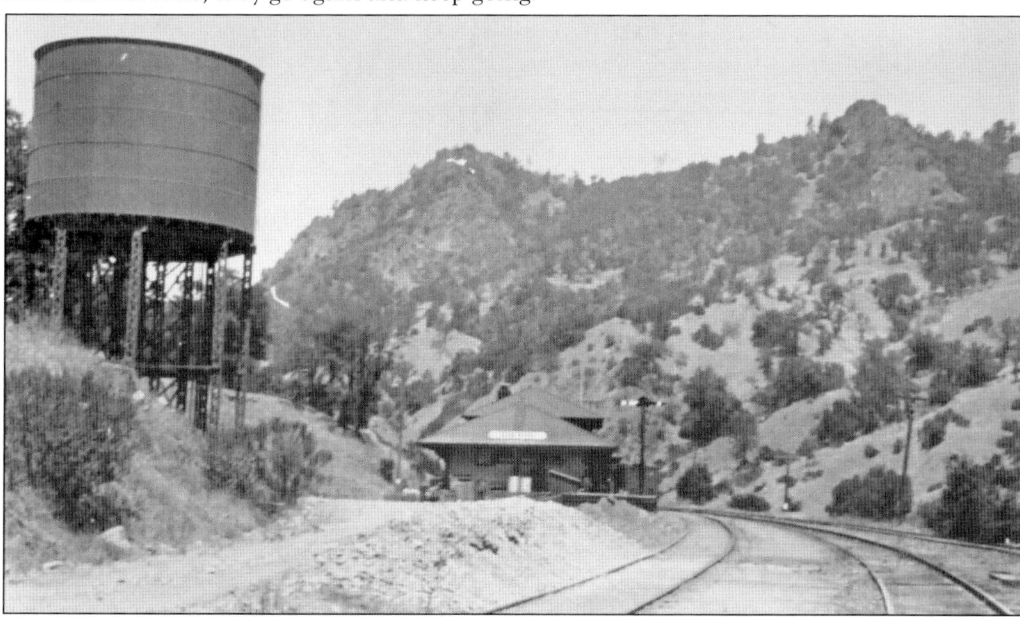

In reminiscences of his 1941 NWP journey, Ted Gruhn wrote, "We passed Spy Rock, a huge rock overlooking the river, and made a stop in Dos Rios to take on and drop off mail and water. Dos Rios was no more than a general store, a few houses and a huge water tank that replenished the locomotive's water supply."

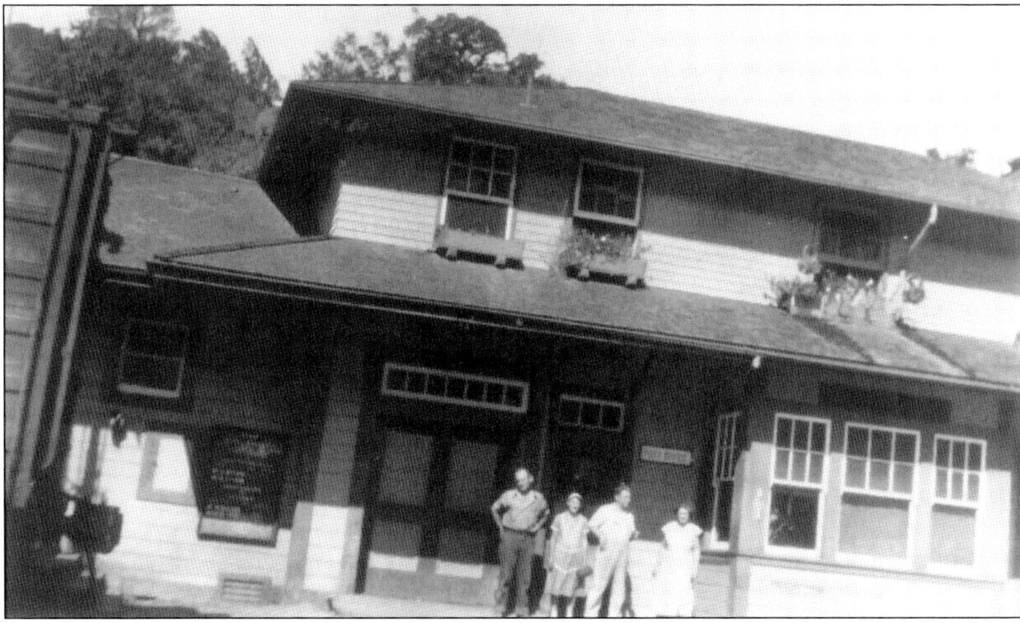

This 1942 photograph shows the Dos Rios depot and post office with, from left to right, husband and wife John and Tess Jesenko, Wilbur Duncan, and Amelia "Nan" Heid. John Jesenko and Heid's husband, Arthur, were members of NWP's Dos Rios section crew, and Duncan was stationmaster. The Dos Rios depot was an example of the hipped-roof variant of Southern Pacific's "Two Story Combination Depot Number 22," a design used in depot construction from 1910 to 1916.

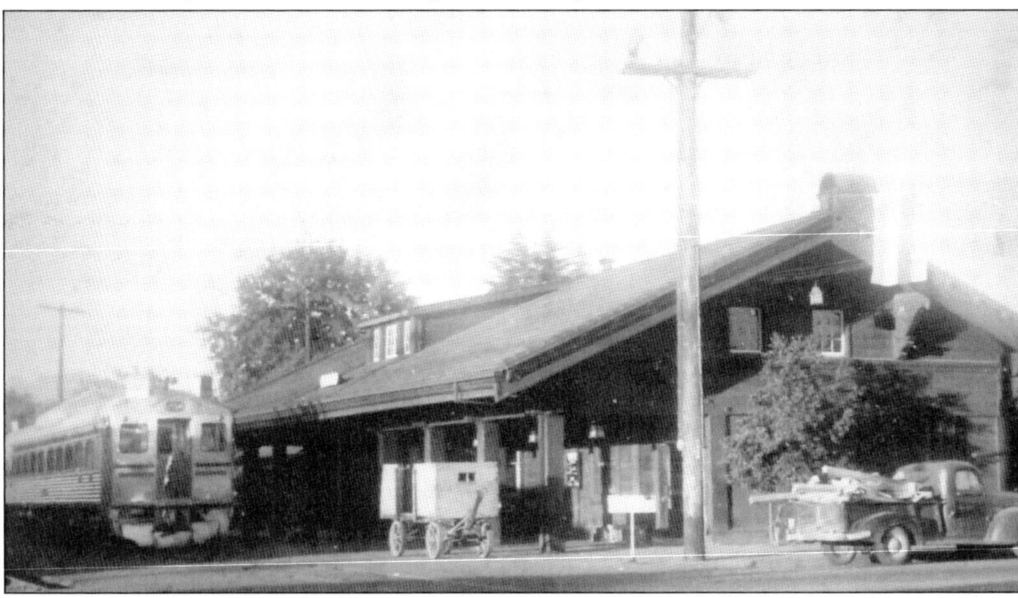

The second Willits depot, built in 1915, is listed in the National Register of Historic Places as "the finest known expression of Craftsman-style railroad architecture in California." The 1942 NWP time book included a Willits Chamber of Commerce article declaring that, "Willits . . . has just been termed 'The Biggest Little City in California' . . . [because] Willits is noted for sponsoring and putting over affairs that would do credit to cities of much greater population." (Courtesy of NWPRRHS.)

Five

Rolling Stock

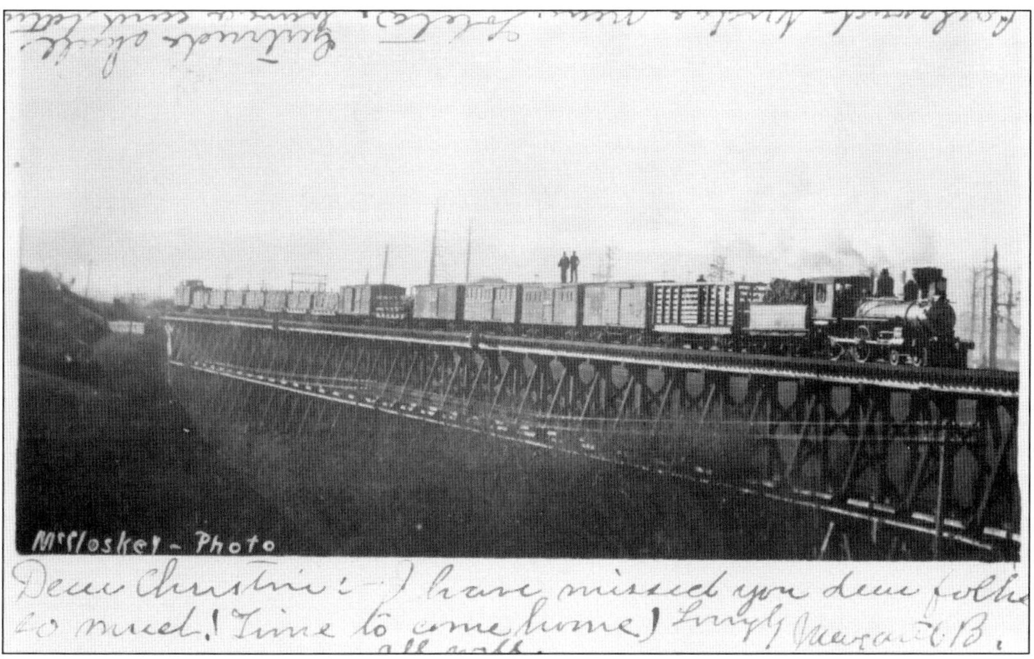

This chapter features locomotives and cars used between Willits and Eureka throughout the Northwestern Pacific's operating years. Much of the information about the rolling stock is from *The Northwestern Pacific Railroad* by Fred Stindt. This image shows NWP No. 2 crossing the Loleta trestle. This engine served the Eel River & Eureka Railroad (ER&ERR) as engine No. 1, the San Francisco & Northwestern as engine No. 1, and, finally, in 1908, as NWP engine No. 2. (Courtesy of HSU.)

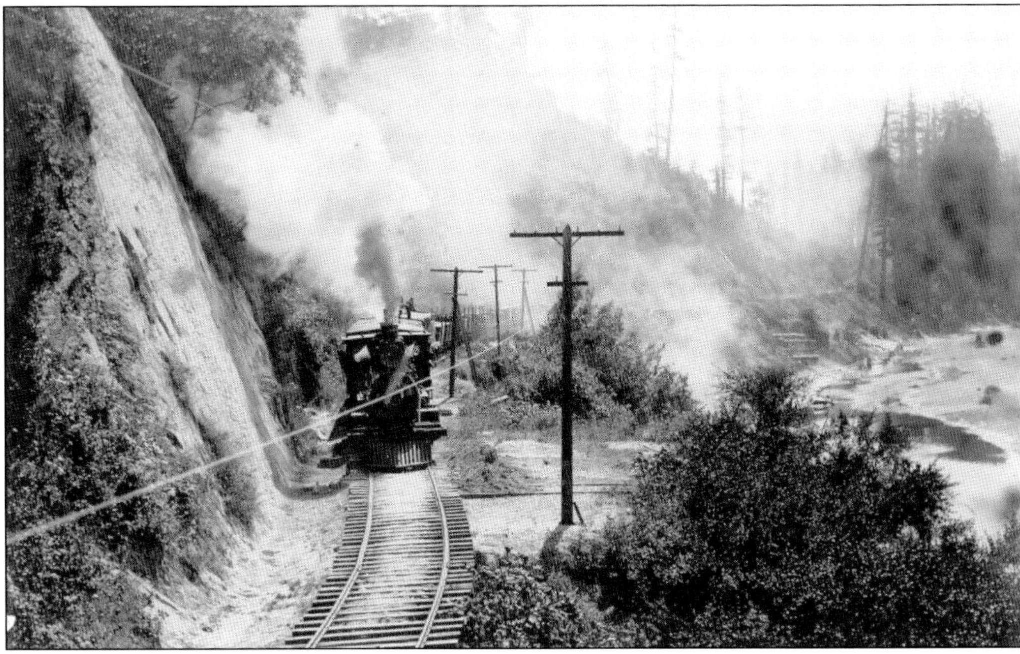

When the NWP formed in 1907, it acquired several engines from ER&ERR, including what became engines numbered 1, 2, 3, and 4. These engines were used from Eureka to Shively and farther south as the line was extended. As older engines, they were retired soon after the golden spike was driven, and some of them—such as No. 2—were used on shorter, less demanding NWP routes.

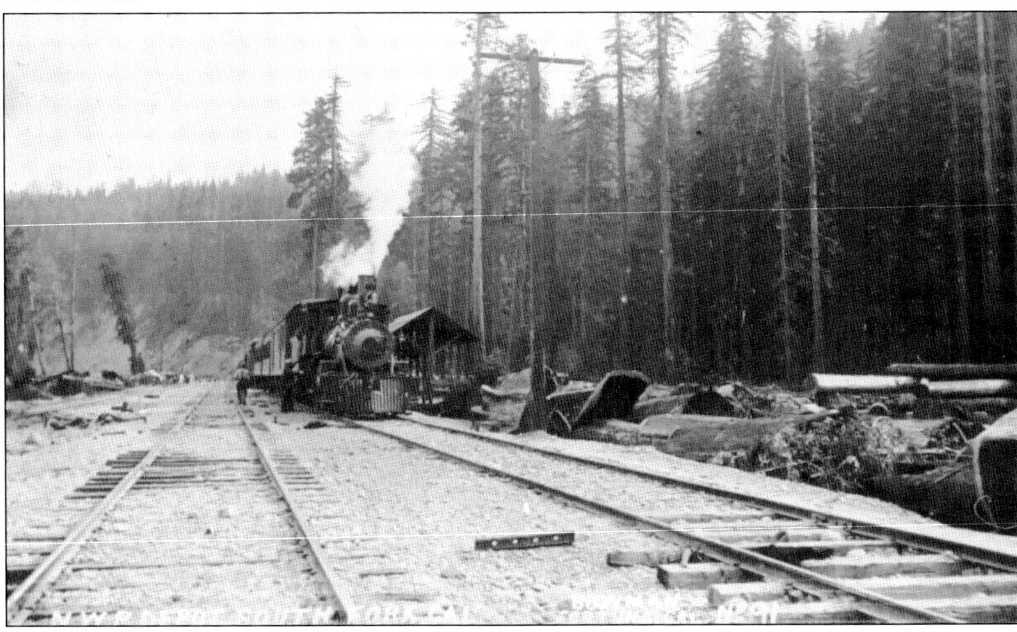

In *The Northwestern Pacific Railroad*, Fred Stindt notes that locomotive No. 3, pictured here at the depot at South Fork, had had multiple owners. The engine belonged to the Los Angeles County Railroad, the Eureka & Klamath, the Oregon & Eureka, and, finally, the NWP in 1911. Built in 1887, it continued to work on the NWP until 1923. (Courtesy of HSU.)

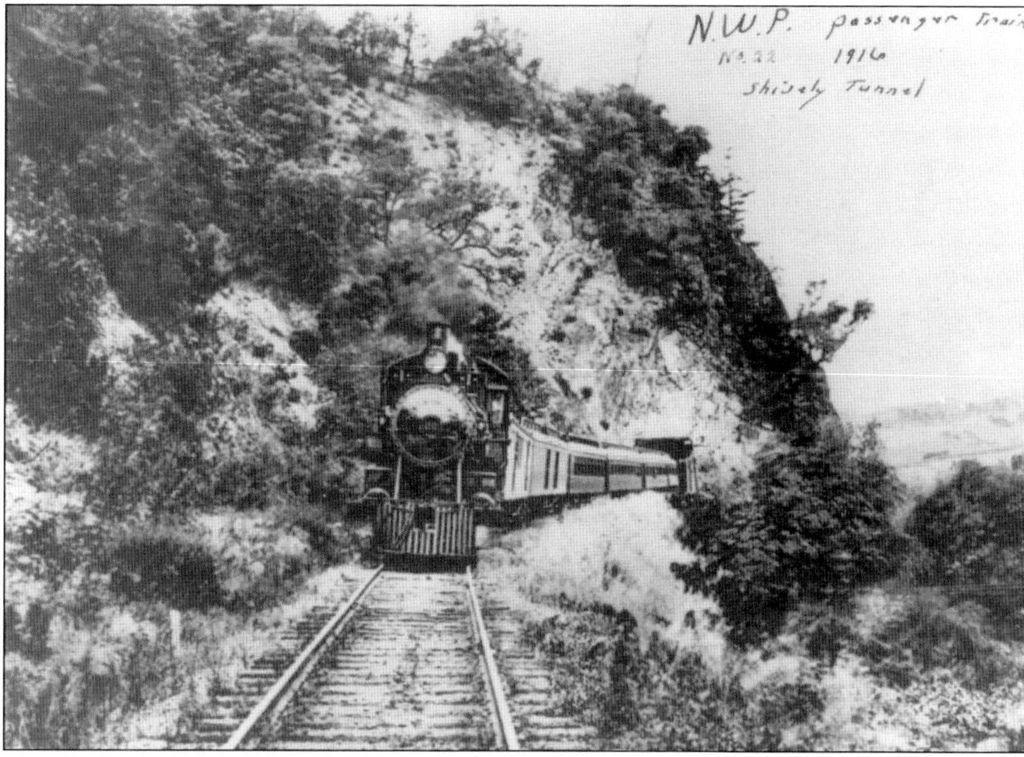

Locomotive No. 22 is shown emerging from Bryan's Bluff Tunnel at Shively. Built in 1908 by the American Locomotive Company, the No. 22 is an example of the eight new engines purchased by the NWP at its inception. This engine served the line for 30 years before being scrapped for parts at the end of the Great Depression.

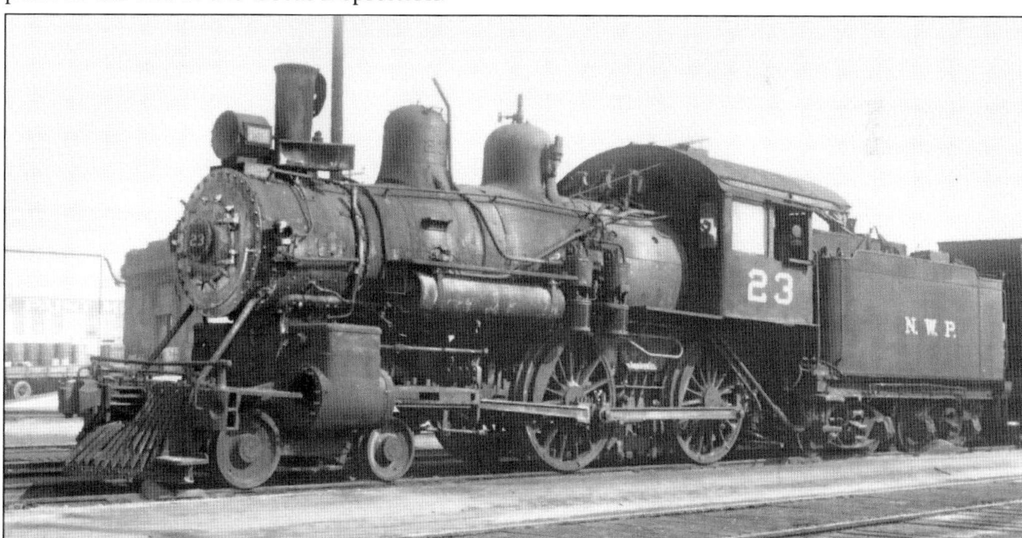

Engine No. 23 was the sister of locomotive No. 22. Purchased by NWP in 1908, it was taken off the route in 1949, making it the last 4-4-0 used on the line. The arrangement of four leading wheels on two axles with four coupled driving wheels was a popular configuration used throughout the 19th century and into the early 20th century.

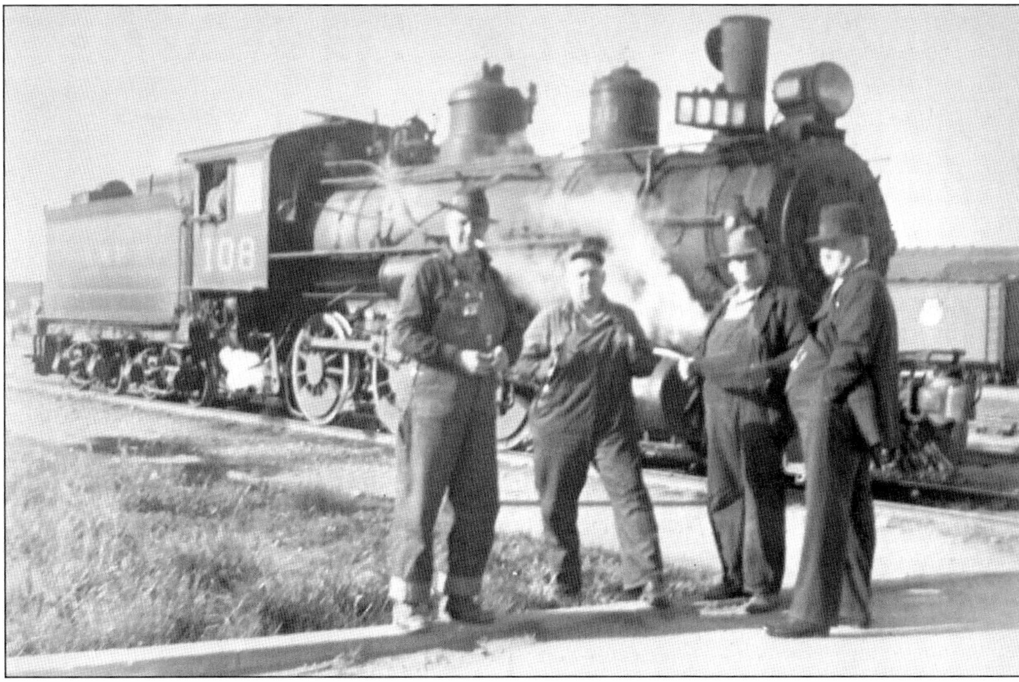

This 1940 photograph shows locomotive No. 108 in Eureka. The men standing in front are identified on the photograph as J. McKay, M. James, C. Moore, and W. Francis. Built in 1904 by Baldwin Locomotive Company, the No. 108 served the San Francisco & Northwestern as No. 23 until 1908. It was used on the NWP line until 1948, hauling freight on the weekdays and passengers on weekends.

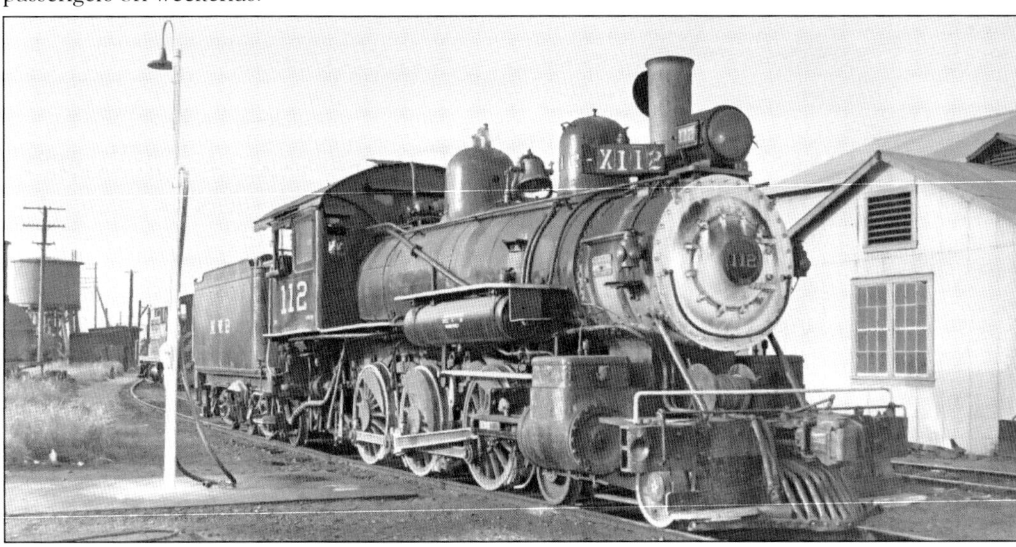

The last surviving steam engine of the NWP, locomotive No. 112, has been restored and is now displayed at the California State Railroad Museum in Sacramento. Built in 1908 by the American Locomotive Company, the No. 112 was used until 1955. A 4-6-0 locomotive, the No. 112 had four wheels on two axles in front with six powered and coupled driving wheels on three axles behind without any tailing wheels. This popular configuration for steam locomotives was also referred to as a 10-wheeler.

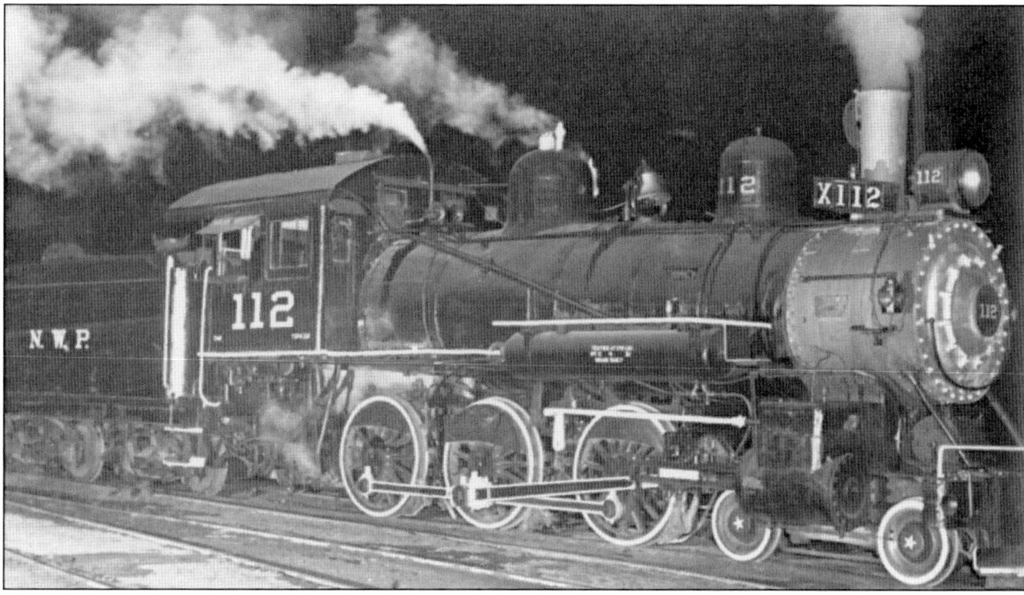

The No. 112 saw use on the entire NWP line and was used to haul both passengers and freight. While working on the southern section of the line at Tiburon in June 1913, it fell into San Francisco Bay when the pier it was on collapsed. The engine was retrieved, repaired, and worked for another 42 years on the line.

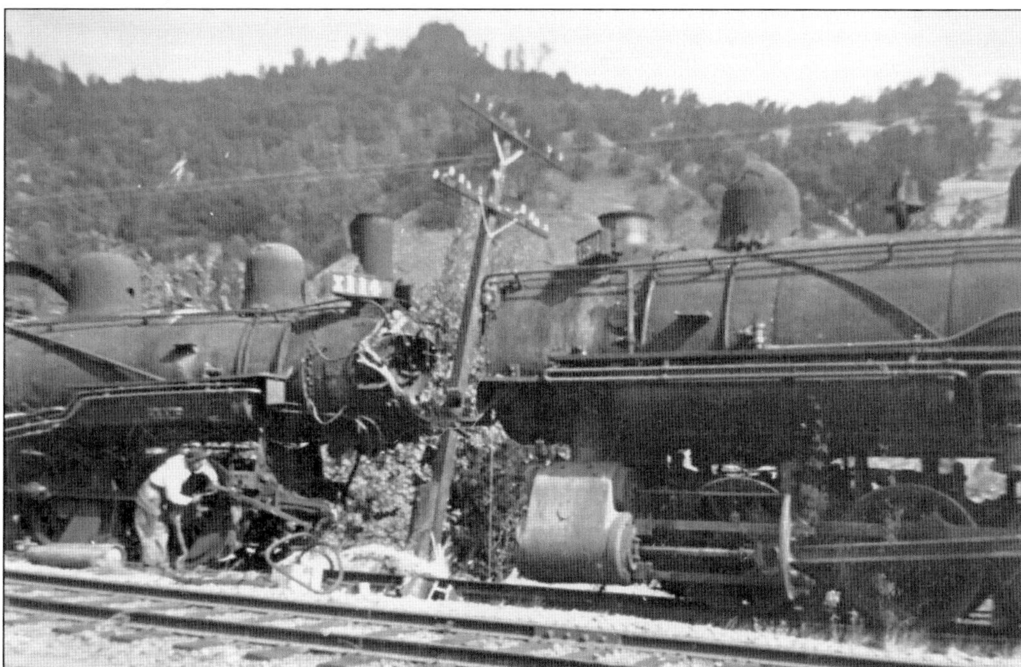

The No. 114, a sister locomotive to the No. 112, was built in 1907 by the American Locomotive Company based on the same plans as those for the No. 112. The No. 114 was less fortunate than the No. 112, however. It is pictured here in 1936 following a collision on the Scotia Bluffs. Ten years later, on September 30, 1946, it was involved in another head-on collision near Dos Rios. The 1946 wreck totaled the No. 114, and it was cut up for scrap iron in 1947.

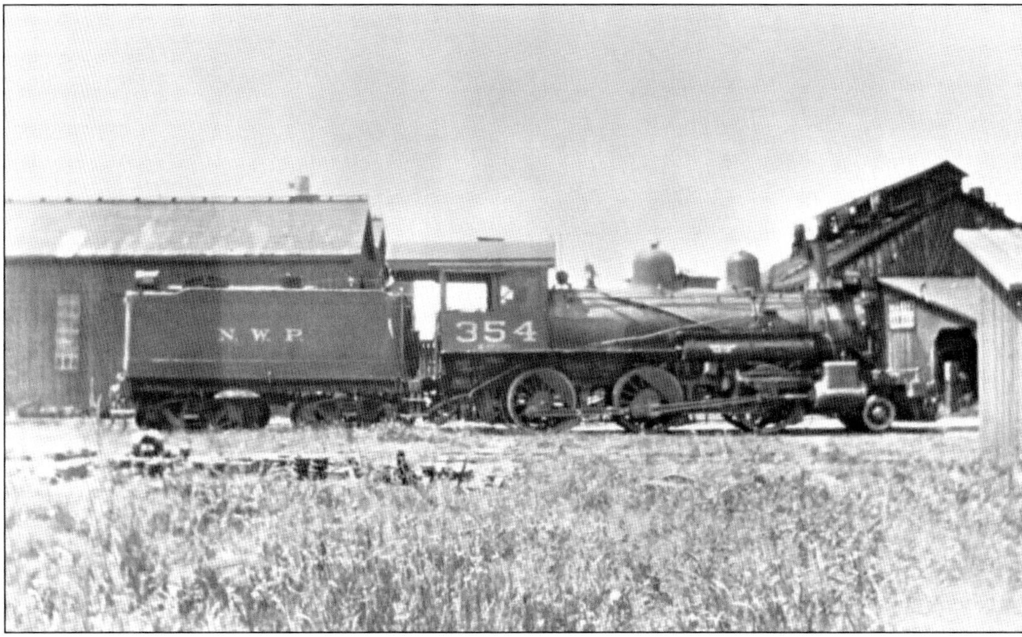

Locomotive No. 354, pictured at the repair yards at South Bay, was originally No. 154 when NWP purchased it from the American Locomotive Company in 1908 along with seven other engines. In 1914, it was renumbered 354, making it the highest numbered engine on the NWP. A 2-6-0, it had two wheels in front on a truck with six wheels powered and coupled on three axles. The No. 354 was retired in 1935.

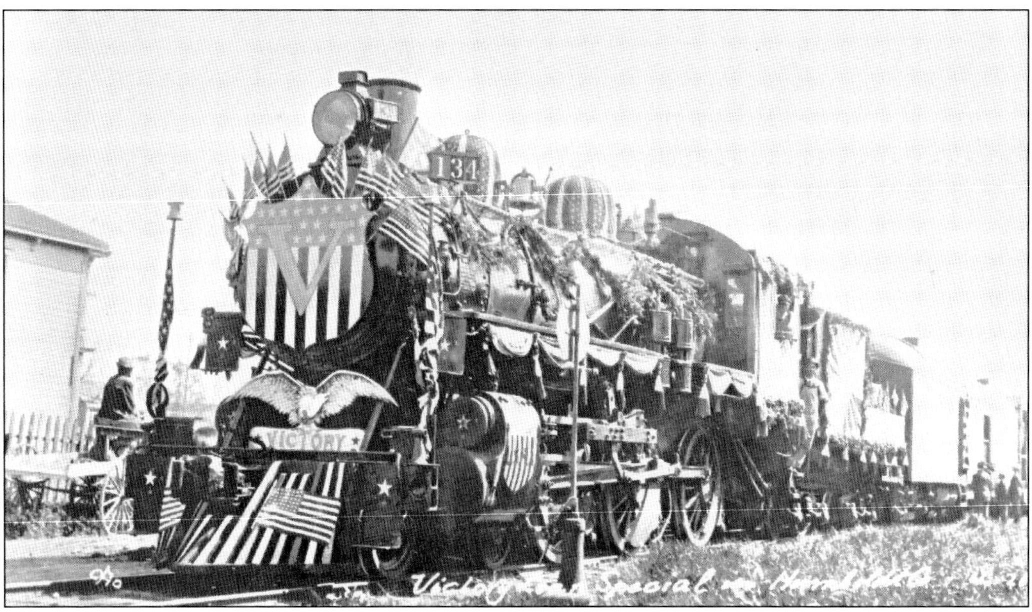

The No. 134 was a 4-6-0 purchased by the NWP in 1912. Built by the American Locomotive Company, a favorite company of the Southern Pacific, the No. 134 featured a longer tender and was heavier than other 4-6-0s on the line. In this photograph taken in Humboldt County after the end of World War I, the No. 134 is decorated as the "Victory Special."

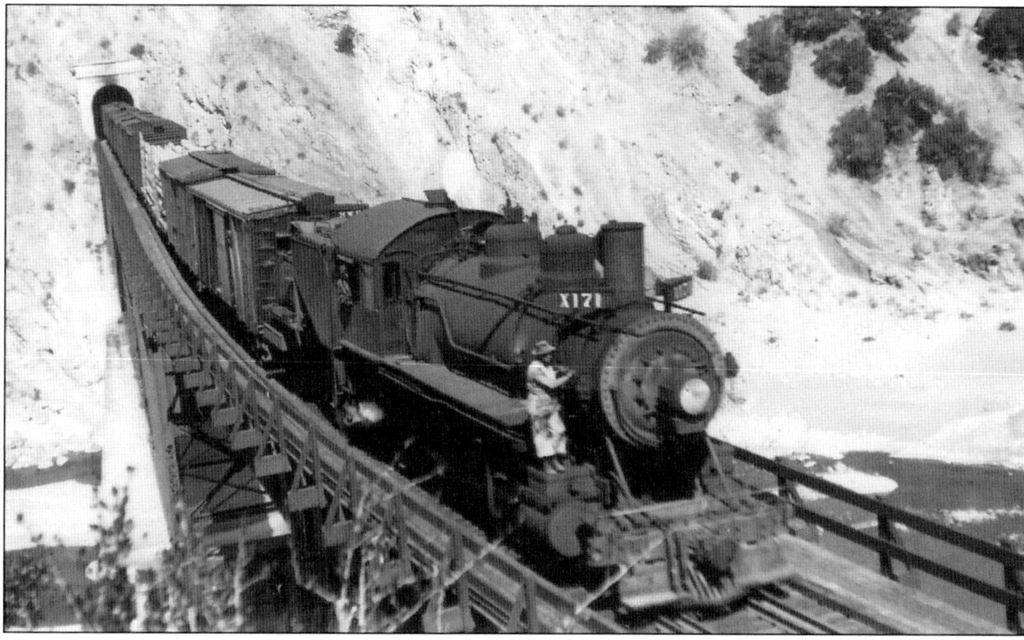

Locomotive No. 171 is pictured exiting the Island Mountain Tunnel onto the bridge crossing the Eel River. Built by Baldwin Locomotive Works of Pennsylvania, the No. 171 was a 10-wheeler steam engine. Originally purchased new by the Las Vegas & Tonopah Railroad and numbered 5, the NWP bought the No. 171, as well as Nos. 170 and 172, when the Las Vegas & Tonopah Railroad was abandoned in 1918. (Courtesy of NWPRRHS.)

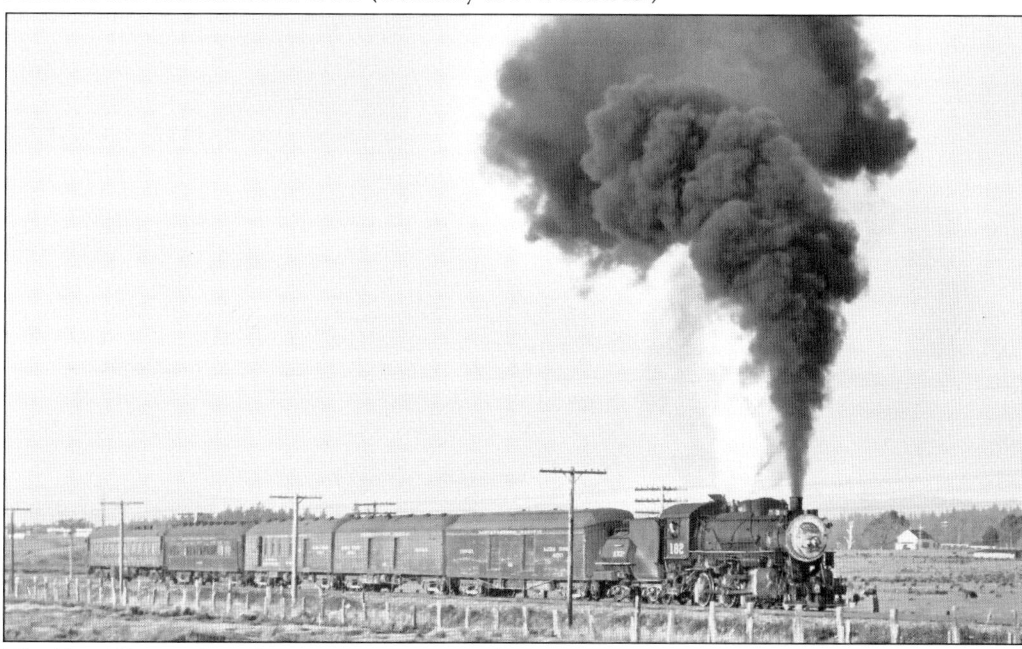

The No. 182, purchased in 1922, was one of the last new engines bought by the NWP. Baldwin Locomotive Works built the engine, which was retired from service in 1955. It is shown crossing the Loleta flats with engineer Ray Barkhurst at the throttle. Barkhurst worked for the NWP for 44 years, traveling between Eureka and Willits.

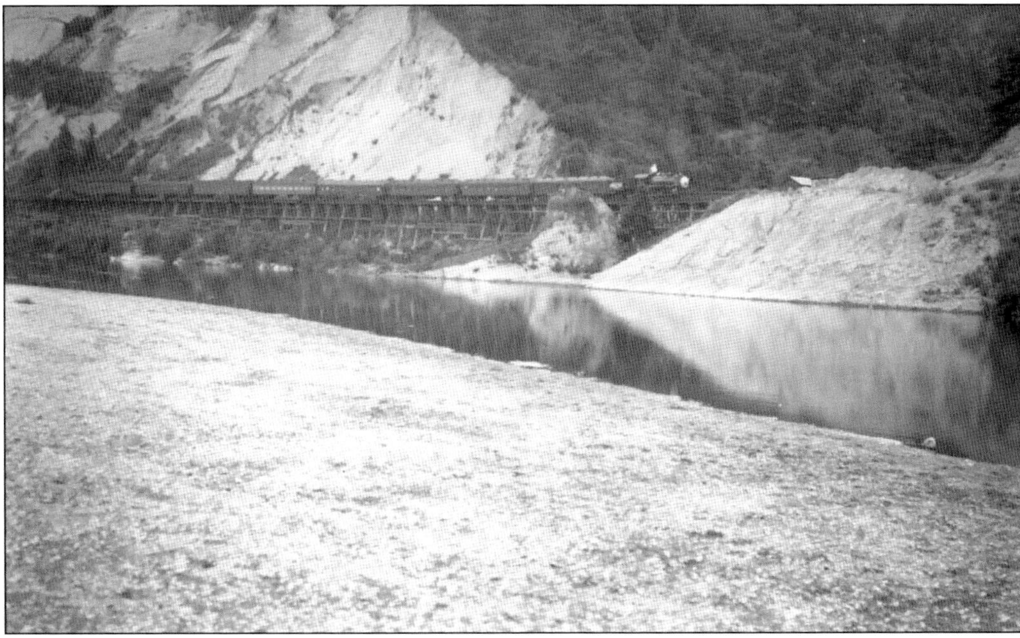

A sister to the No. 182, engine No. 183 is shown crossing the bridge at Nanning Creek along the Scotia Bluffs in the 1950s. Like the other steam engines included in this chapter, the No. 183 was a 4-6-0. The No. 183 was retired in 1955.

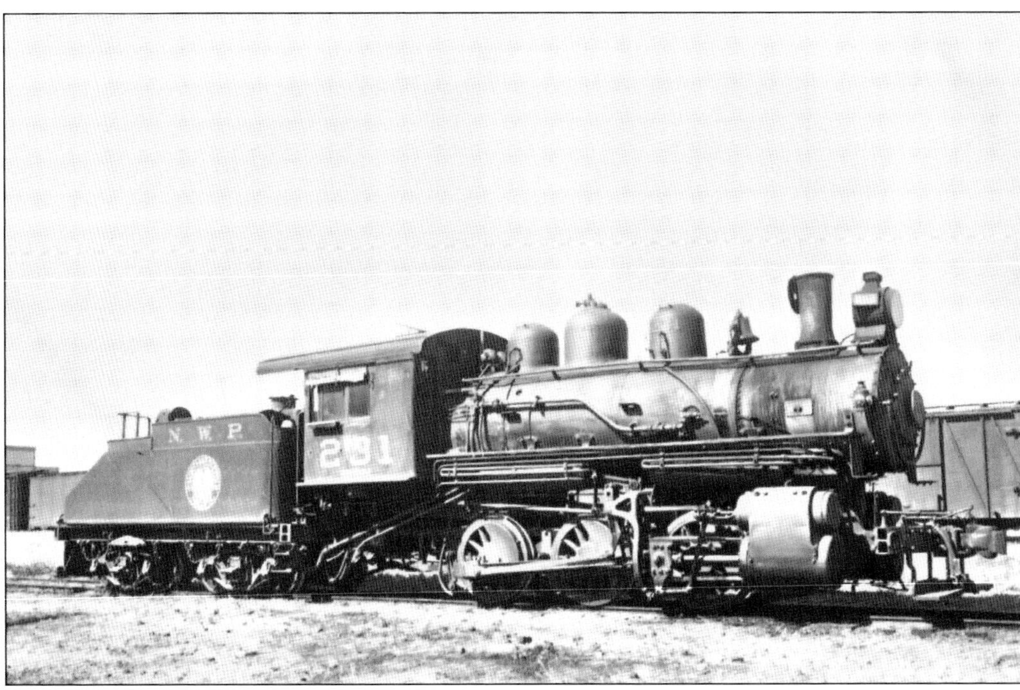

Engine No. 231 was a switch engine purchased in 1914. Switch engines moved cars at sidings to create new trains. The No. 231 featured a 0-6-0 wheel arrangement, distinguishing it from engines used to pull loads. With no leading wheels, it instead had six powered and coupled driving wheels on three axles that moved the engine; it did not have trailing wheels.

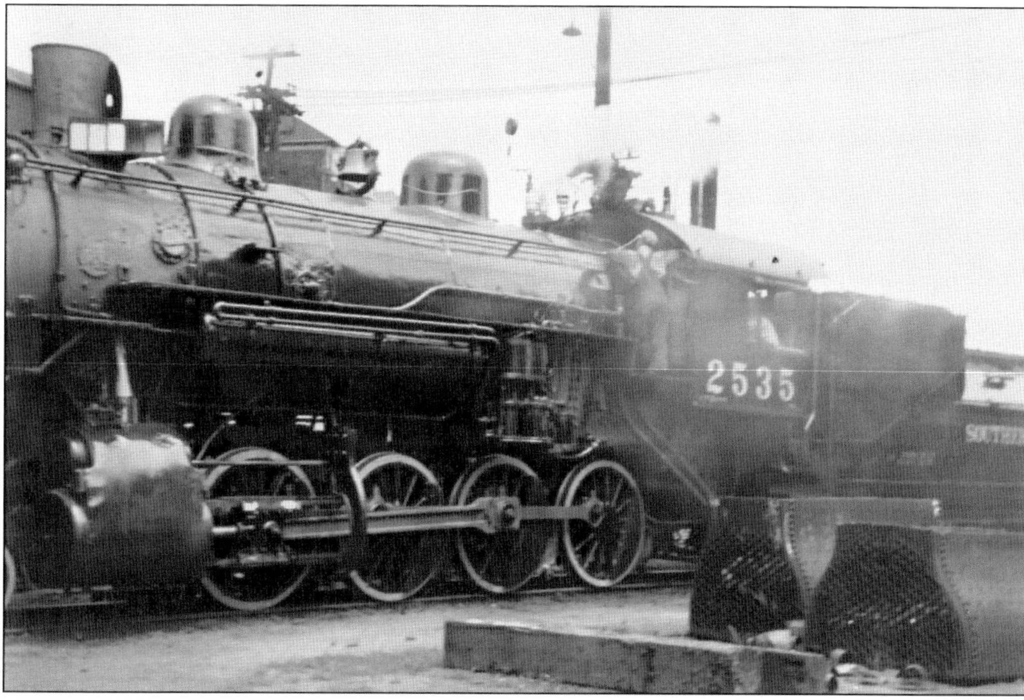

Engine No. 2535, a steam-powered 2-8-0 built by Baldwin Locomotive Company, was used by the NWP from July 1934 until October 1951. The 2-8-0 configuration was referred to as a "consolidation engine" and was one of Baldwin Locomotive's most popular designs. In this image, the No. 2535's crew is working on the locomotive prior to departure.

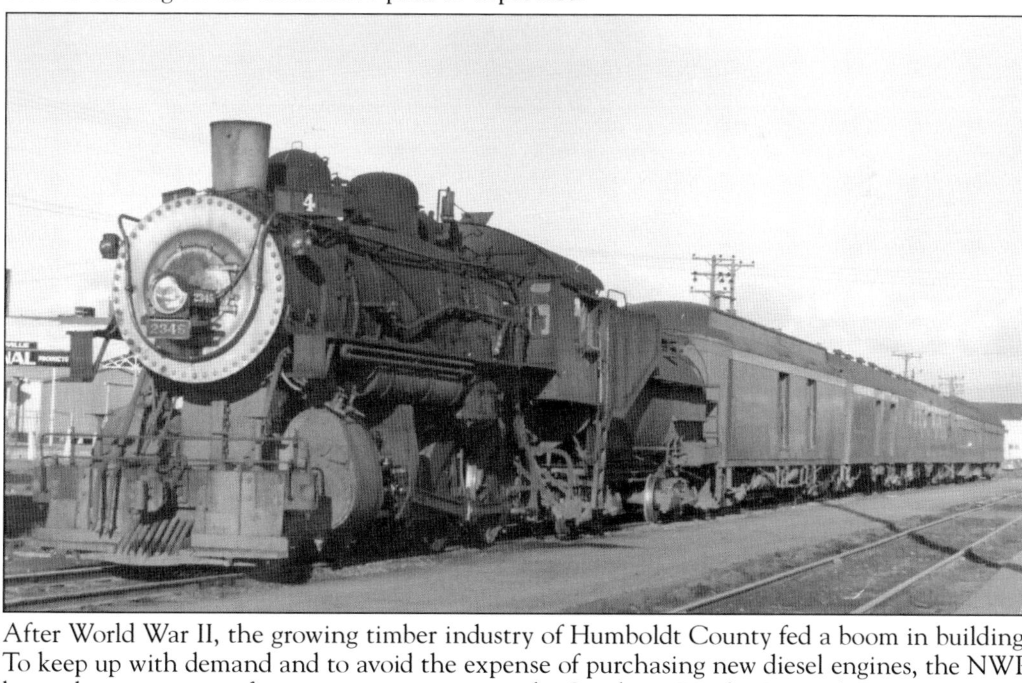

After World War II, the growing timber industry of Humboldt County fed a boom in building. To keep up with demand and to avoid the expense of purchasing new diesel engines, the NWP began leasing engines from its parent company, the Southern Pacific. Here, the No. 2345 waits to load passengers in Eureka. The NWP leased the No. 2345 from May 1953 until August 1954.

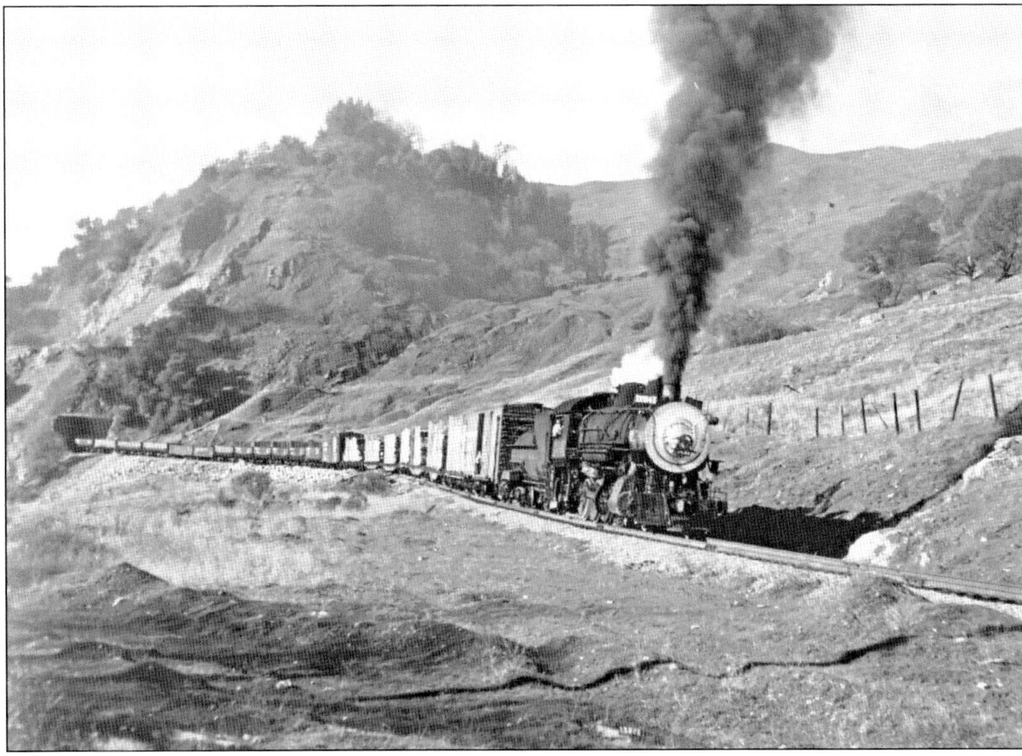

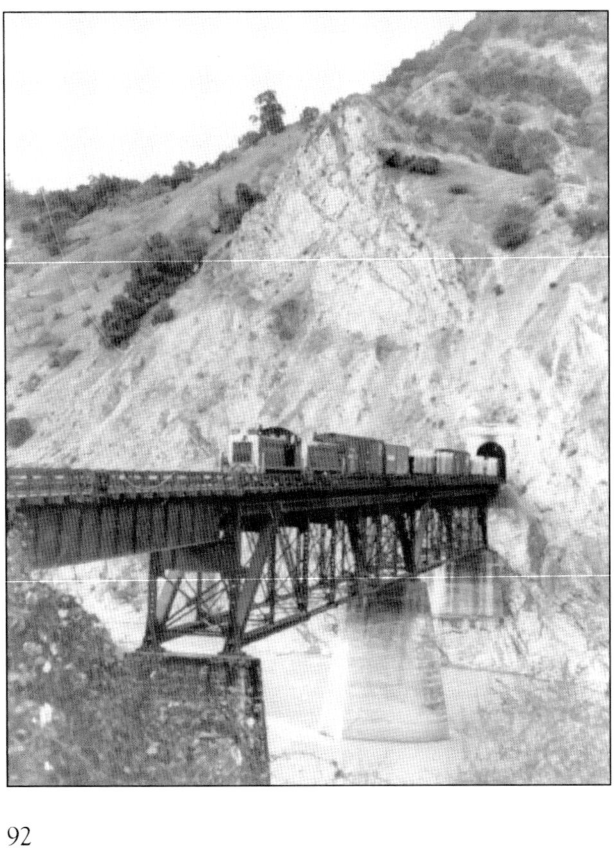

The No. 2541 was leased for just one year, from July 1952 until July 1953. Here, the No. 2541 is pictured south of Cain Rock on its way to Kekawaka. The longer loads created by increased demand for lumber required the additional power offered by diesel engines. During this time period, steam engines were used on short runs, while diesels did long hauls. The NWP first used electric-diesel locomotives in 1952.

In 1951, the Southern Pacific acquired a new series of locomotives from Electro Motive Diesel. The locomotive was combined with a rear unit for additional power in a "cow and calf" pairing in which the second engine was operated remotely from the first engine. These locomotives were assigned to work on the NWP. In this image, Locomotive No. 4603 and "calf" No. 4703 are crossing the bridge at Island Mountain.

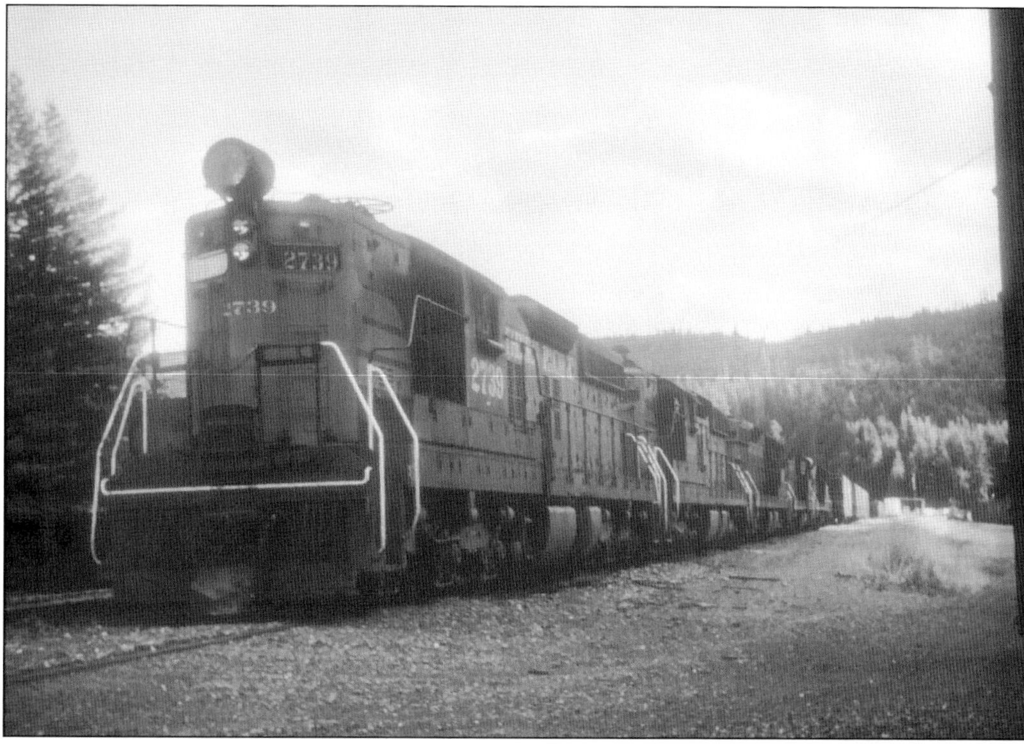

The SD-7s were another workhorse engine model used on the Southern Pacific. Built by General Motors' Electro-Motive Division in 1952 and 1953, the SD-7 featured six axles and was used as a road switcher to create new trains. Locomotive No. 2739 is pictured here at South Fork in the mid-1960s.

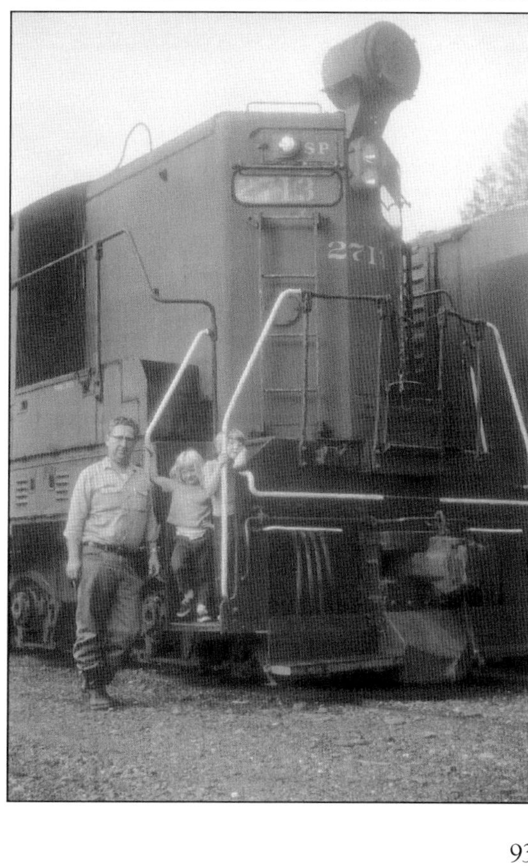

Locomotive No. 2713, another SD-7 engine, is pictured at South Fork. In this image, California Department of Forestry (CDF) ranger Harry Pritchard, who was elected Humboldt County District Two supervisor in 1980, is inspecting the engines along with his two daughters, Susan (left) and Karen. The CDF rangers inspected locomotives for carbon buildup on the stacks, since engines sprayed glowing embers that could cause forest fires.

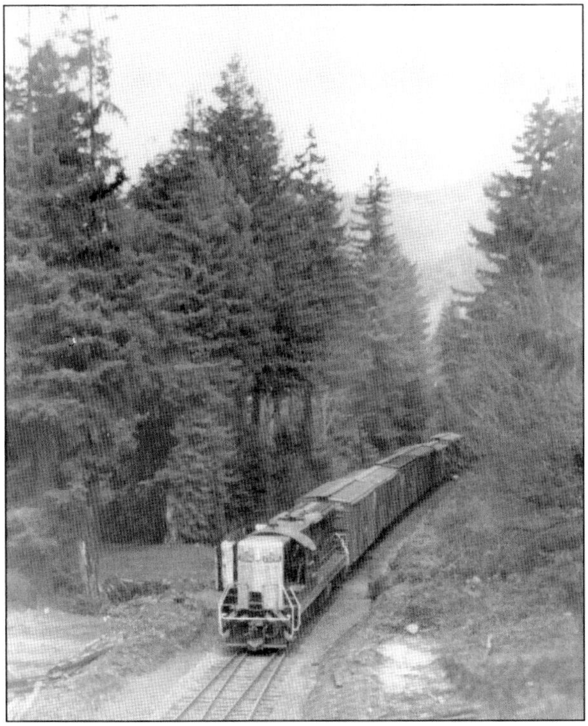

The No. 5266, a road switcher engine built in the early mid-1950s, is shown near South Fork. The No. 5266 was a diesel electric engine built by Baldwin Locomotive Works between 1950 and 1952. Named AS-616 by the company, it could produce 1,600 horsepower and rode on three axle trucks. Southern Pacific purchased 51 of the 214 locomotives produced by Baldwin.

The No. 5260 is pictured below near Shively. One of the 51 Baldwin AS-616s purchased by the Southern Pacific, the No. 5260 had the distinction of being the first radio-equipped diesel engine operated on the NWP line. One reason the Southern Pacific purchased so many of the AS-616s was that the six-motor arrangement allowed for better traction at lower speeds.

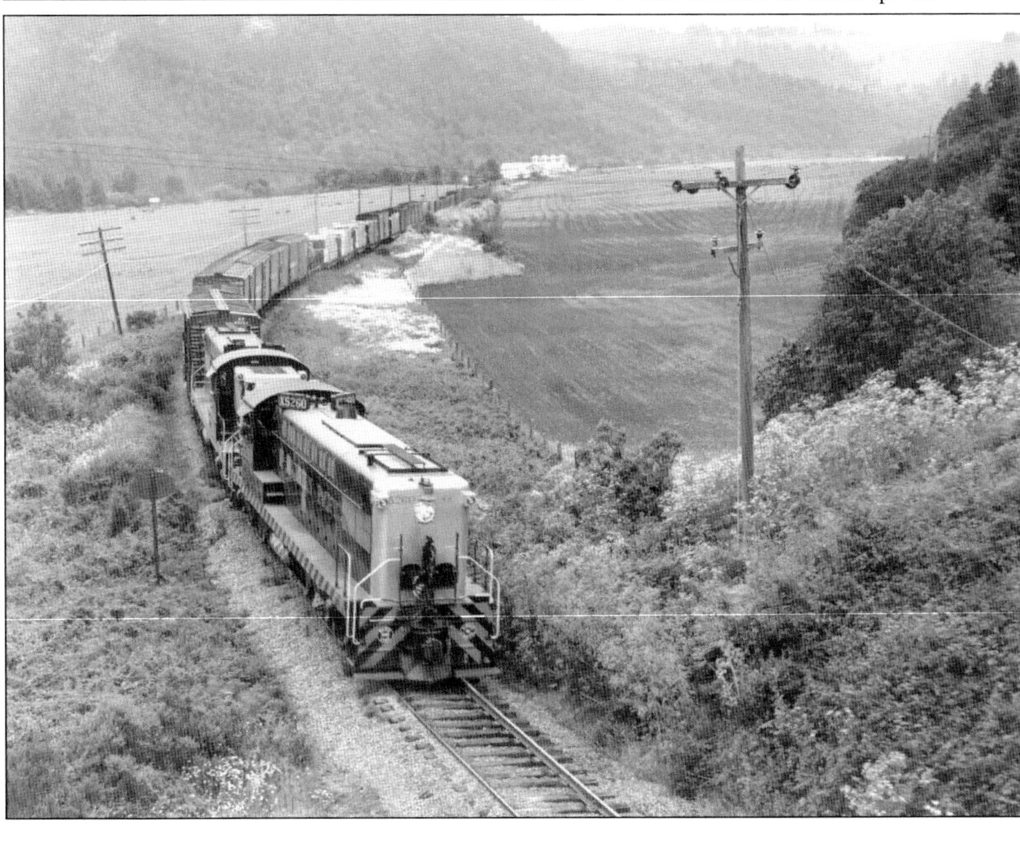

The SD-7 diesel was made by General Motors' Electro-Motive Division and was very desirable to the Southern Pacific because it was geared for steep grades like the ones found on the NWP line. Here, unidentified NWP workers pose with locomotive No. 5328. The SD-7 model was only made for one year—between 1952 and 1953—but Southern Pacific utilized the engines for four decades.

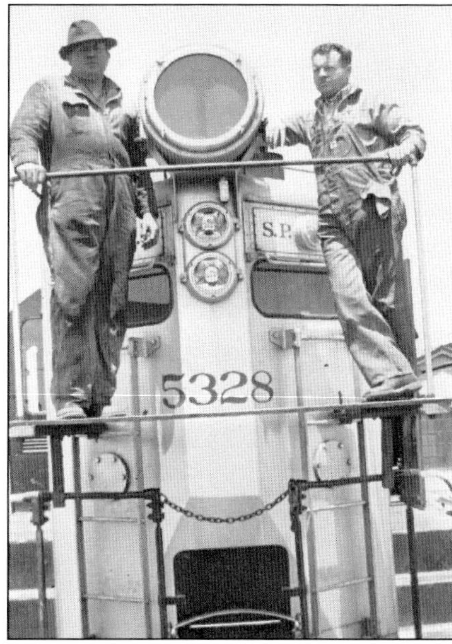

The No. 8442 is another locomotive from General Motors' Electro-Motive Division. The locomotive, identified as an SD40 model, went into production in 1966 and became a very popular style for all railroad companies since it produced 3,000 horsepower and reduced the number of engines required to haul heavy loads. The No. 8442 is pictured below in Eureka.

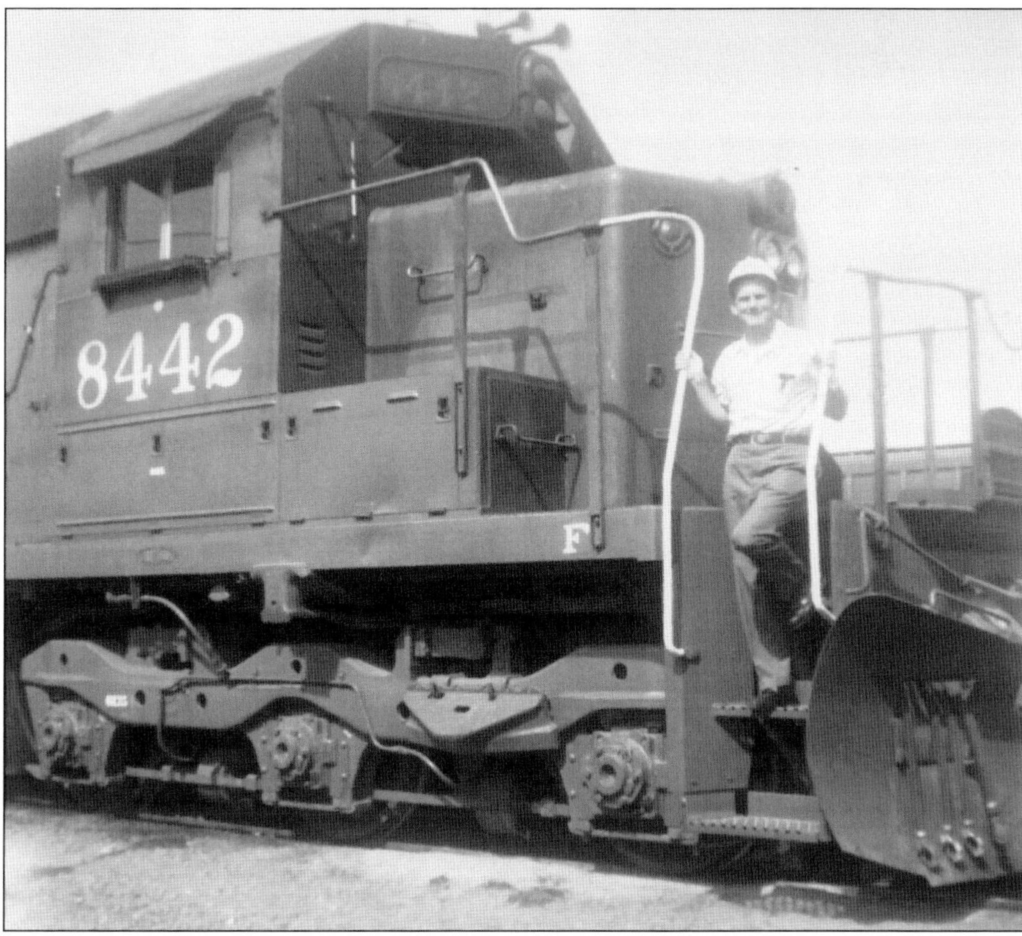

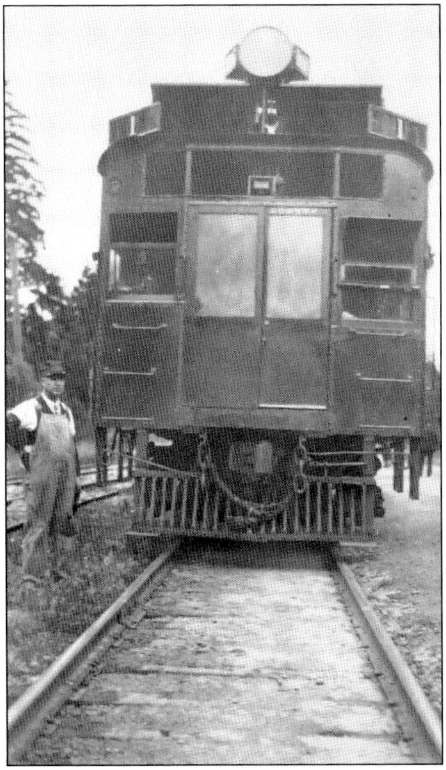

In addition to the numerous locomotives operated on the line, the NWP also ran self-propelling passenger cars that made electricity from either a diesel or gasoline generator. The cars were originally used on short lines, but during the Great Depression, they were utilized on the main line to Eureka. The car pictured at left was one of the early passenger cars originally used in the San Francisco Bay Area. Since they were less costly to operate and capable of towing a baggage car, these cars were popular during the summer as they took vacationers to destinations along the line. Below is the "Budd" car, which was named for its builder and had a capacity of 68 passengers. The Southern Pacific logo is visible on its door; after SP purchased the car in 1954, they leased it to the NWP in 1959.

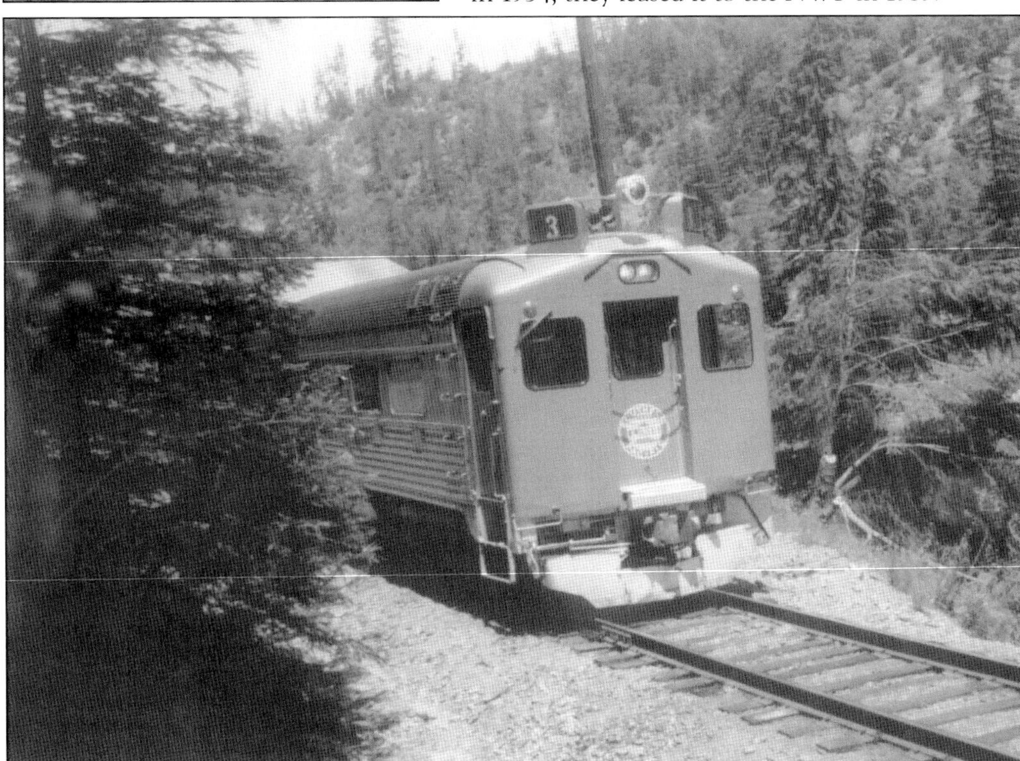

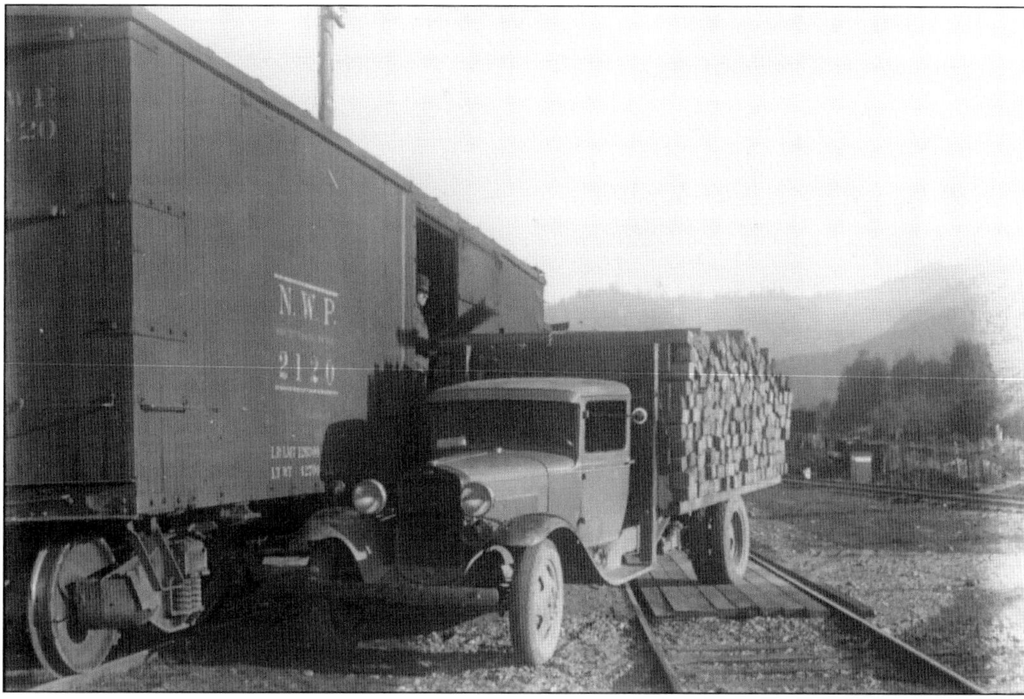

The NWP used many different boxcars and railcars to haul the "red gold" (redwood lumber). In this 1920s image, boxcar No. 2120 is being loaded with railroad ties in southern Humboldt County. The split products industry was based on the ease of splitting redwood into many different products, including railroad ties. Ties varied in weight from 100 to 300 pounds each and, as shown here, were loaded by hand. (Courtesy of HSU.)

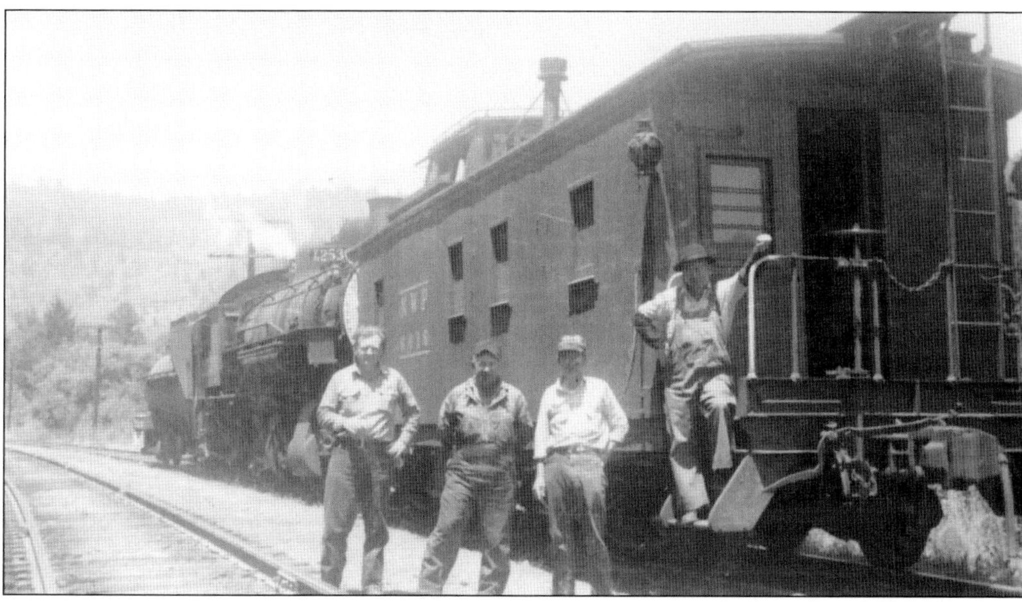

The NWP also used a great variety of cabooses. Caboose No. 6016 (earlier numbered 16) is pictured here with her crew in Alderpoint in 1949. Now under private ownership, caboose No. 16 was built in 1911 and—like most cabooses of the time—was made of wood.

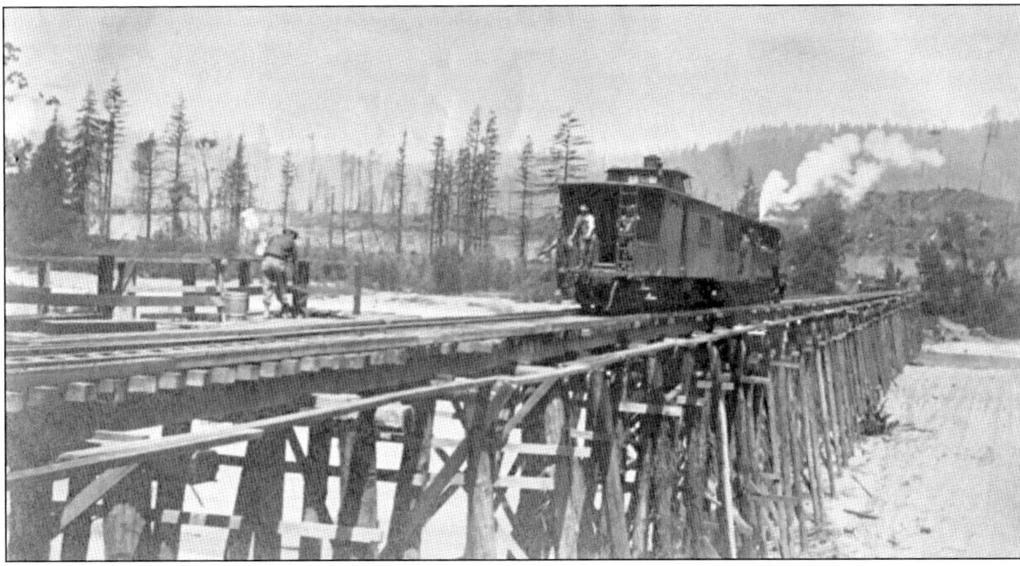

Caboose No. 13 (later renumbered 6013) served the NWP for 60 years. It was one of four cabooses purchased in 1909 from the Standard Steel Company. Caboose No. 13 was sold when the Federal Railroad Administration banned the use of wooden cabooses in 1971. In 2003, it was moved to the Mendocino County Museum in Willits, where it was restored by the NWPRRHS and is now on display.

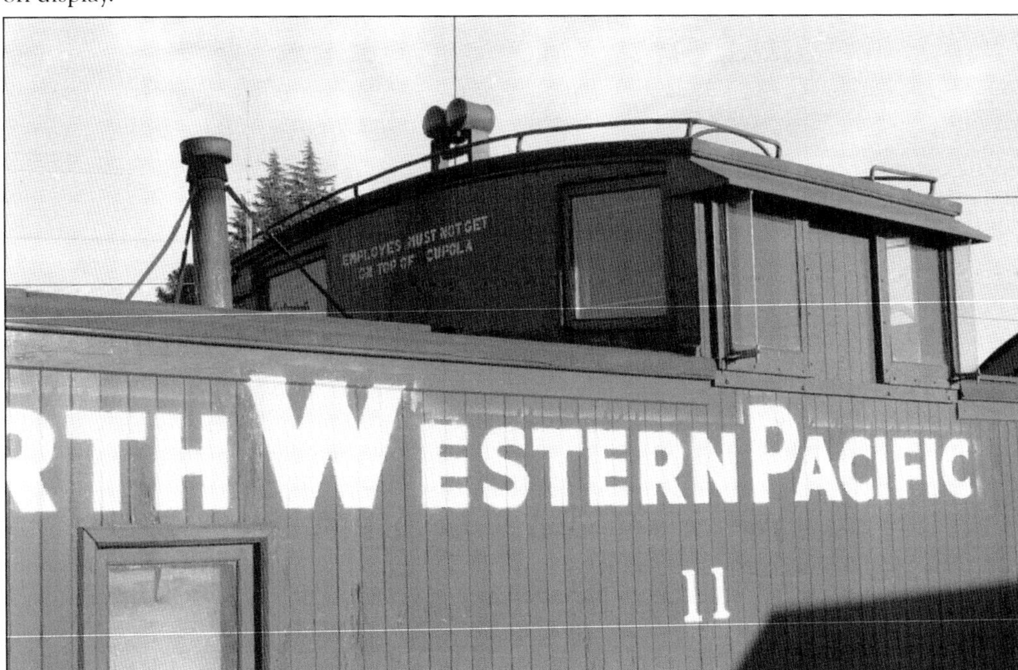

Built in 1909, Caboose No. 11 features a wooden cab and frame and was retired in 1970. That year, G&R Metals of Eureka purchased the caboose and presented it as a Christmas gift to J. Sturgis of Eel River Sawmills. After serving as the shipping office for Eel River Sawmills for over 30 years, the Noble family bought the caboose and donated it to the City of Fortuna. The caboose is now restored and is displayed beside the Fortuna Depot Museum. (Courtesy of NWPRRHS.)

Six

Disasters along the Line

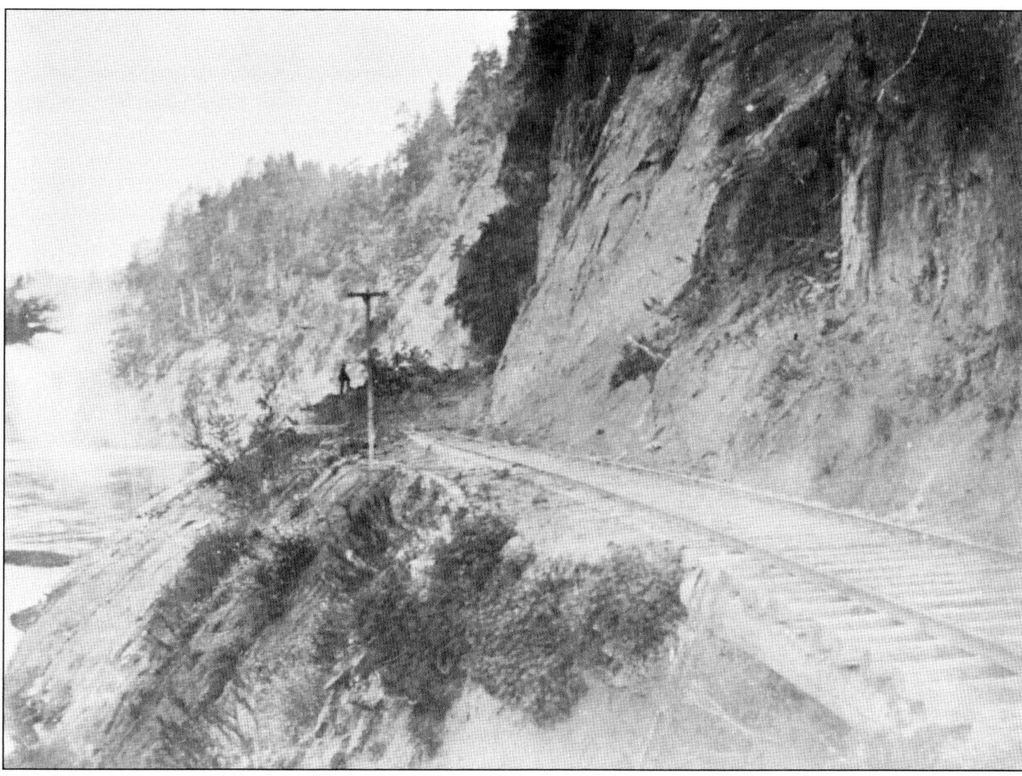

Landslides plagued the Northwestern Pacific from its inception in 1907 until its closure in 1984. In 1914, a young engineer stated the following in the *San Francisco Chronicle*: "We have just 108 miles of slide"—the length of the line between Shively and Willits was 108 miles. Landslides constantly damaged the line and caused several deaths during the railroad's operation.

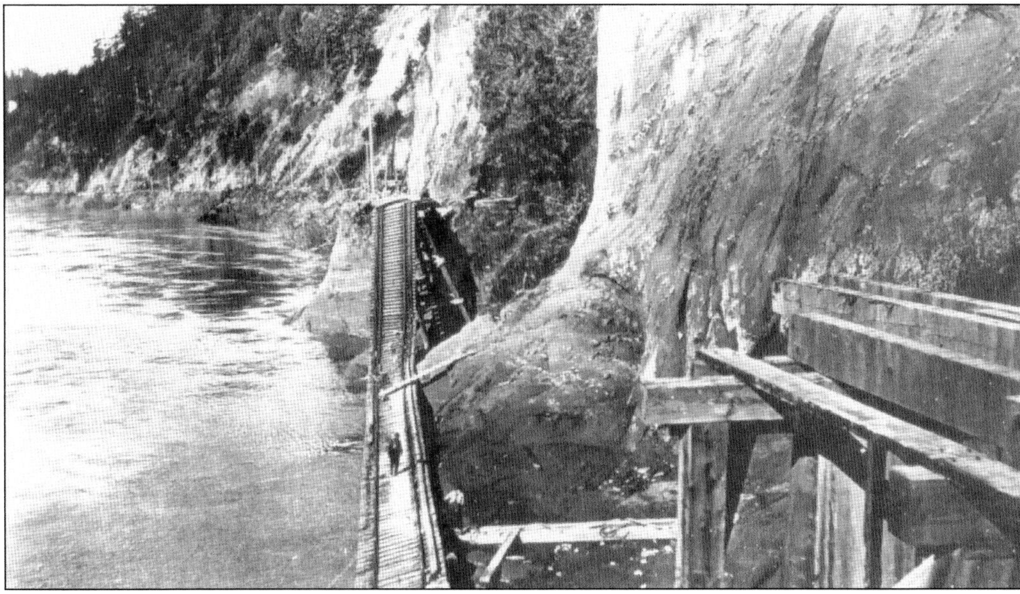

In 1913, heavy rains and flooding triggered a large landslide that carried away seven belts (sections) of the Nanning Creek Bridge on the Scotia Bluffs. Passengers walked south across the fallen ties and slide material to meet a train that had been in Shively, allowing train service to continue. Note the gentleman on the ties below the slide.

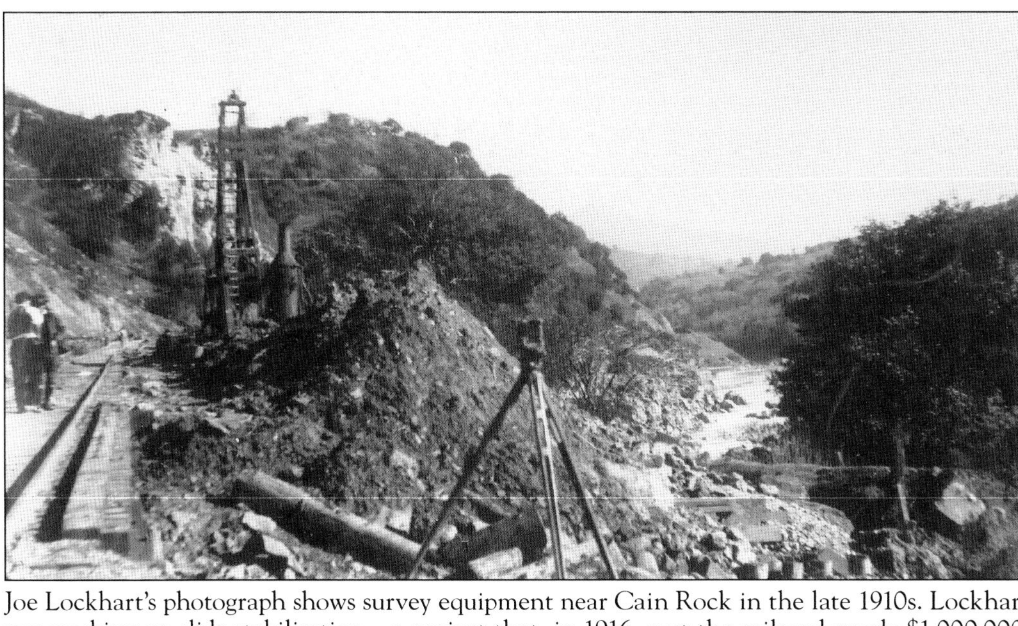

Joe Lockhart's photograph shows survey equipment near Cain Rock in the late 1910s. Lockhart was working on slide stabilization—a project that, in 1916, cost the railroad nearly $1,000,000. J.W. Williams, chief engineer for the entire line, explained the cost as follows: "For 100 miles along the road there are great movements of earth, like glaciers."

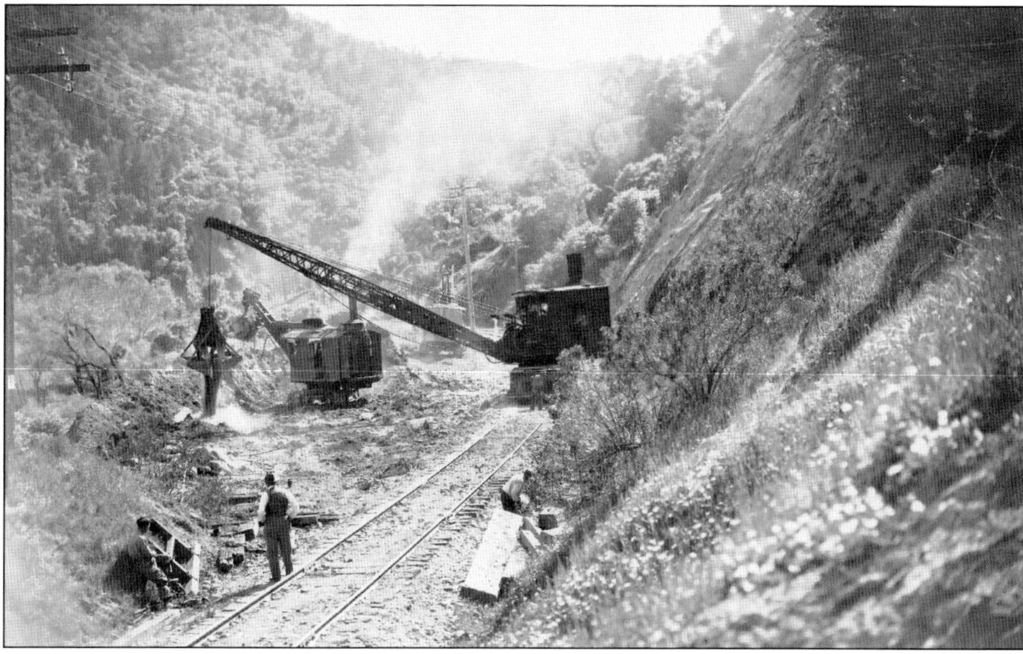

1935 saw heavy rainfall in the spring, with Willits receiving four inches more than average by April. A large slide at milepost 186, north of Bell Springs, closed the line intermittently for several days. According to the *Ukiah Republican Press*, "as fast as the dirt was cleared away, new slides came in and again covered the tracks."

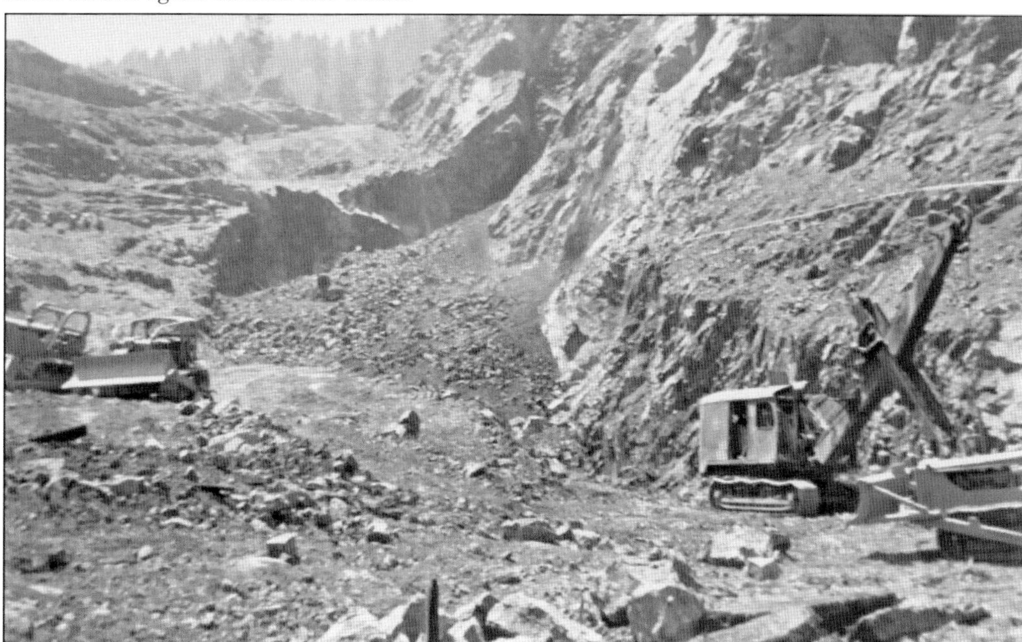

Crawler shovels were gradually replaced with tractor crawler dozers in the late 1940s. Pictured here are three Caterpillar D8 2U series dozers and a power shovel. Regardless of the technology used, clearing a slide was dangerous work, as mud or rockslides could engulf both machines and operators.

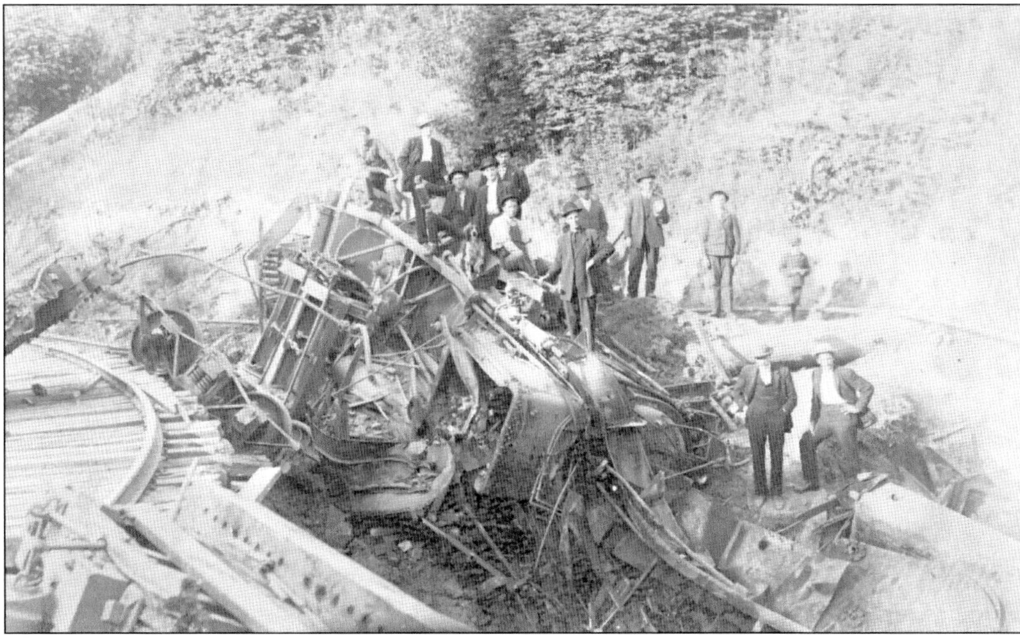

Derailments and collisions were other types of disasters on the NWP. Derailments were often caused by slides, leading to delays on the line as the train was righted. Frequently, as shown in this photograph by Fortuna's Spesert Photography Studio, the rails were twisted and required replacement. Many people visited the accident sites to see the damage and pose with the wreckage.

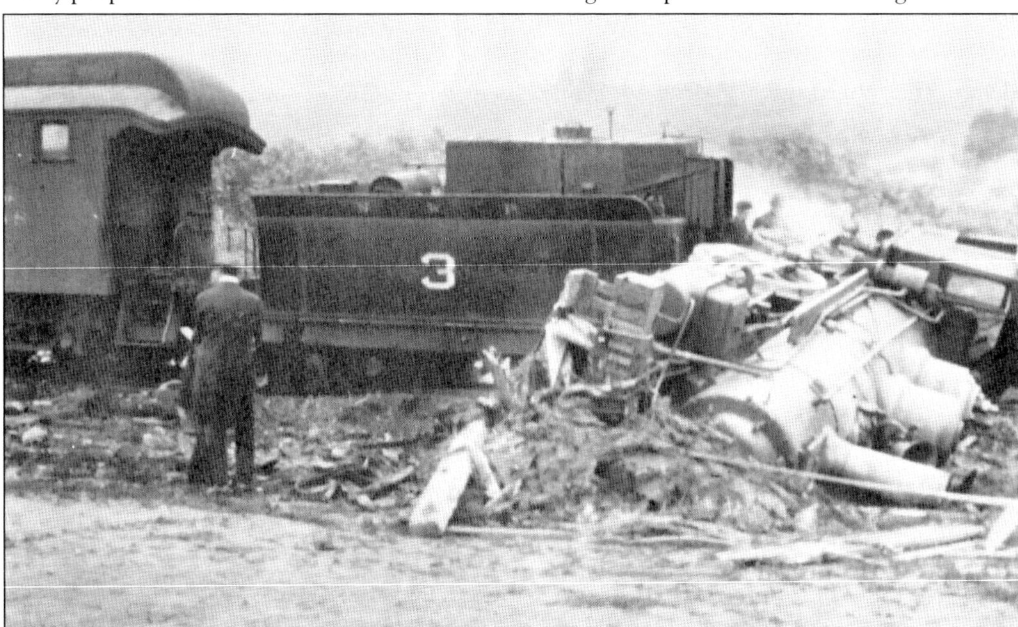

Some wrecks were caused by factors such as operator error, faulty rails, or—in one early 1920s wreck—a cow. This is the wreck of locomotive No. 3. The NWP purchased No. 3 from the Oregon & Eureka Railroad in 1911 for use on the northern section of the line before the golden spike was driven. After this wreck, it continued to serve the NWP as a stationary boiler at Willits until 1923.

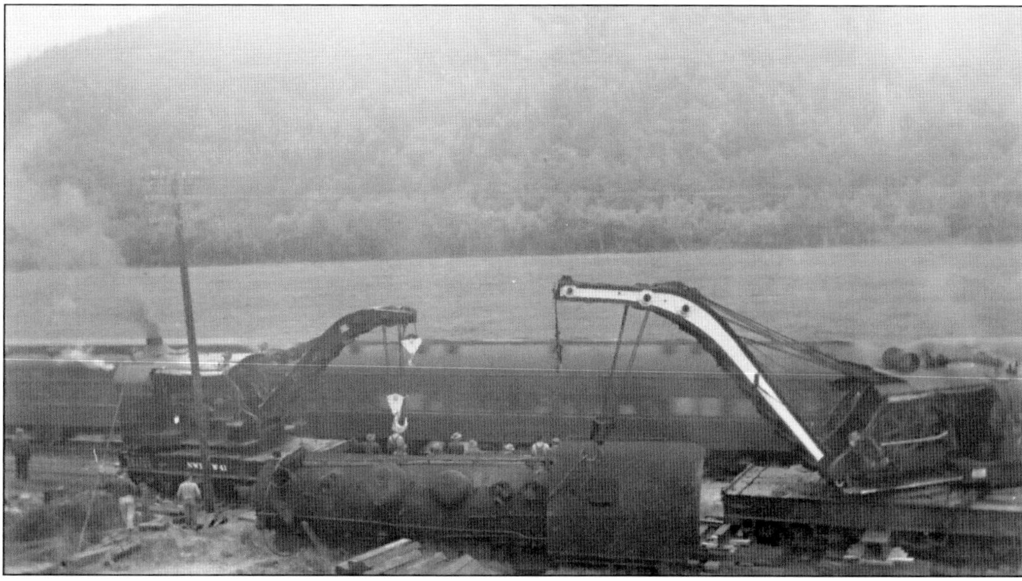

A passing passenger train delays work on the righting of locomotive No. 180 in this December 1948 photograph. Two cranes were required to lift the 196,500-pound engine. The cranes' crews are watching the passenger train as it goes by. The cranes, which were mounted on railroad cars, were highly mobile and could be taken to where they were needed.

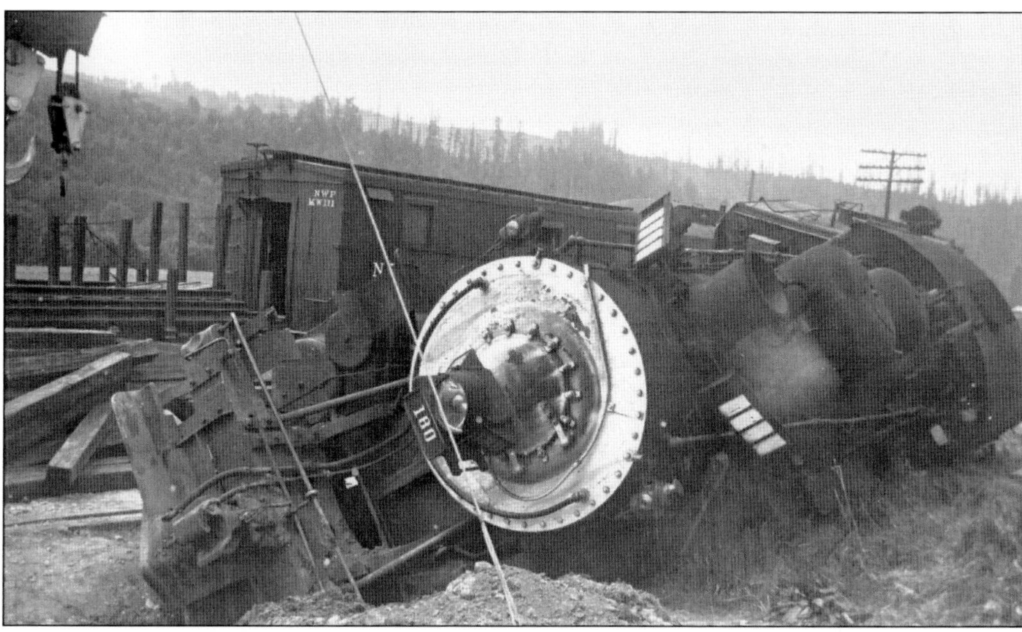

Locomotive No. 180 did not remain in service for long after this derailment. The engine, built by the American Locomotive Company, was retired in August 1952. The arrival of new, more powerful diesel engines made it financially unsound to rebuild the 1914 engine, as the NWP had done with many engines before.

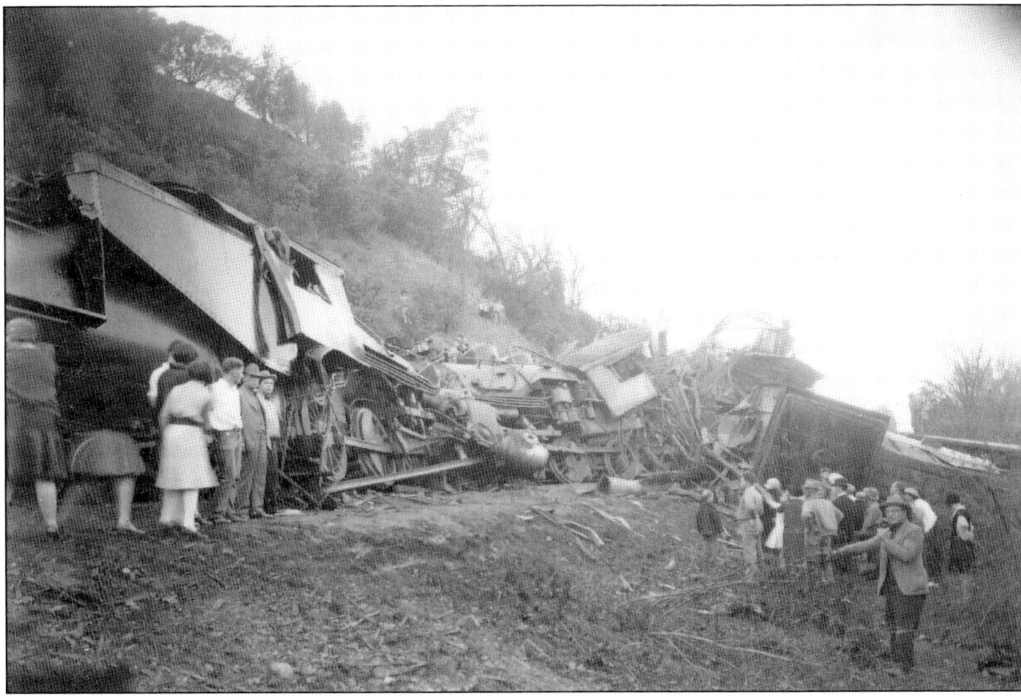

Locomotives Nos. 184 and 141 were involved in a crash near Largo, south of Ukiah, in 1929. The freight train headed by the No. 184 collided head-on with the No. 141 hauling a passenger train south from Eureka. The crewmen killed on the No. 184 were engineer George Cunard and fireman P.L. Landre. George Bradley Jr., engineer of the No. 141, was also killed, while 32 passengers and other crew were injured. Though badly damaged, both locomotives were repaired.

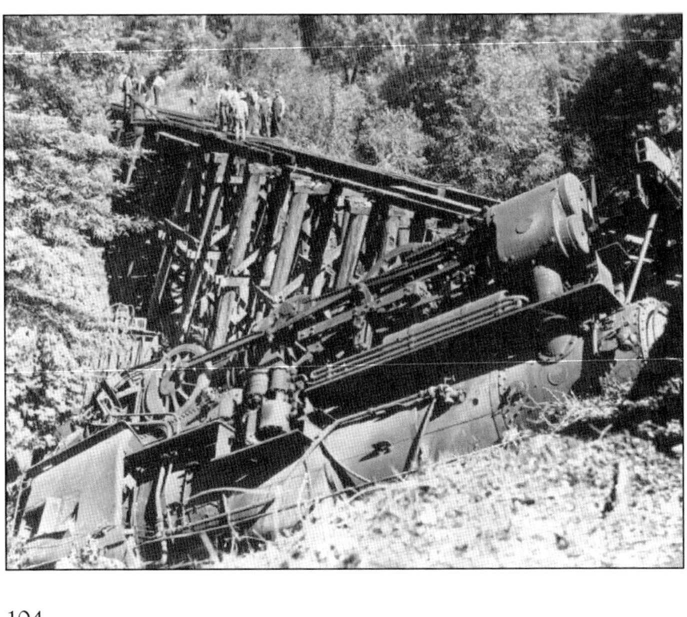

On August 6, 1937, a fire caused another fatal wreck. The No. 182, sister engine to the No. 184, was hauling freight northbound when, near Shively, the engineer saw a "terrifying view of the bridge on fire," according to the *Ukiah Republican Press*. "The burned timbers gave way with a roar and sent the engine plunging 30 feet into the gorge . . . the tragedy wiped out the engine crew and a brakeman." These men were engineer Ed Weatherby, fireman Carl Bartlett, and brakeman George Still. (Courtesy of HSU.)

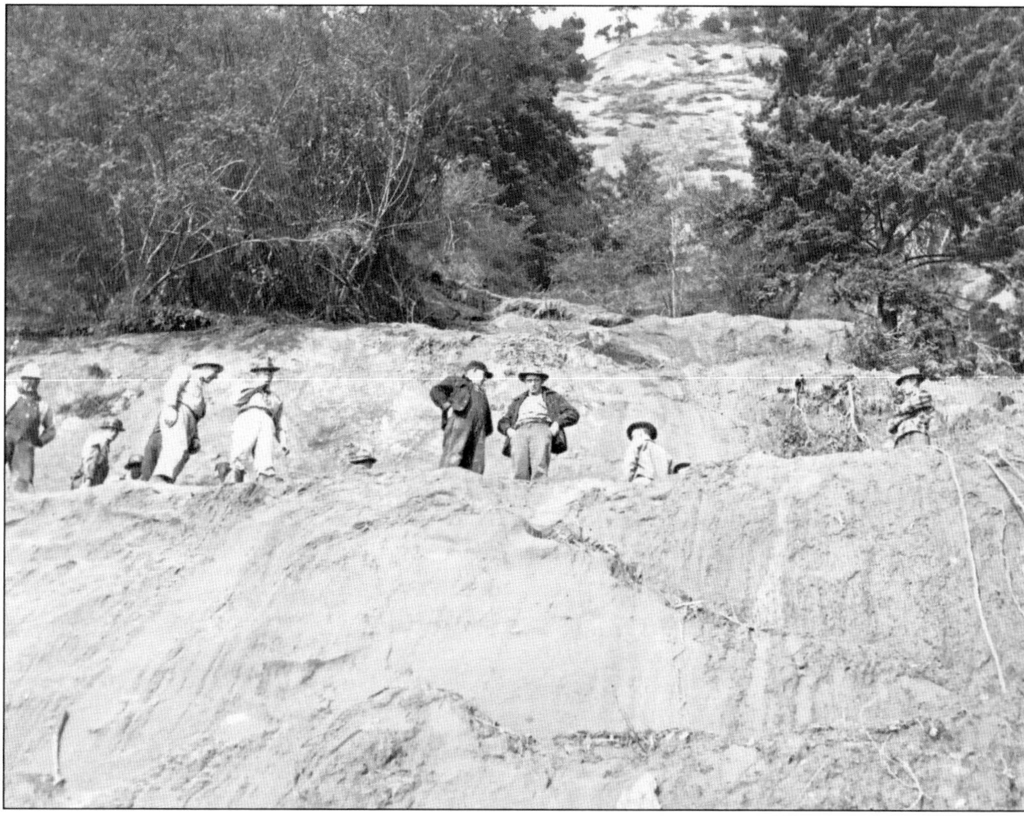

The No. 184, which was involved in the 1929 wreck at Largo, had another fatal wreck in 1953 and was demolished. The No. 184, by then relegated to serving as a work train, and its crew were sent out to repair a slide reported along the Scotia Bluffs after four inches of rain had soaked the hillsides. *The Fresno Bee The Republican* reported that after the No. 184 had been detached from the work train and as crews started to work on the first slide, a "tremendous mass of rock and earth crashed down the bluff" and sent the engine "hurtling over a 45-foot embankment." Three men were killed in the wreck, which occurred a mile north of Nanning Creek; a memorial dedicated to engineer D.G. Liscom, fireman T.R. Porter, and brakeman J.H. Aure now stands next to the Fortuna Depot Museum. A fourth man, Jesus Sanchez, escaped the wreckage by clinging to a bridge piling.

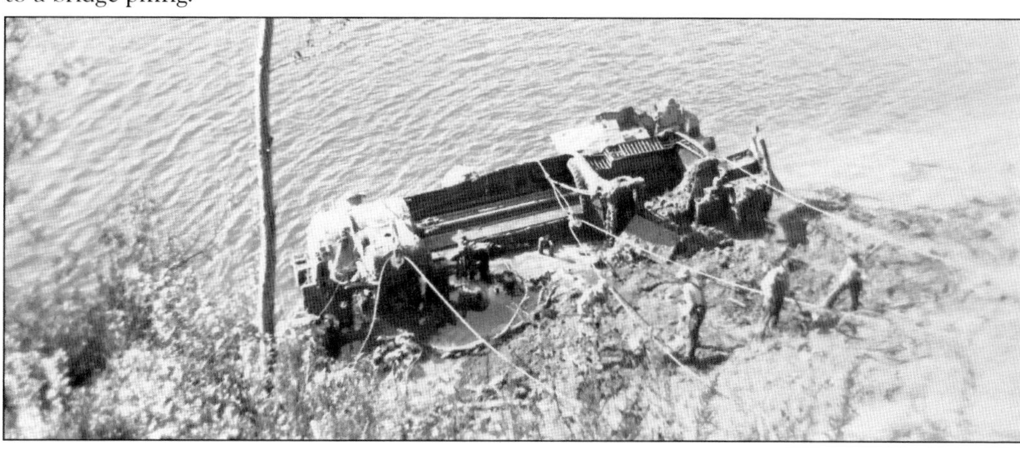

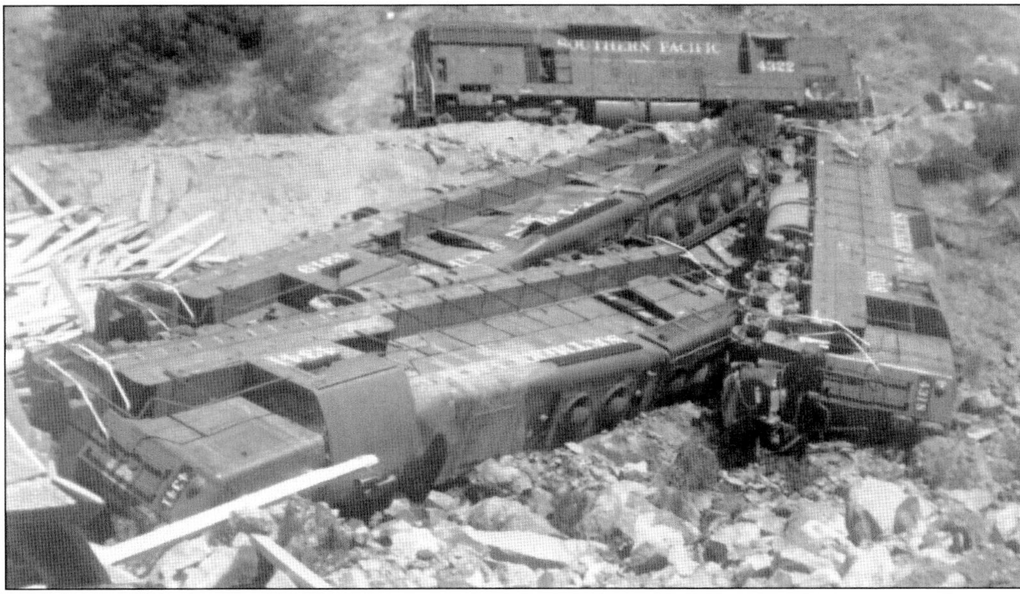

In the 1950s, a series of wet winters caused numerous slides on the northern section of the NWP. In the early months of 1958, slides caused frequent closures of the line, and in March, a seven-car derailment occurred near Kekawaka south of Alderpoint. The *Humboldt Standard* reported: "The southbound train left Eureka . . . hauling 70 cars loaded with lumber from local mills. NWP reports said the derailment started about 15 cars behind the engine. Considerable track was torn up in the accident." In April 1958, two other trains were derailed in the Eel River Canyon. George Morrison, vice president and general manager of the NWP, told the *Humboldt Standard* that "the canyon is so wet it is almost impossible to keep the tracks open. In order to serve shippers we will continue to keep the trains going, but it will be a gamble."

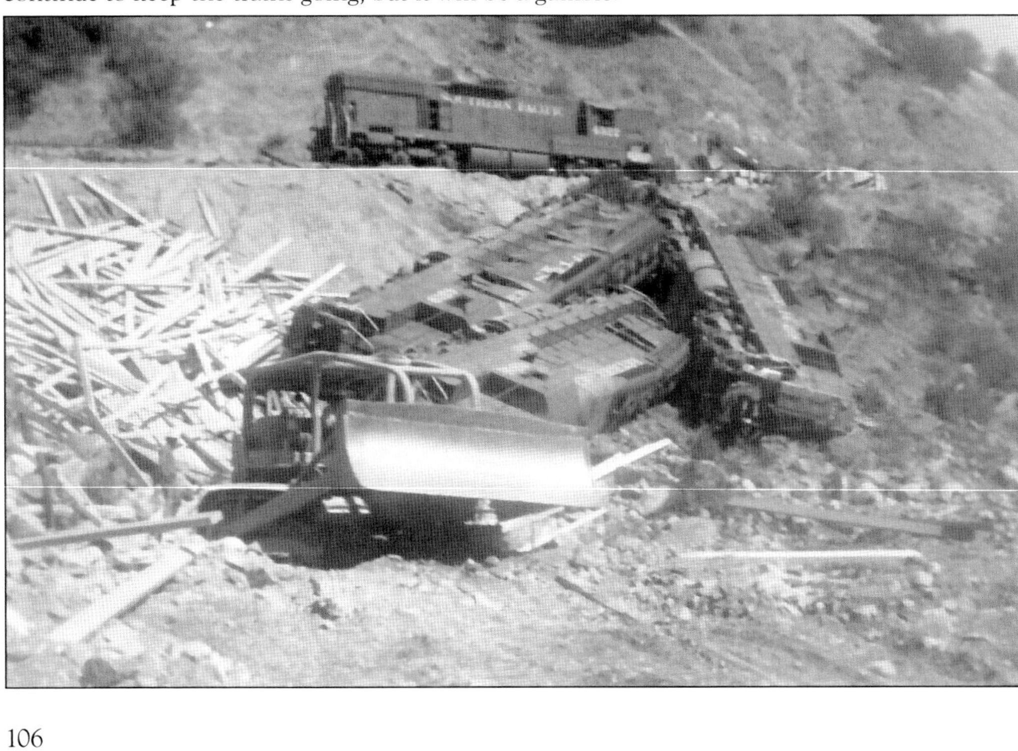

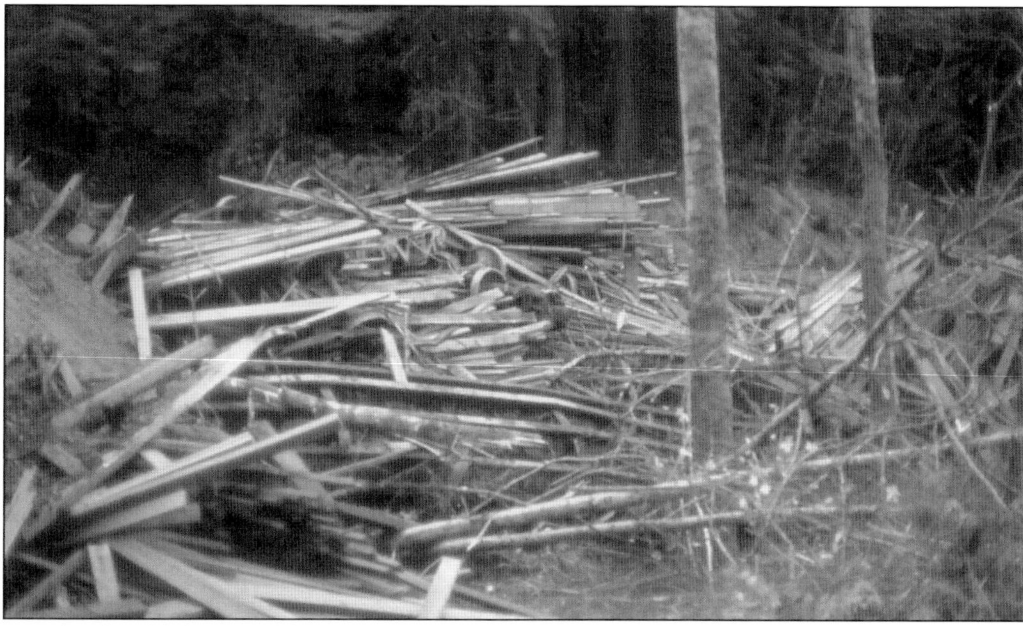

Another landslide caused four locomotives and 16 cars to derail in November 1963 a mile south of South Fork. The *Humboldt Standard* reported: "Engineer Richard Knife saw the slide ahead but the momentum of the train, with all but one car loaded, made it impossible to stop in time." The impact of the collision forced the lead locomotive into a slough of the Eel River. Water rapidly filled the cab, but Knife and fireman Henry Lovett were able to break a window and escape. To retrieve the locomotive, NWP hired a salvage rigging expert from Portland, Oregon. A week after the wreck, the lead locomotive remained partially submerged in the slough, although cranes retrieved the other cars and locomotives. The line was closed for only one day, as a spur was built around the scene of the wreck. (Both courtesy of HRIA.)

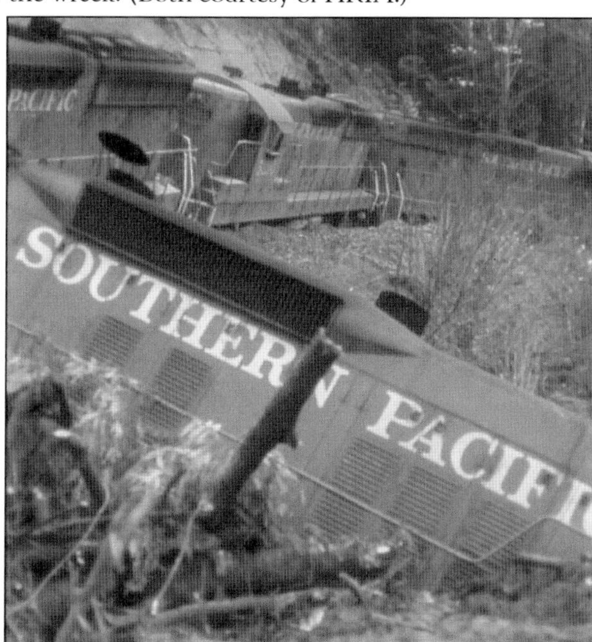

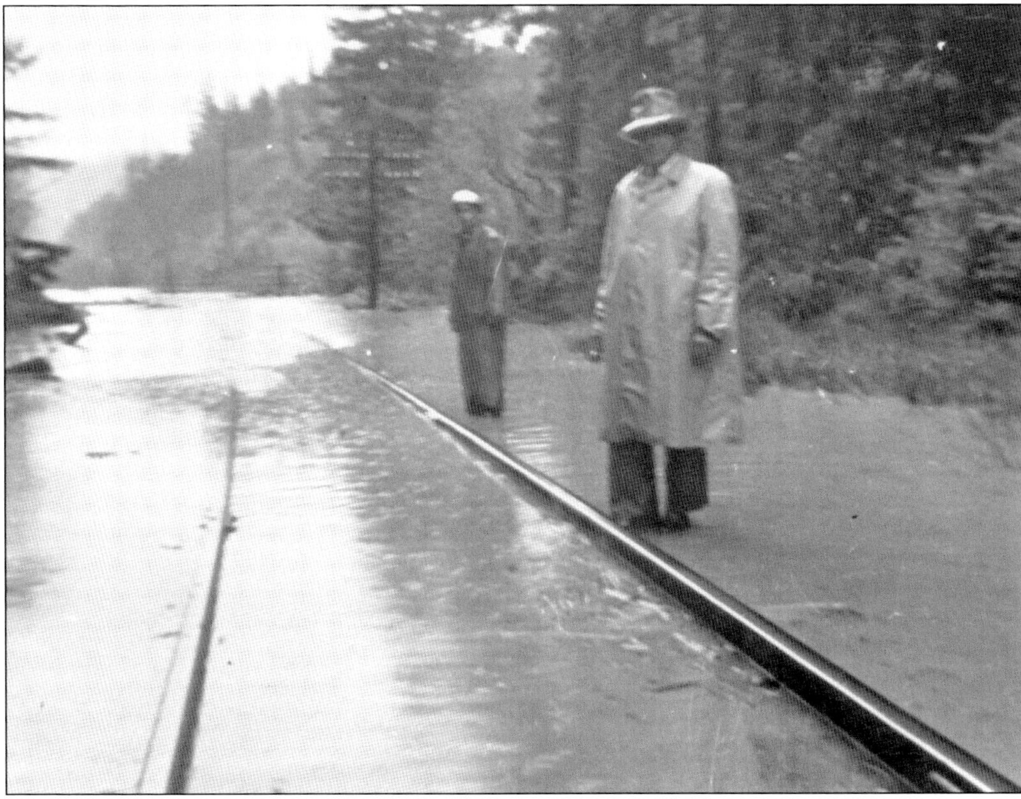

After the 1913 flood forced the rebuilding of much of the newly built line, the railroad experienced few problems from high water in the first half of the 20th century. This changed, however; in this image, line inspectors stare at the rising water on December 21, 1955. On the back of this photograph, they recorded, "Milepost 246, (near Shively) 11 am water covered track 10 pole lengths in three hours."

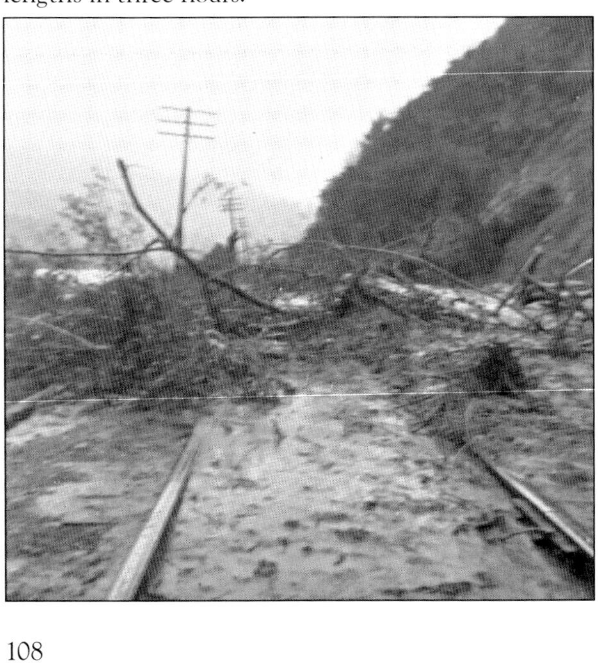

In December 1955, as floodwaters receded, inspectors found more damage along the line. This slide at milepost 244, south of Shively, came in before 9:00 a.m. as the floodwaters rose. The waterlogged line required extensive repairs, especially regarding slide removal, by maintenance crews, but the line reopened in early 1956.

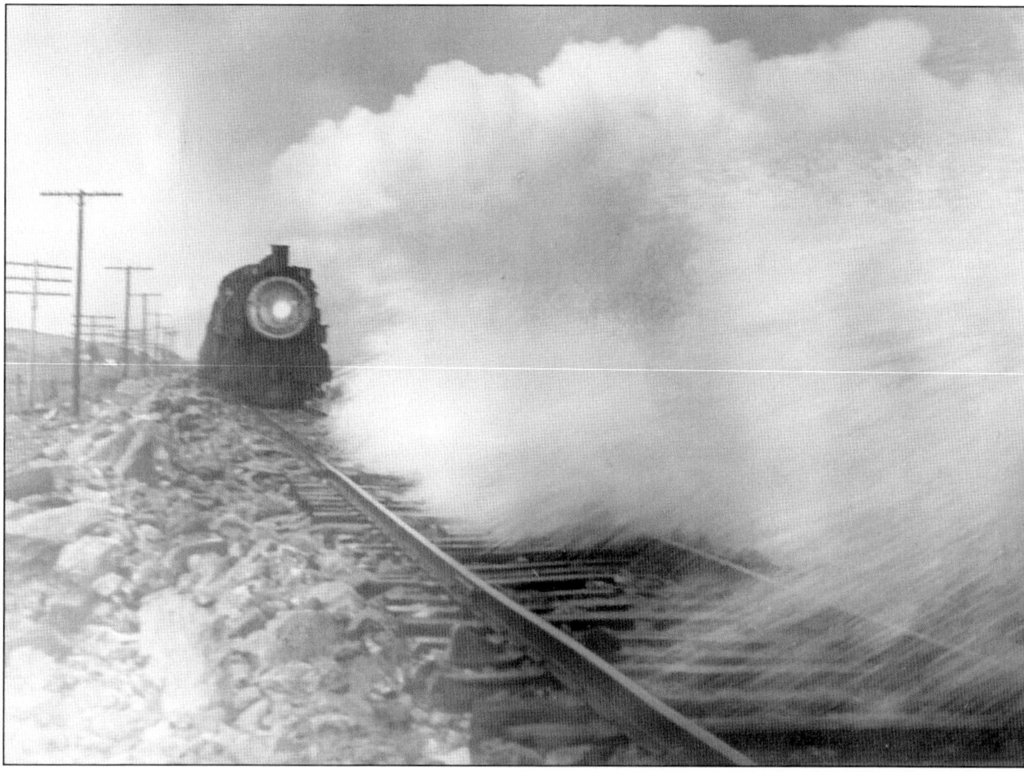

An unanticipated side effect of Humboldt Bay jetty construction in the 1880s was the focusing of wave action from the mouth of the bay onto the shore directly across from the entrance. During high storms, ocean waves pounded the shoreline and eroded the land, including the edge of the railroad. Buhne Bluff, directly across from the opening, was once a 500-foot-tall bluff. After jetty construction, the bluff eroded to just slightly above sea level. The railroad combated the waves' erosive power between Fields Landing and Eureka, where the line hugs the shoreline. Starting in the 1930s, workers placed riprap and rocks to protect the line, but winter waves frequently covered the line, creating dramatic images—like these—when trains rolled through the waves. Tidal effects were most noticeable following repairs to the jetties in the mid-20th century.

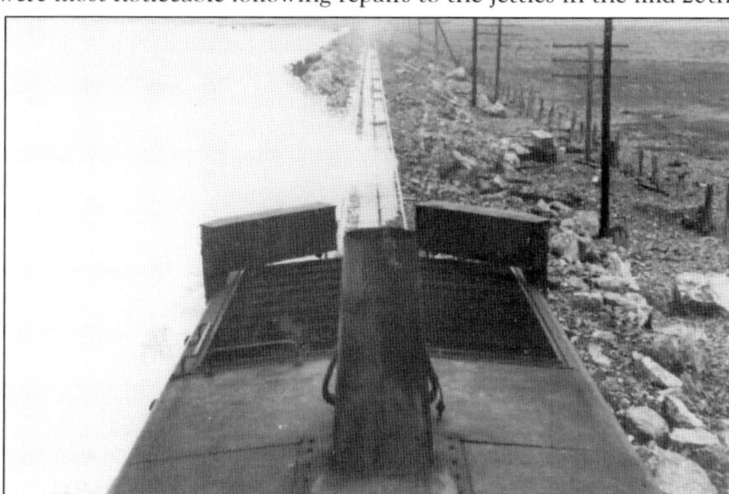

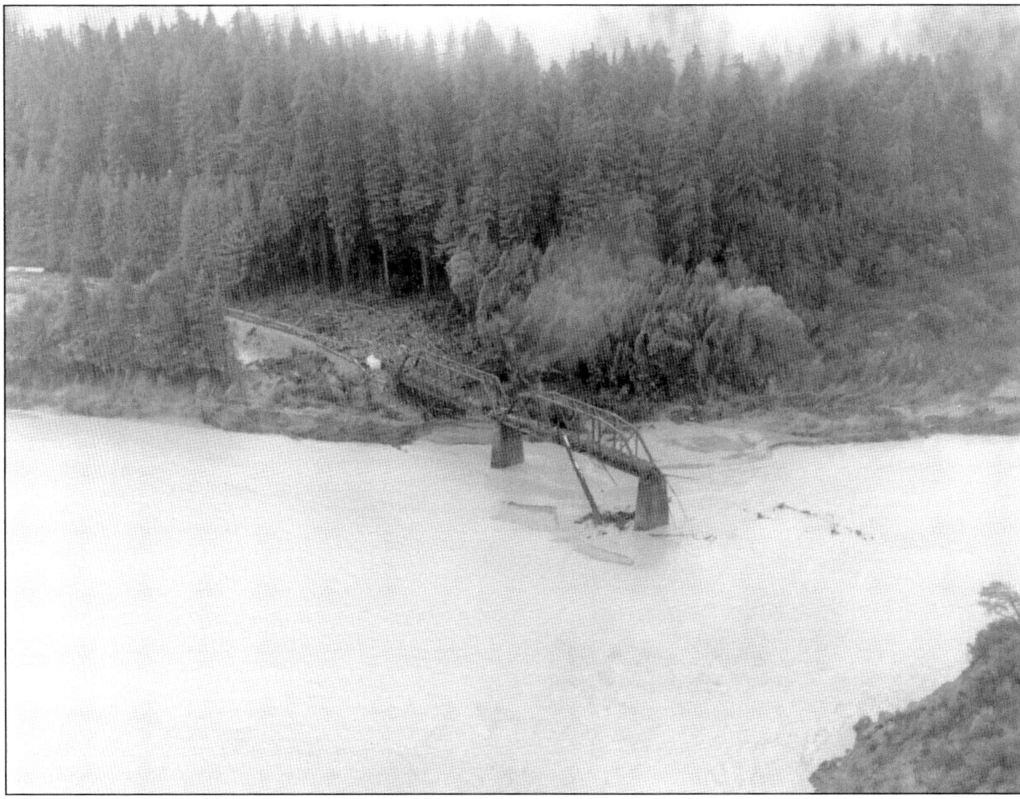

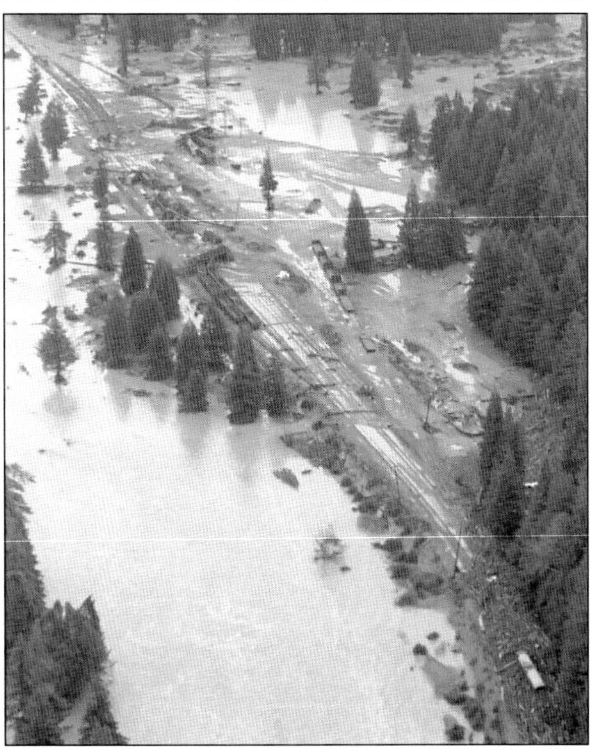

One of the greatest disasters for the NWP was the 1964 flood. In December of that year, a wet snowfall was followed by heavy warm rains, flooding rivers in northern California. The Eel River crested above the tracks on the bridge at Dyerville, as illustrated by debris left on the bridge. Two spans of the bridge were washed away, and the bridges at Island Mountain and Cain Rock were also heavily damaged.

At the community of South Fork, south of the Dyerville Bridge, the river crested 21 feet above the tracks. Tanker cars were upset, and railroad cars were pushed downriver; their remains are still observable during the summer. Thirty-thousand gallons of gasoline spilled from the tankers forced a six-week quarantine of South Fork. Mud and debris, deposited as the river receded, added to the massive cleanup. (Courtesy of Greg Rumney.)

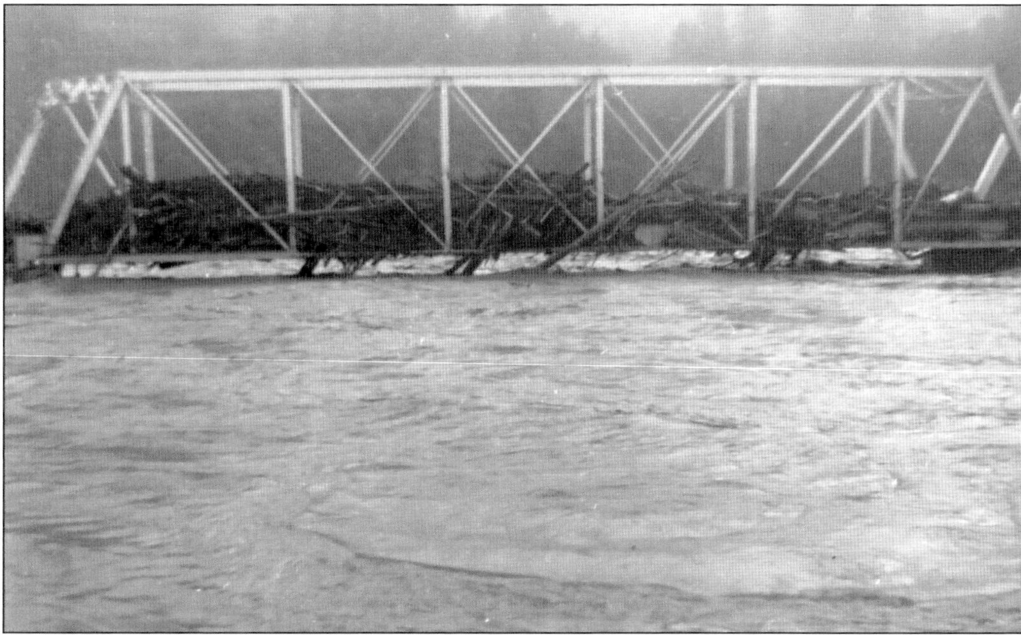

The damage from the 1964 flood was much more extensive than what occurred after the 1955 flood. Miles of track were washed away throughout the Eel River canyon. In some places, only canyon walls remained. Tunnels were jammed with debris, as was the Cain Rock Bridge (pictured); during the summer months, this bridge crosses 63 feet above the river. Officials estimated that it would cost nearly $7 million—half the cost of building the route in the 1910s—to repair the line.

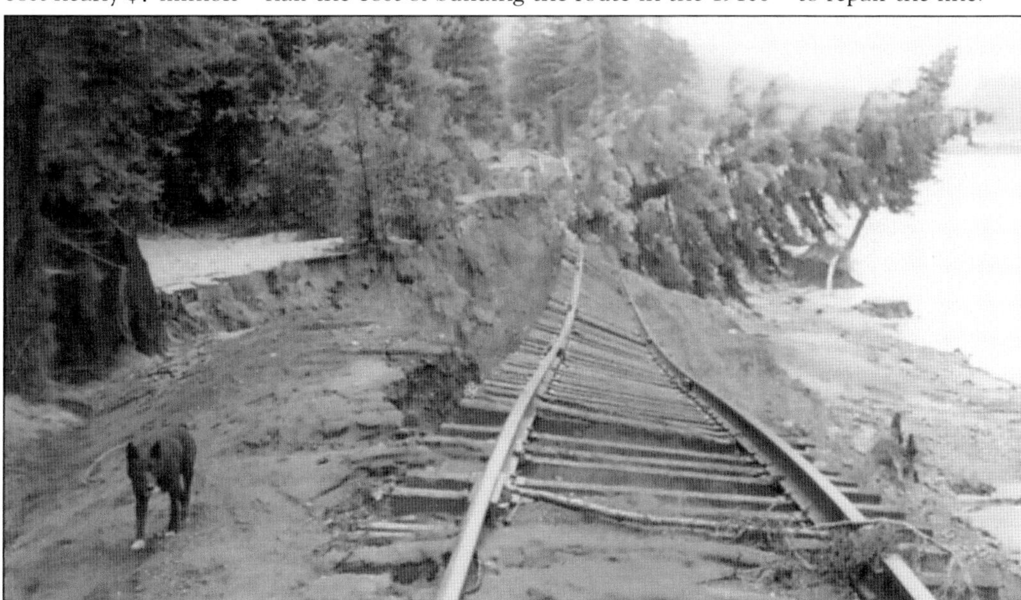

NWP hired Morrison-Knudsen Company to do major repairs on the damaged line, including re-laying 100 miles of track and rebuilding the roadbed. Morrison-Knudsen official Orile Joiner told the *Humboldt Standard* that, "damage done on the Scotia Bluffs was not as serious as that upstream in the Alderpoint area, and other canyon sections." NWP crews also worked on rebuilding efforts. Ultimately, more than 800 people worked on the repairs.

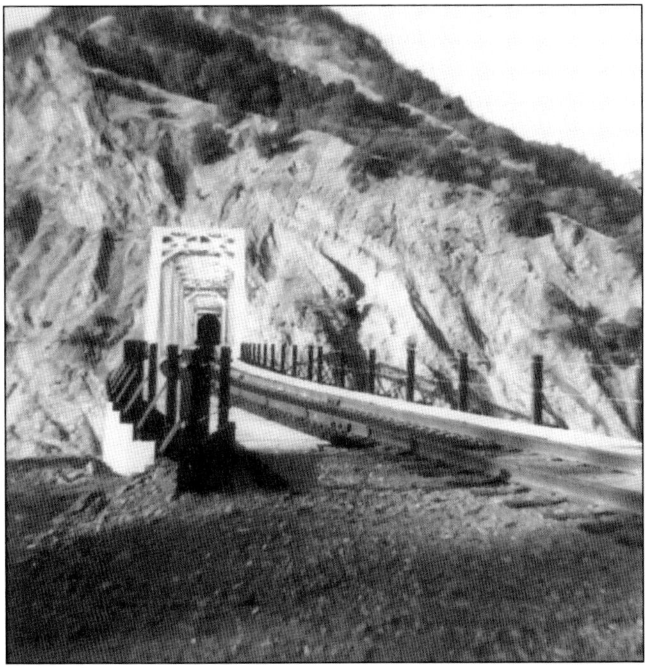

After the 1964 flood, rebuilding costs rose to $10 million. NWP built camps similar to the ones used during construction at Spy Rock, Island Mountain, and Kekawaka. In another action similar to the original construction, work was divided into 22 work sites in order to expedite repairs. The rebuilding efforts required over 500 pieces of equipment, including locomotives to haul supplies and trucks to supply remote locations. The image at left shows the bridge at Island Mountain after it was rebuilt.

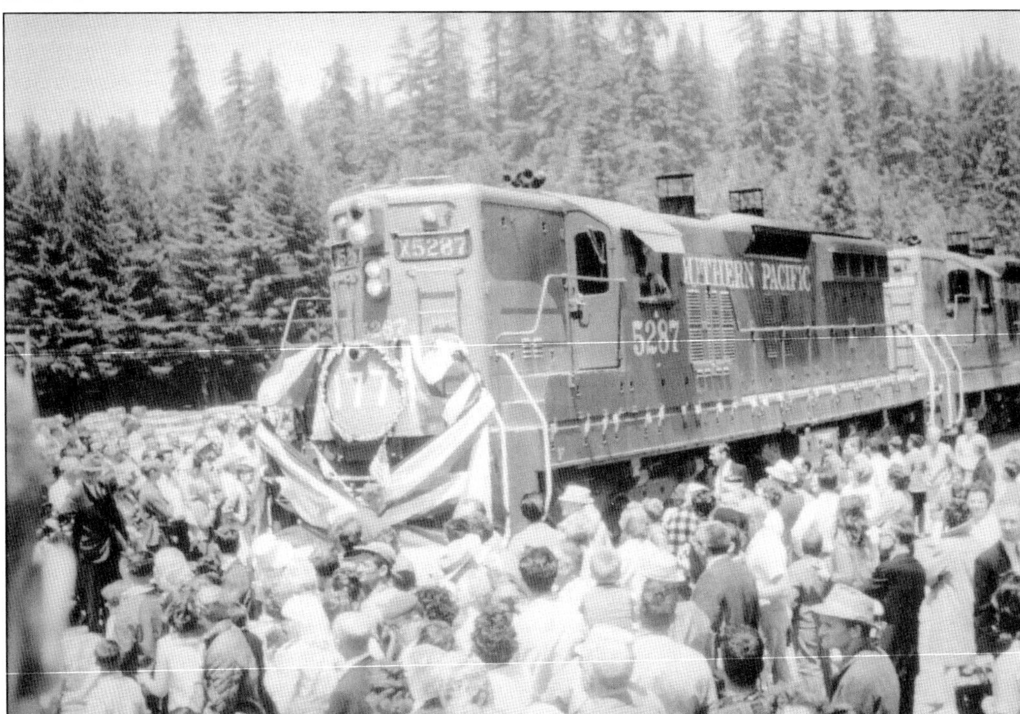

Given the Herculean nature of the repairs, NWP officials decided to rededicate the railroad with a ceremonial re-driving of the golden spike. Ceremonies were held at South Fork on June 16, 1965. Reports estimated that 3,500 people attended the dedication. Afterward, a 70-car train pulled out of the station, hauling the first load of lumber transported south since December 1964. (Courtesy of NWPRRHS.)

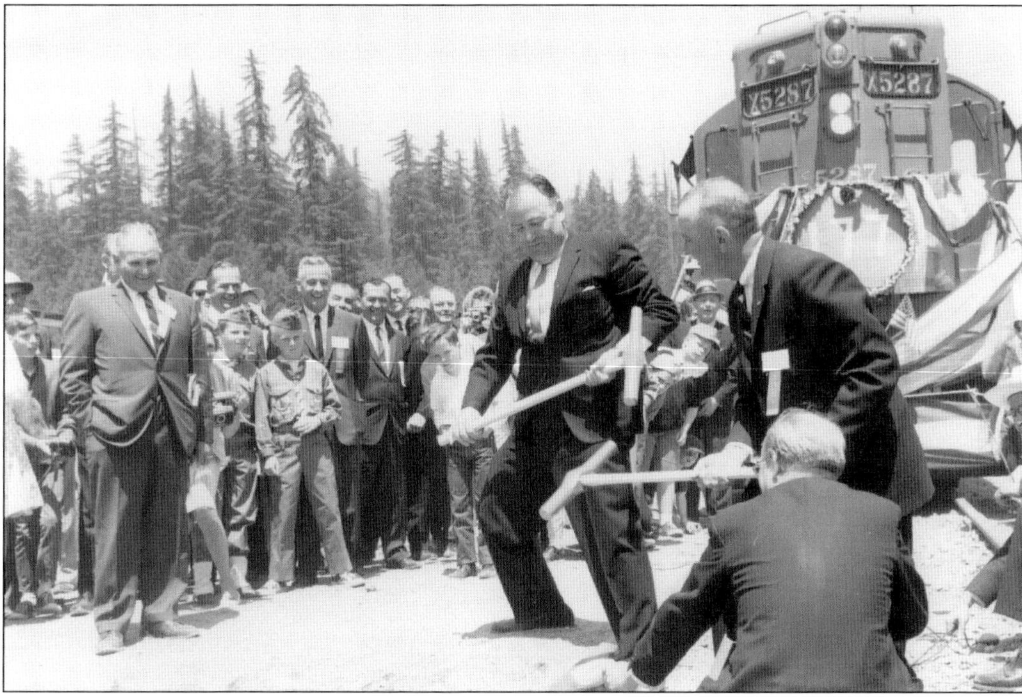

US representative Don Clausen (right) and B.F. Biaggini, president of the Southern Pacific, drove the same golden spike used at Cain Rock in 1914. Both men gave speeches, with Clausen commenting that he "wished the line of steel would never again be cut." At this time, the Humboldt lumber industry was valued at $160 million, and the railroad was vital to meeting shipping needs. (Courtesy of HSU.)

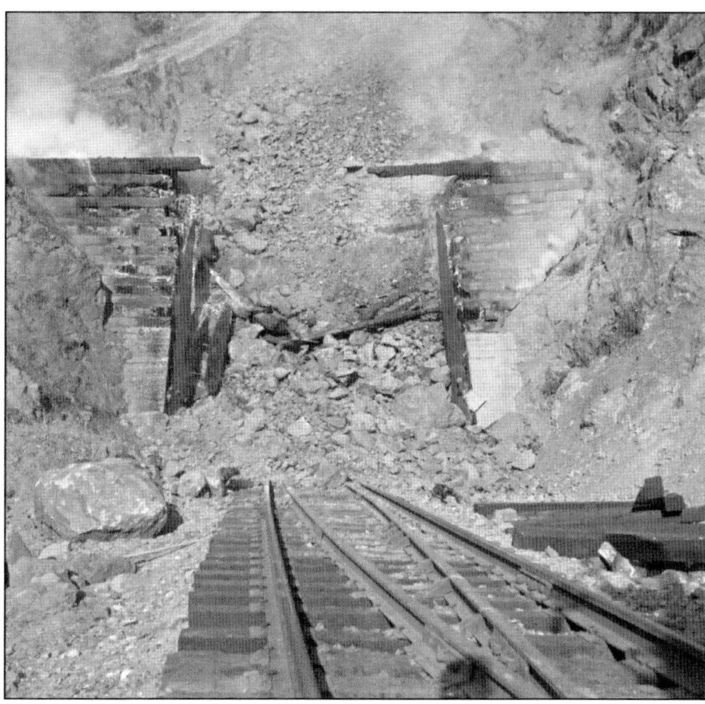

Tunnel fires presented a different kind of disaster for the NWP. Forest fires could ignite the timbers of a tunnel, sometimes collapsing the ends of it. The cause of this 1955 fire at Tunnel No. 31, located between Alderpoint and Fort Seward, is unknown. Tunnel fires were dangerous, because they could burn for long periods of time even after the ends collapsed.

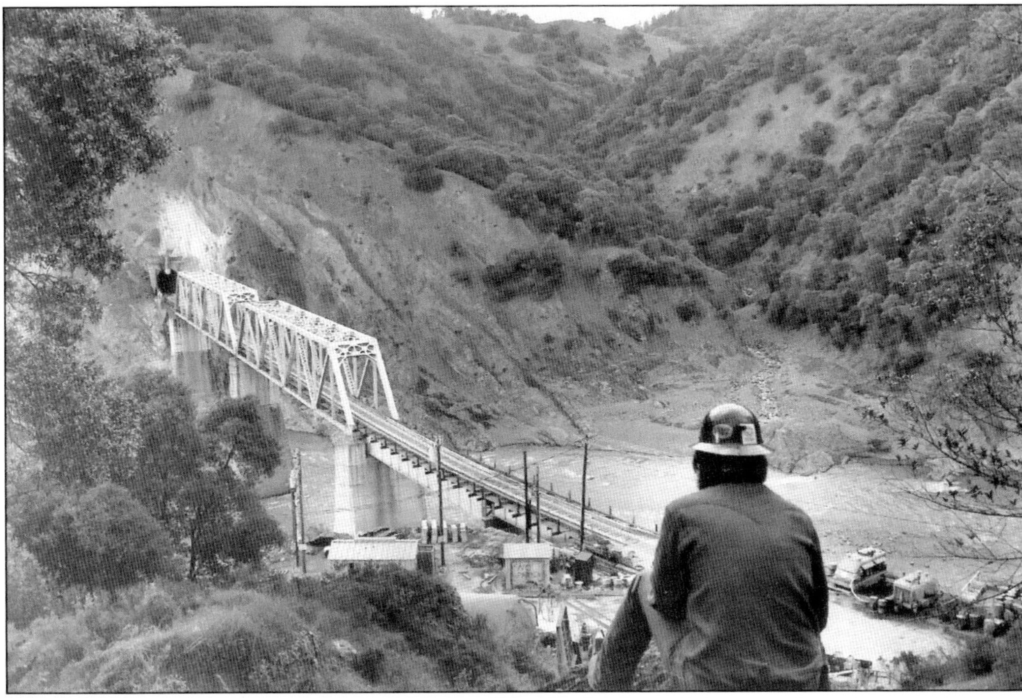

In 1978, a fire in the mile-long tunnel at Island Mountain caused the complete closure of the line for more than a year. On the "railroaders' nostalgia" discussion board on the website trainorders.com, a member of the crew who was present on September 6, 1978, recalled receiving a call from NWP district superintendent Hi Fowler. Fowler informed the crew member of "a report of heavy smoke coming from the mouth of tunnel 27." The tunnel, which was lined with dry redwood timbers, burned out of control, creating its own draft and burning hot enough to fracture rock 300 feet above the roof of the tunnel. Workers tried both water and foam to suppress the fire, but neither were successful. Even after the tunnel was sealed at both ends to starve the fire of oxygen, it continued to burn for two weeks, and workers could not begin repairs until the rocks cooled. (Both courtesy of NWPRRHS.)

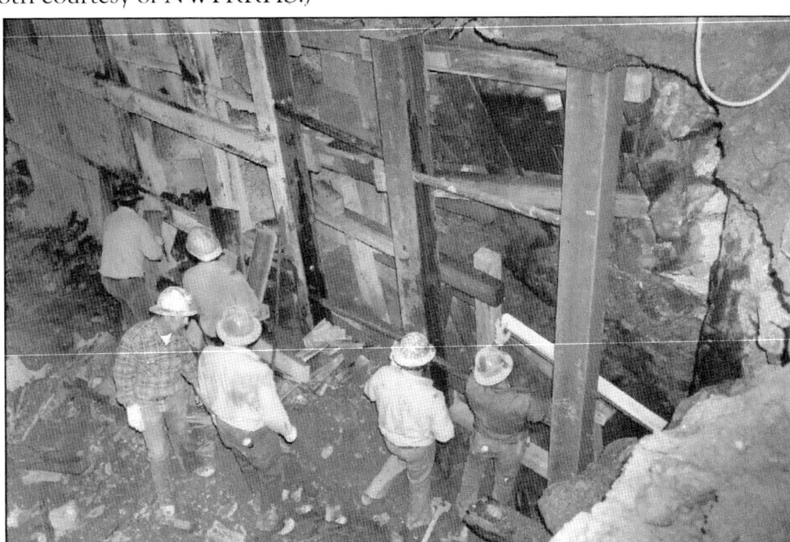

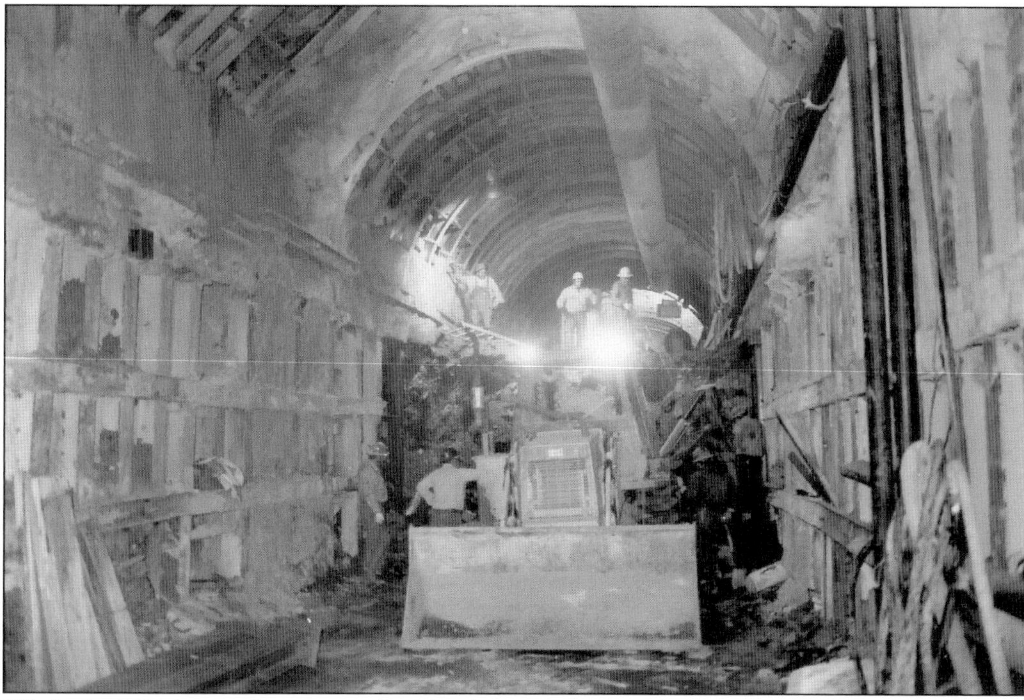

While the 1978 fire was burning in the Island Mountain tunnel, the NWP and its parent company, the Southern Pacific, considered options that included closing the railroad. California congressman Don Clausen and other politicians fought to keep the line open, and NWP ultimately hired Morrison-Knudsen Company to rebuild the tunnel. An article in a 1979 edition of *EM-Kayan Magazine*, an in-house magazine for the company, described the massive operation: "M-K's work consists of reopening a 1,600-foot-long section of the tunnel at its midpoint that is completely plugged with caved in earth and boulders, requiring careful excavation procedures." Crews lined the tunnel with "shotcrete"—concrete shot from high-pressured air guns—to prevent additional fires. Work was done from both ends, with work camps at either end of the tunnel. The project cost $19 million, more than the original cost of the entire line. (Both courtesy of NWPRRHS.)

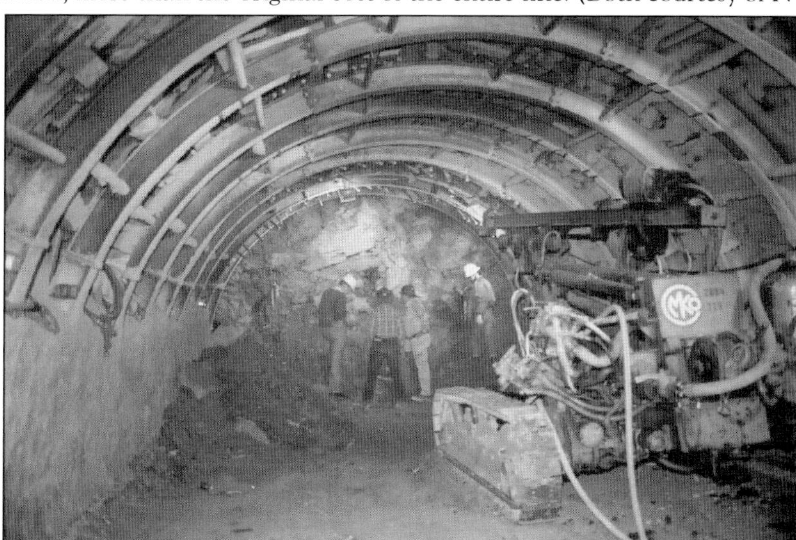

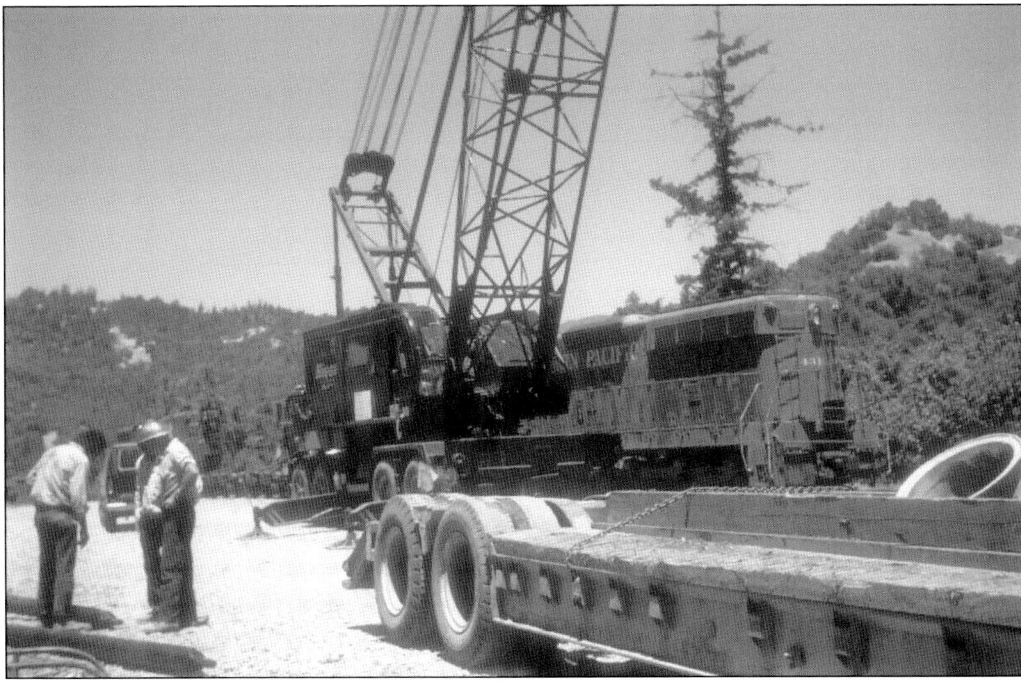

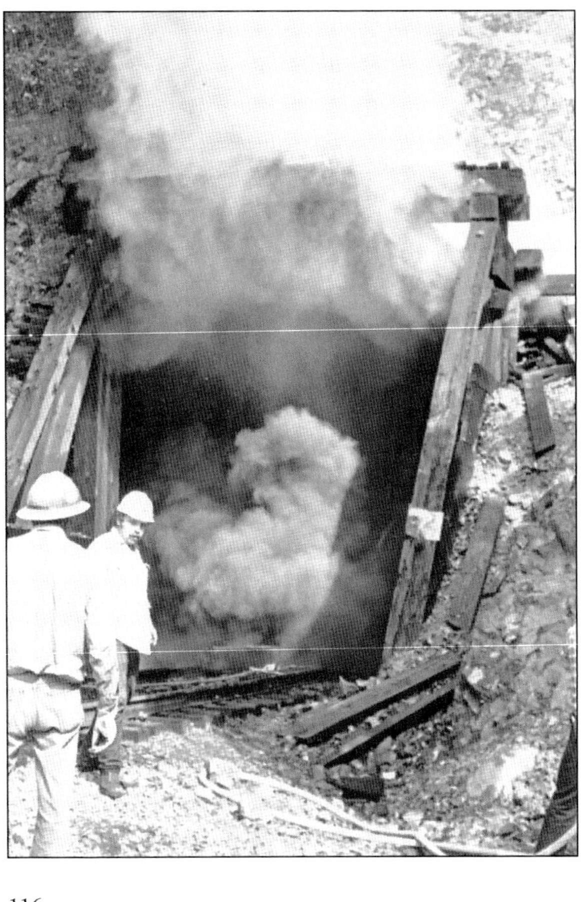

With the indefinite closure of the line, valuable rolling stock sat unused in Eureka. The locomotives, leased from Southern Pacific, cost the NWP $200,000 a month. In April 1979, the Humboldt County Board of Supervisors granted permission to move eight locomotives by truck on county roads from Alderpoint to Covelo. At Alderpoint, the 200,000-pound engines were taken off their wheels and lifted by heavy cranes onto waiting lowboy trailers reinforced with extra axles.

A tunnel fire near Longvale on September 11, 1983, contributed to abandonment of the line north of Willits. Although NWP crews began repairs, a quarter of the maintenance staff was laid off in October 1983, effectively abandoning the line. Despite a short respite from the Interstate Commerce Commission, which opposed closure, the final NWP trains rolled in August 1984.

Seven

Decline and Legacy

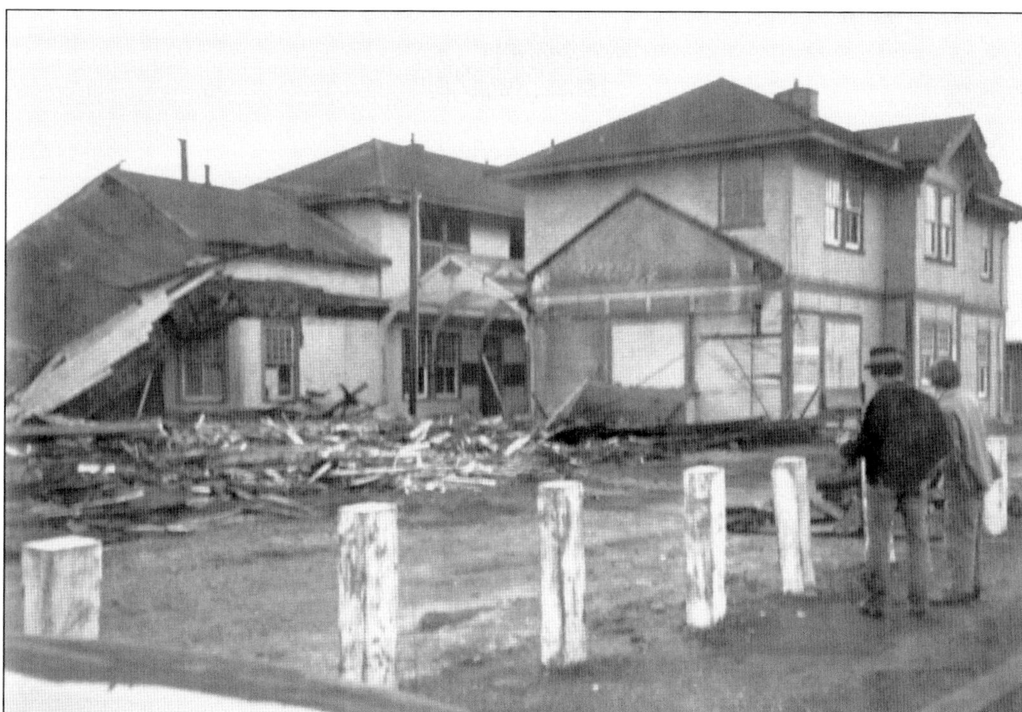

A relic of Eureka's railroad history was lost when the 70-year-old depot was demolished in January 1971. Area historian/journalist Andrew Genzoli wrote in the *Times-Standard* that elements of the depot were saved from "the salvage or burning piles"—portions of the waiting room and "other finishings . . . have been sent to Nevada, where they will be incorporated in a restoration . . . too bad something of this nature can't be done here at home."

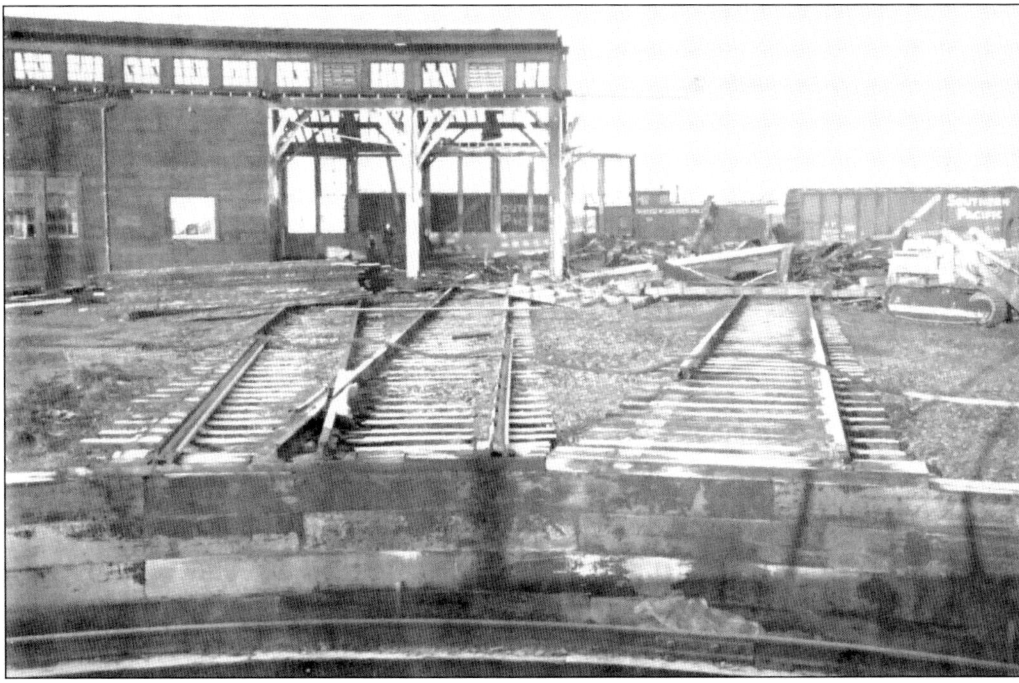

Two weeks after the January 1971 demolition of the Eureka depot, the roundhouse was torn down. This (and the image on page 117) are from the photograph album of P.E. Bandy, a Northwestern Pacific engineer who documented these melancholy moments near the end of Eureka's NWP history. The Eureka rail yard is now a problematic environmental cleanup site, and its future uses are the focus of vigorous and frequently bitter debate.

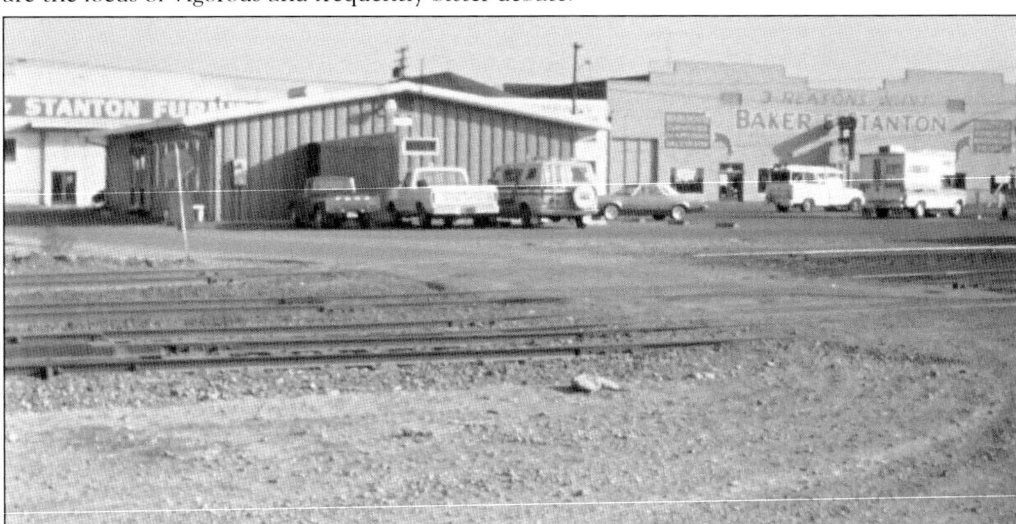

An *Arcata Union* editorial depicted Eureka's replacement depot as a slap in the face for the railroad's timber industry customers. The irate writer reported that "the new building, located in what was the north parking lot of the old station on Second Street, is made of METAL!" Highlighting the interdependence of the railroad and timber industries, the editorial predicted that "without the mills, the Southern Pacific would have to close the line so fast we would hardly know what happened."

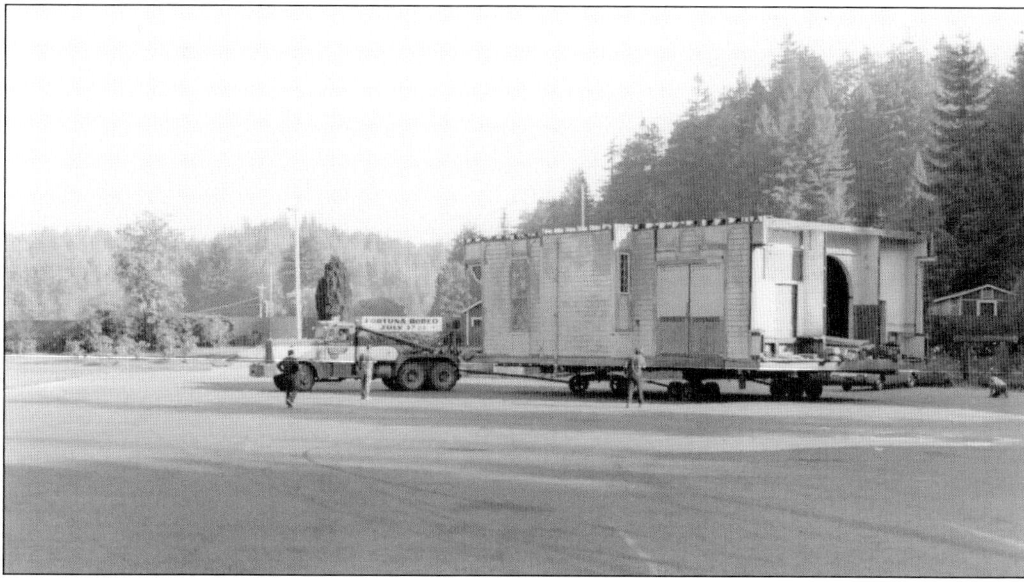

Fortuna's depot barely escaped the fate of its counterpart in Eureka. Shortly before the building's scheduled demolition, a citizens' group—led by Fortuna City Council member Beth Rundell—convinced the city to purchase the historic structure for renovation and future use as a local history museum. In October 1974, the depot was moved across town to a new home in Rohner Park. At the museum's grand opening on July 4, 1976, Andrew Genzoli spoke of the depot's central role in the life of the community in his keynote address, "The Heart of an Old Depot." The building's former location is shown below shortly after the depot's crosstown voyage. The photograph below shows the house (at left) used by the Eel River & Eureka Railroad (ER&ERR) as a home for the depot's stationmaster and his family.

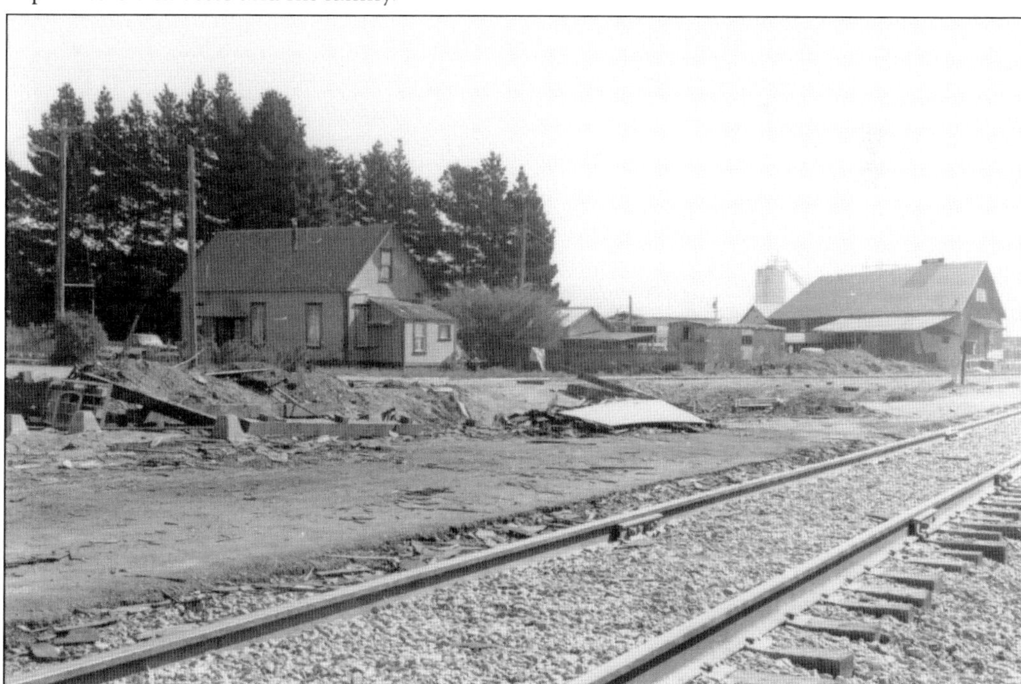

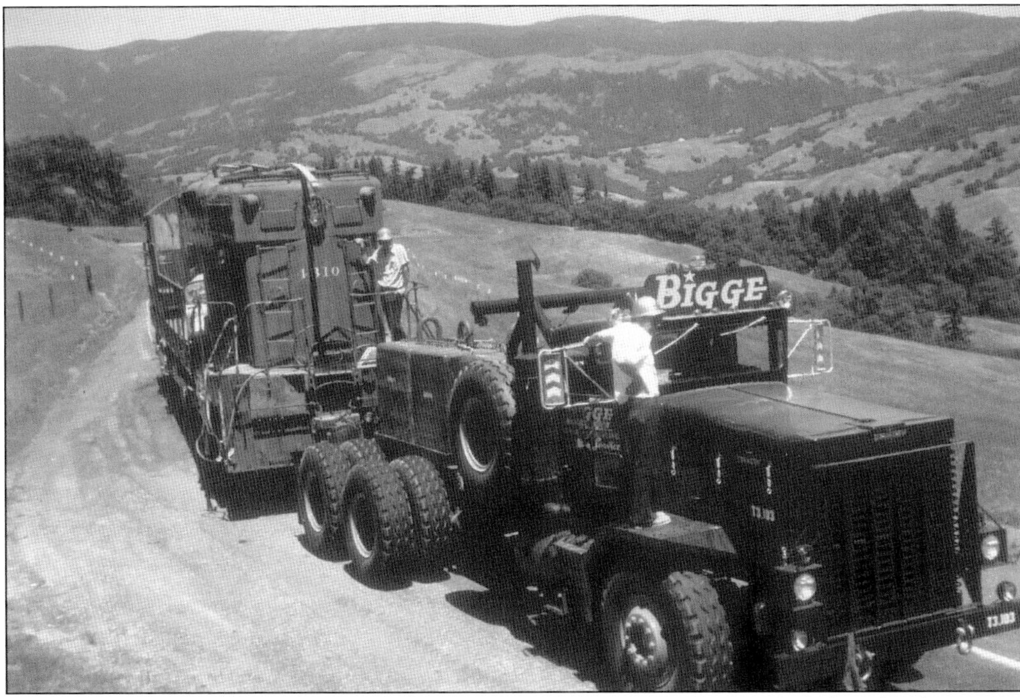

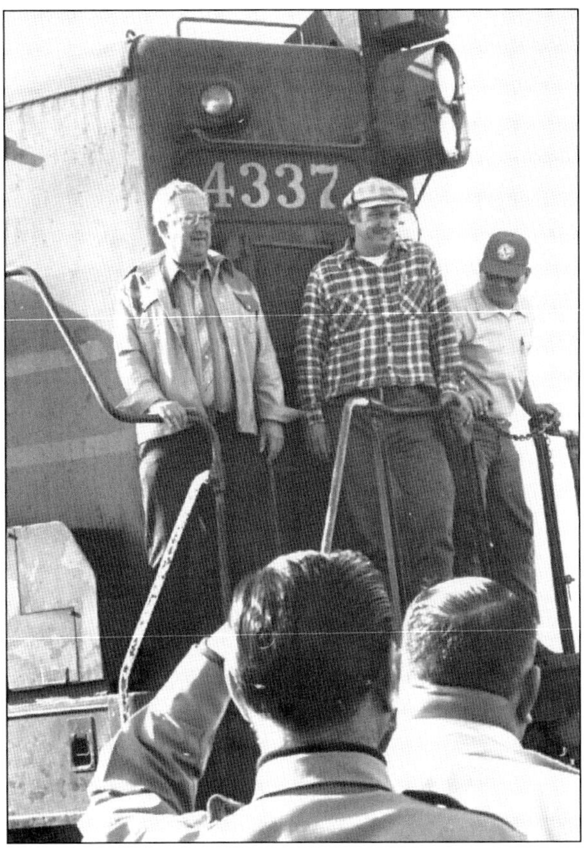

In June 1979, after the Island Mountain tunnel fire, the evacuation of locomotives over 30 miles of steep, winding country roads took two days per trip, with the heavy-duty trucks driving at top speeds of around five miles per hour. Fourth District county supervisor Danny Walsh grimly predicted in various newspaper articles that the removal indicated that Southern Pacific's pledges to not abandon rail service north of Willits were "PR hype."

On December 7, 1979, Eureka welcomed—with some fanfare—the first northbound train from Willits since the Island Mountain tunnel fire. Pictured here on locomotive No. 4337 are, from left to right, Humboldt County District 2 supervisor Harry Pritchard, an unidentified Southern Pacific official, and engineer Earl Wahlund. Two engines hauled approximately 250 empty freight cars to take shipments of lumber and other products from, according to the *Arcata Union*, "the transportation starved Northcoast."

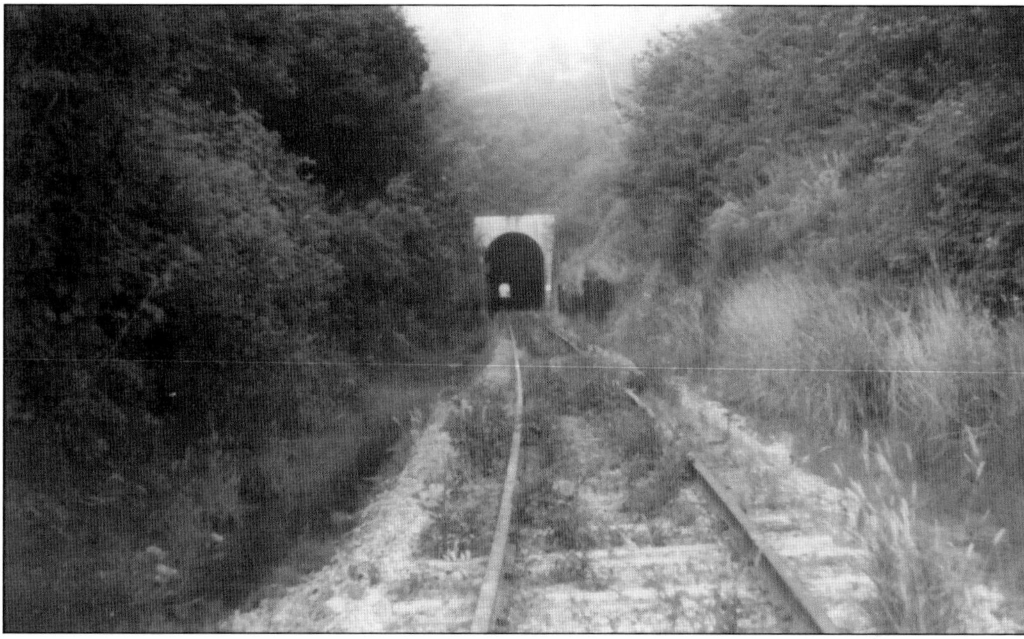

This photograph from the Francee White collection was taken by George Jesenko in July 1984 and shows the east portal of Tunnel No. 40, at Loleta. At this time, the Loleta Tunnel— completed by the ER&ERR in the summer of 1884—was almost precisely a century old. This tunnel is one of the better-preserved relics of the area's railroad past thanks to extensive renovation by the NWP in 1960.

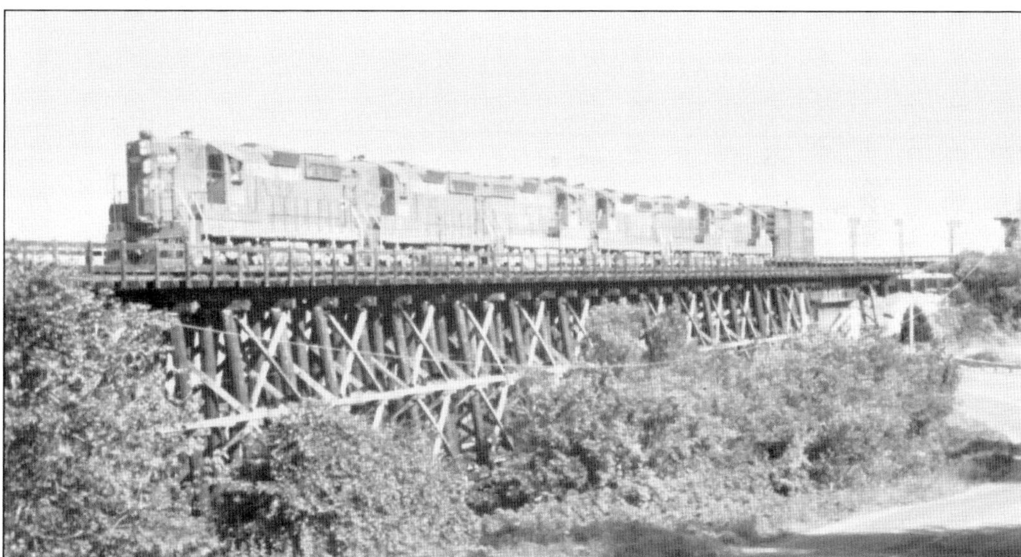

LOLETA TRESTLE (LASTTTRAIN OF LOADS ON NORTH END

The "last train of loads" pulled out of Eureka two days before a controversial $1,200-per-car shipping surcharge took effect on Monday, July 18, 1983. The *Times-Standard* quoted John Miller, lawyer for the Pacific Lumber Company, as saying, "The fight . . . is over, certainly in regard to the surcharge . . . on Monday, the line, in essence, will be abandoned." Railfan Gene Poon photographed this and the following five images, all of which are from the Francee White collection.

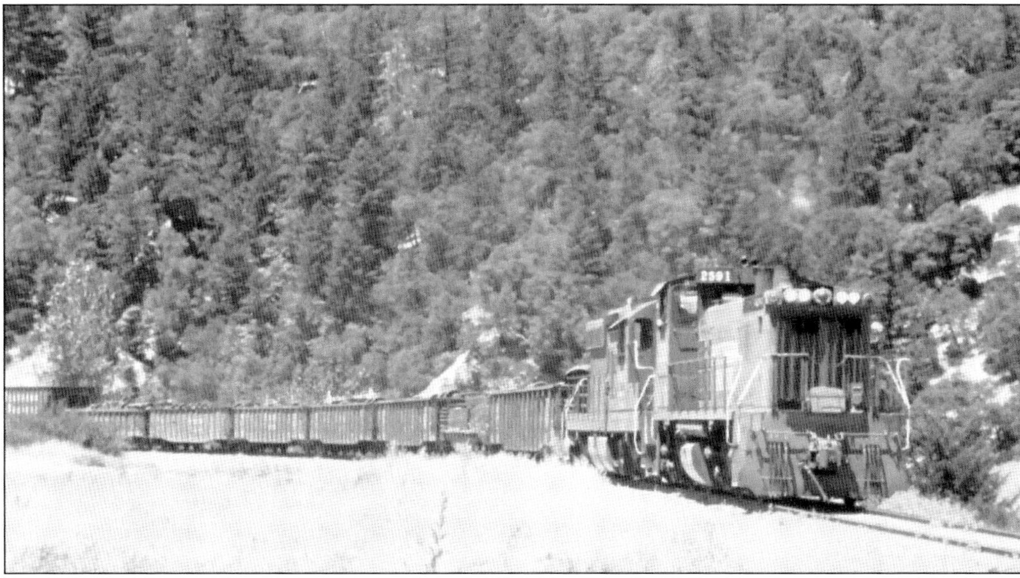

Freshman California congressman Doug Bosco was among many north coast residents who bitterly resented the Interstate Commerce Commission's decision not to overturn SP's $1,200 surcharge. The *Times-Standard* reported Bosco's condemnation of Southern Pacific as follows: "The real villain is the railroad, which proved that it pays more attention to profit and loss statements than to people." This July 1983 photograph was taken at Alderpoint.

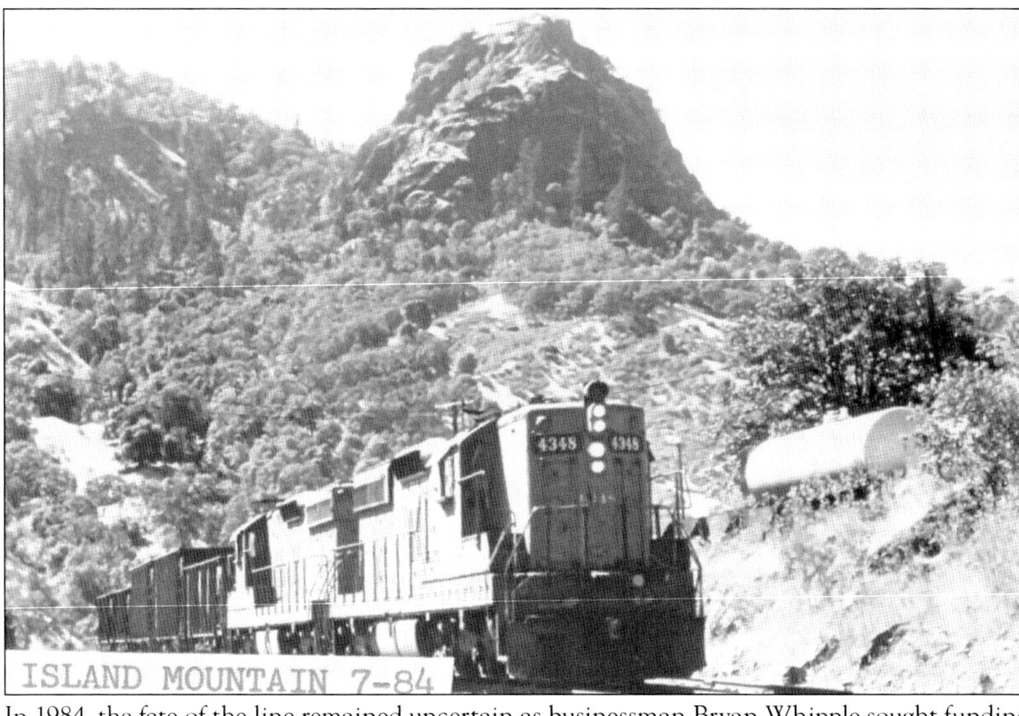

In 1984, the fate of the line remained uncertain as businessman Bryan Whipple sought funding to purchase the NWP's northern division. Whipple, a former Southern Pacific executive from Santa Rosa, had been negotiating the purchase since May 1983. This image shows one of the last NWP trains on the northern end as it passes Island Mountain.

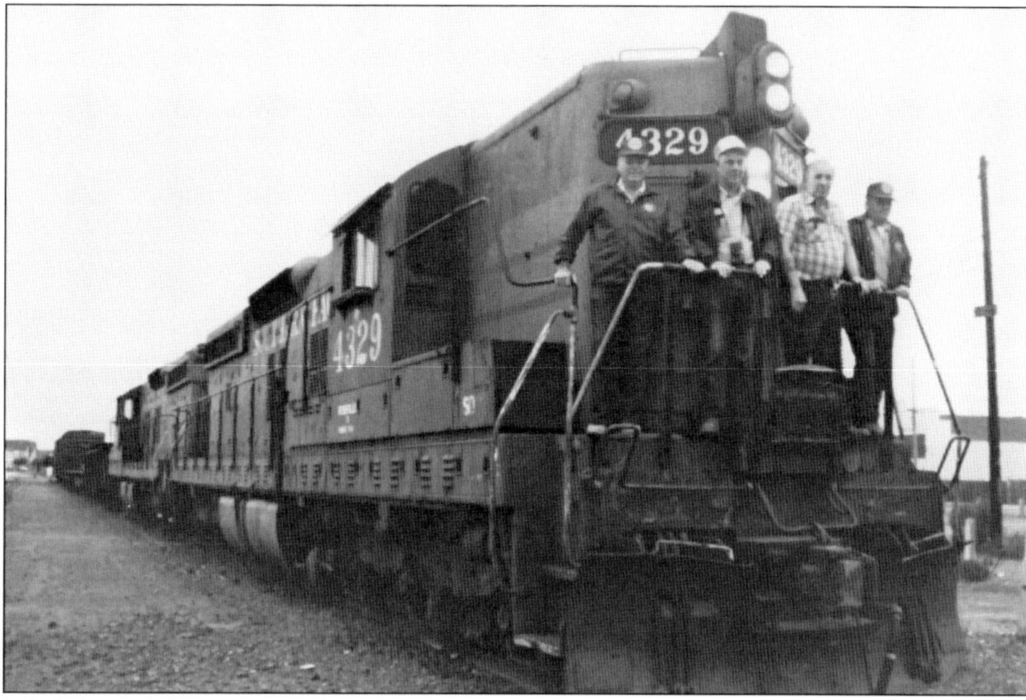

Labeled "NWP last train out of Eureka 8/25/84," this photograph shows, from left to right, brakeman Bailey Cooksey, conductor William Dusick, brakeman George Bodiroga, and engineer Earl Wahlund. Reserve engineer Terry Ballard (not pictured) was the fifth crew member. On August 27, 1984, two days after this photograph was taken, the northern end of the NWP line changed hands from Southern Pacific to Bryan Whipple's Eureka Southern Railroad.

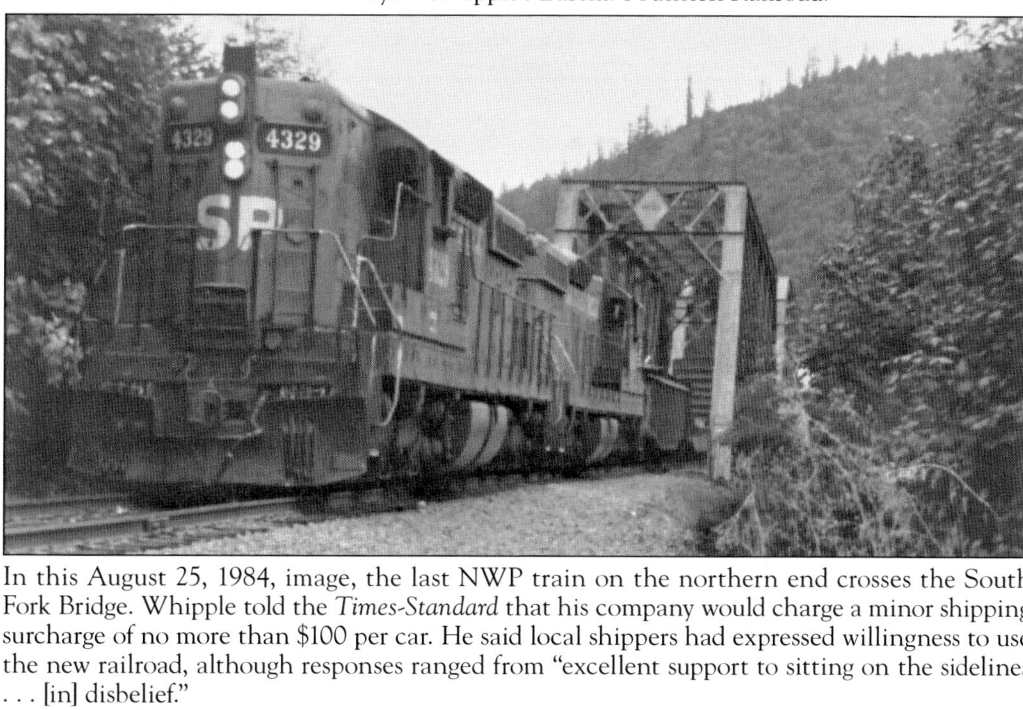

In this August 25, 1984, image, the last NWP train on the northern end crosses the South Fork Bridge. Whipple told the *Times-Standard* that his company would charge a minor shipping surcharge of no more than $100 per car. He said local shippers had expressed willingness to use the new railroad, although responses ranged from "excellent support to sitting on the sidelines . . . [in] disbelief."

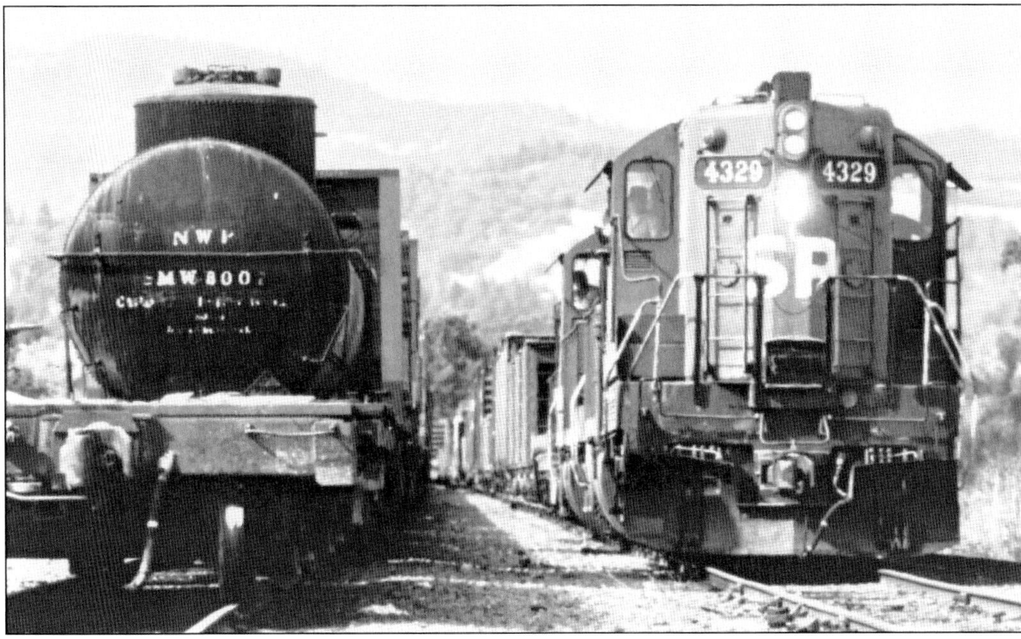

In this image, the last NWP train from Eureka is arriving in Willits on August 25, 1984. It had been just under 70 years since the jubilation of October 1914, when the *San Francisco Chronicle* proclaimed that "all California joins with the citizens of Eureka and the dwellers in the north coast counties in their celebration . . . what San Francisco helps Humboldt County celebrate today is an event of significance comparable to the opening of a transcontinental line."

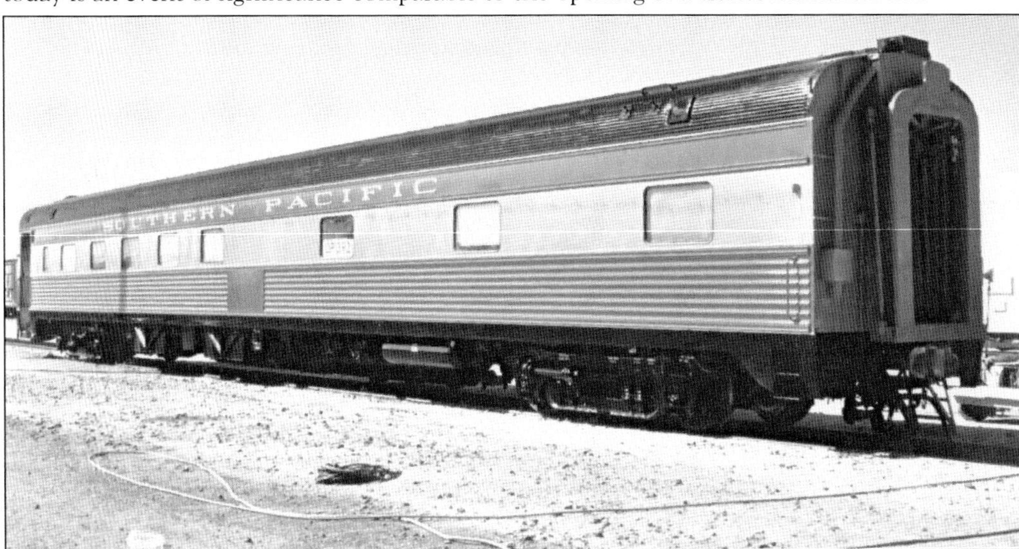

This leased Southern Pacific passenger car was repainted in the red, orange, and black coloring of Bryan Whipple's Eureka Southern Railroad. The Eureka Southern ran its first freight and passenger trains in November 1984. In June 1985, the railroad launched the North Coast Daylight Willits-to-Eureka excursion train. In the *Times-Standard*, Eureka mayor Fred Moore enthusiastically hailed the new ventures as follows: "We need this railroad . . . if we lose this railroad we'll start losing population."

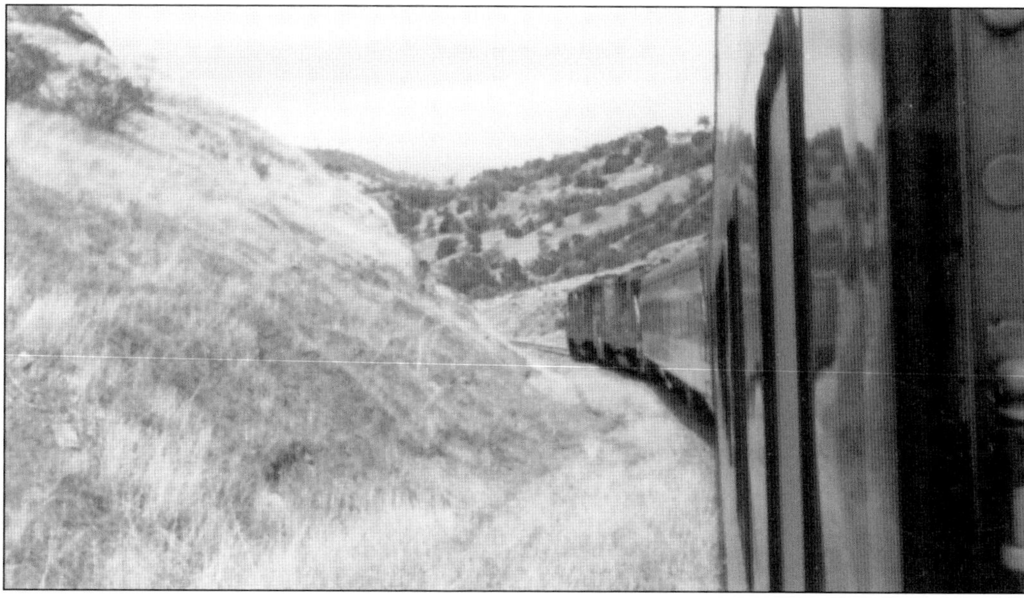

Notwithstanding such optimistic headlines as "New county railroad lights up the tunnel for business and politicians" (from the *Times-Standard*), the Eureka Southern Railroad filed for bankruptcy in December 1986. Service continued until a 1991 earthquake and landslide closed the line. After the line was sold to the North Coast Railroad Authority in 1992, it operated as the North Coast Railroad but finally went out of service in 1995. This November 1984 image from the Francee White collection shows a Eureka Southern passenger train near milepost 186.

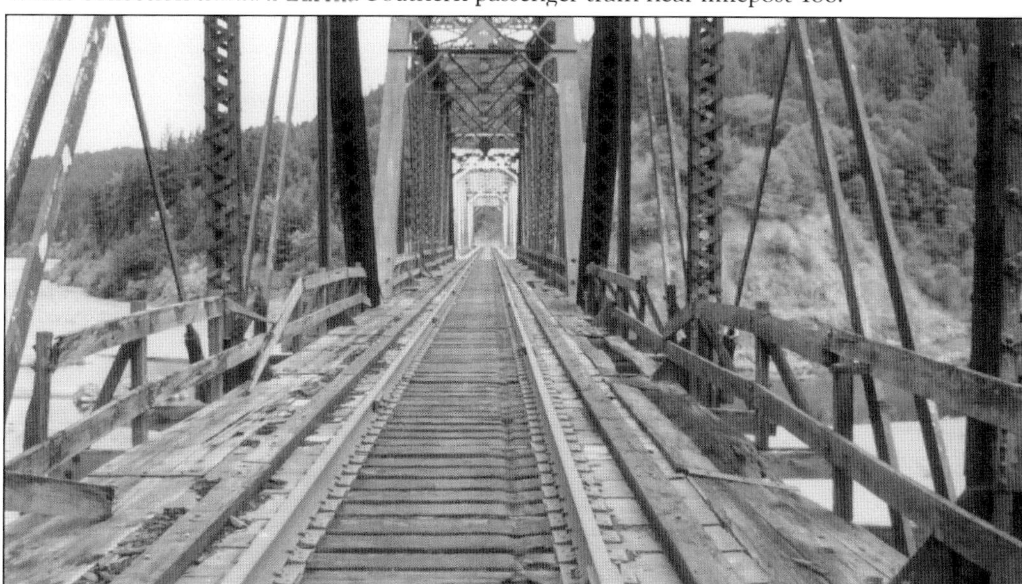

The dilapidated South Fork railroad bridge, pictured here in 2001, shows that lack of repairs in the decades since the railroad's closure have fulfilled concerns expressed in an August 1984 *Ukiah Daily Journal* article about erosion, landslides, and decay of railroad infrastructure leading to "the inevitable washout of NWP track in the Eel River Canyon." Those who hope to reopen the railroad will have to confront challenges at least as great as those faced by its builders a century ago. (Courtesy of HRIA.)

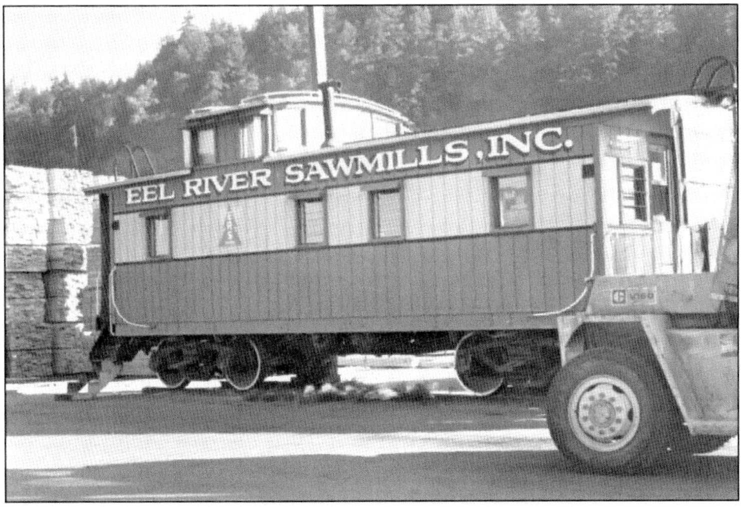

During its three decades as a shipping office for Eel River Sawmills, located south of Fortuna, NWP caboose No. 11 was a beloved landmark along Highway 101. Inquiries and offers to purchase the caboose became so frequent that the sawmill's staff developed a form letter that provided information on No. 11's history and politely stated that it was not for sale.

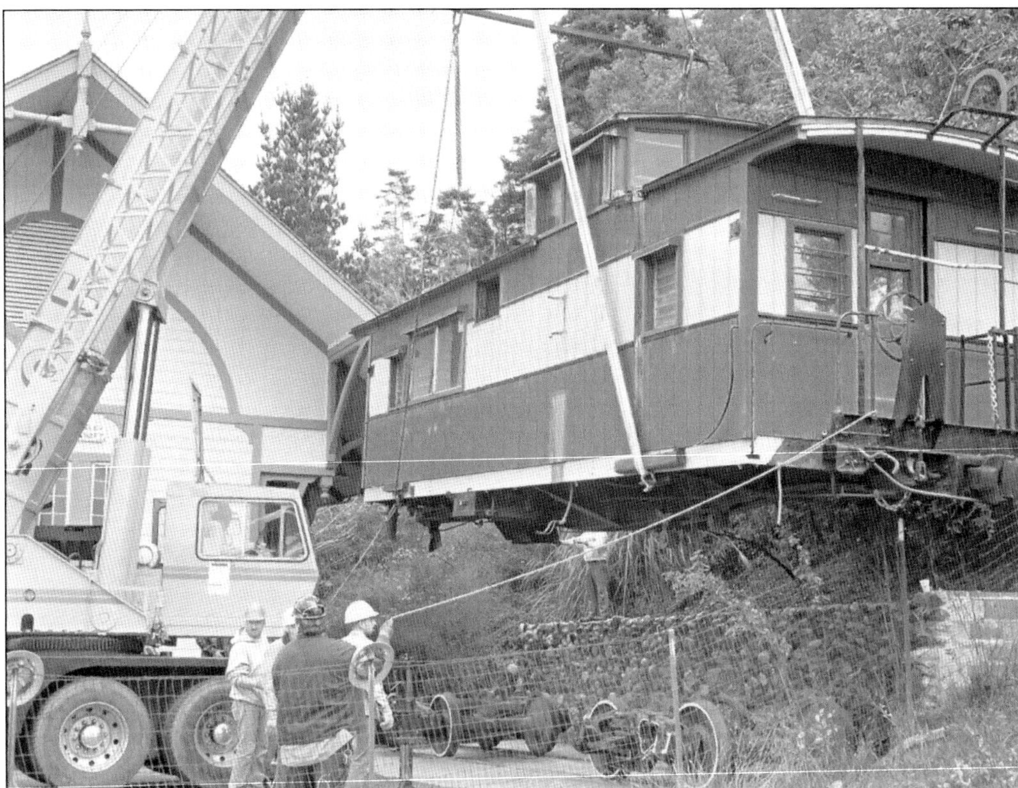

After the 2006 closure of Eel River Sawmills, the Noble family purchased caboose No. 11 at auction and then donated it to the Fortuna Depot Museum in memory of Mary Snell Noble. Transporting the caboose to its new home involved a Fortuna Rodeo Association grant, labor by city staff and volunteers, the use of two trucks donated by Wendt Construction, and a crane supplied and operated by North Coast Fabricators. In this image, John Crotty, the Fortuna Parks and Recreation Department director at the time, is facing the camera.

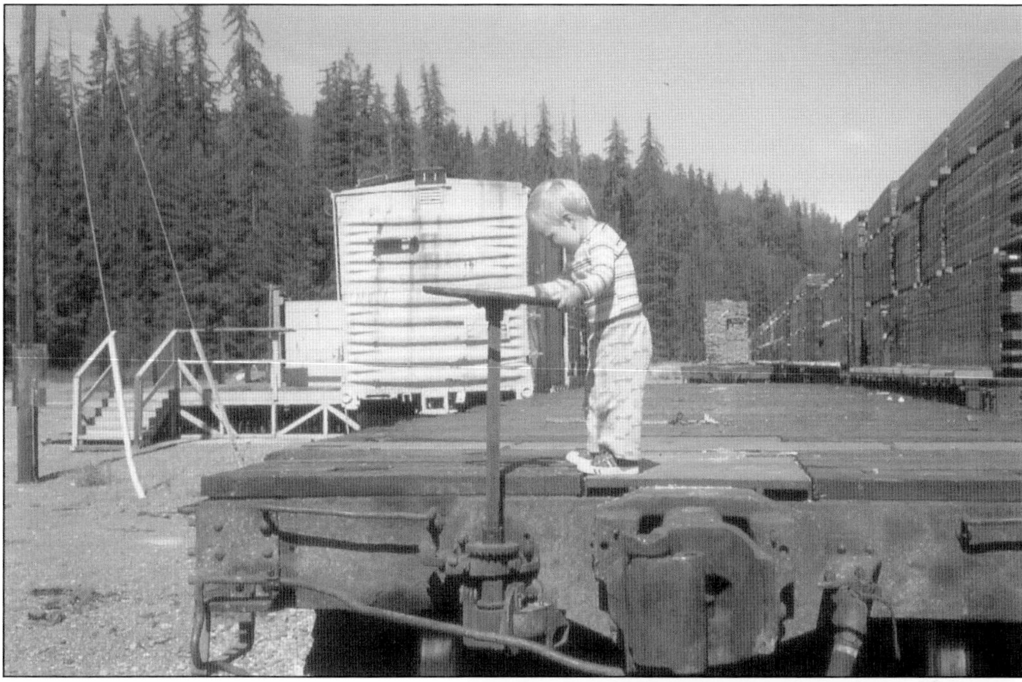

The romance of the rails lives on for countless children, former railroad employees and their descendants, and lovers of history. In this c. 1978 image from South Fork, young David Stockton indulges in the timeless joy of playing with trains. Along northern stretches of the old NWP, nostalgia mingles with a longing to bring back the railroad and recapture some of the dreams of prosperity that accompanied the line's completion in 1914. (Courtesy of HRIA.)

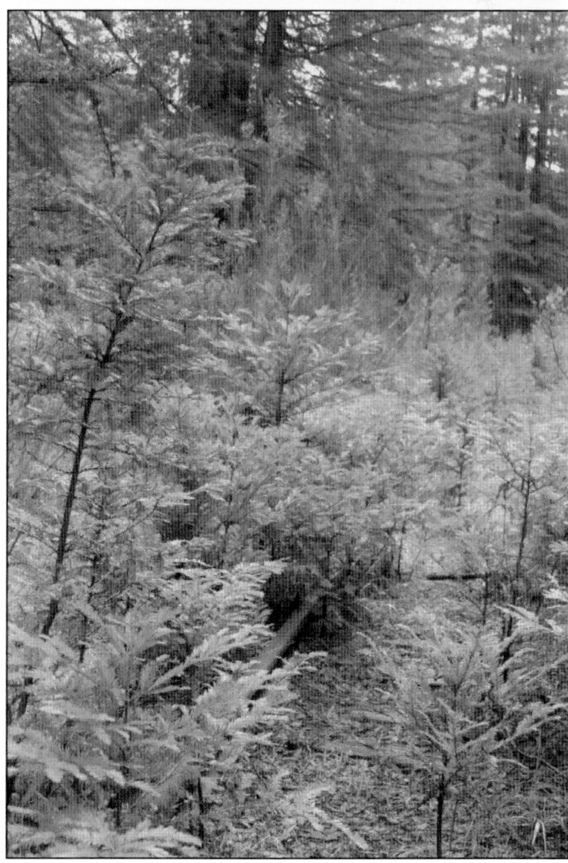

In this image, redwood saplings grow between the ties of rails built to harvest the "red gold." The crumbling remnants of this once-vital railroad can be seen as memorializing the determination, ingenuity, labor, and perseverance of those who constructed the line and maintained it through its century-long history. These rails can symbolize the dream to once again link this isolated region with the potential commerce of the outside world. While the debate continues on future usage of the line, the forests quietly continue to reclaim their own.

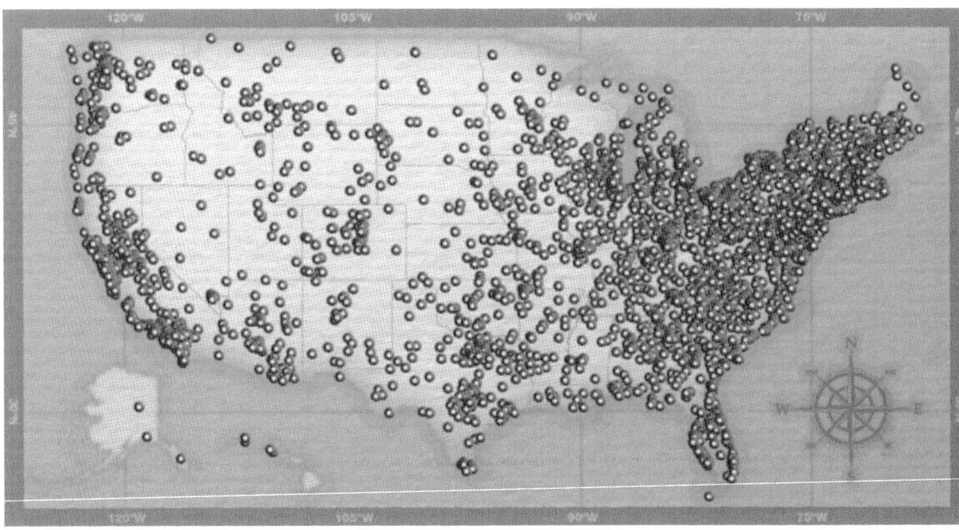